LABOR'S PARTISANS

LABOR'S PARTISANS

ESSENTIAL WRITINGS ON THE UNION MOVEMENT FROM THE 1950S TO TODAY

A *DISSENT* ANTHOLOGY

EDITED BY

NELSON LICHTENSTEIN AND SAMIR SONTI

THE
NEW
PRESS

NEW YORK
LONDON

Requests for permission to reproduce selections from this book should be made through our website: https://thenewpress.com/contact.

Published in the United States by The New Press, New York, 2025
Distributed by Two Rivers Distribution

ISBN 978-1-62079-881-8 (hc)
ISBN 978-1-62097-892-4 (ebook)
CIP data is available

The New Press publishes books that promote and enrich public discussion and understanding of the issues vital to our democracy and to a more equitable world. These books are made possible by the enthusiasm of our readers; the support of a committed group of donors, large and small; the collaboration of our many partners in the independent media and the not-for-profit sector; booksellers, who often hand-sell New Press books; librarians; and above all by our authors.

www.thenewpress.com

Composition by Dix Digital Prepress and Design
This book was set in Palatino Linotype

Printed in the United States of America

10 9 8 7 6 5 4 3 2 1

Contents

Part V: What Is to Be Done?

**Part VI: The *Dissent* Tradition, Then and Now:
A Roundtable Discussion on the Labor Movement and
Democratic Socialism**

LABOR'S PARTISANS

Introduction:
Socialism Is the Name of Our Desire

To be a radical in the first half of the twentieth century meant that one was almost always a union partisan, an advocate for and sometimes a participant in the great struggles and strikes that gave rise to the set of powerful unions that did so much to transform working-class life in the years of the Great Depression and after. Socialists, Communists, Trotskyists, advocates of a Christian social gospel: they all believed that trade unionism was but the first step the working class would take in its own emancipation and in the liberation of all humanity from ancient hierarchies and prejudices. "The earth shall rise on new foundations," announced "The Internationale," composed in 1871 by a French communard. "We have been naught, we shall be all."

Dissent was a socialist magazine steeped in this ethos. Yet by the time Irving Howe, Lewis Coser, and a handful of comrades founded the quarterly periodical in 1954, such a faith had been sorely tested. If the Great Depression made clear that American capitalism could generate an economic crisis that would shake society to its very roots, the prosperity generated by World War II seemed to demonstrate that Keynesian statecraft could stabilize the beast. In this context of strong economic growth and rising incomes, not to mention an ideological chill wrought by the McCarthyist witch hunts, many intellectuals grew skeptical of both the desirability of social transformation and the willingness of supposedly privileged U.S. workers to make any sacrifices for it. "More and more writers have ceased to think of themselves as rebels and exiles," the editors of the once radical *Partisan Review* wrote in 1952, and instead "now feel closer to their country and its culture."[1] Looking back, it hardly seemed the most propitious time to initiate any sort of project on the left.

What was more, if the mass strikes and insurrections that gave rise to the Russian Revolution had seemed to validate a Marxist understanding of how capitalism might be overturned, the Stalinist regime that followed led radicals in the United States and elsewhere to reconsider the path a working class must take toward its own true liberation. Indeed, the "Russian question" stood at the heart of much left-wing politics in the Depression decade and after. While hundreds of thousands of Communists in the United States and elsewhere celebrated the new regime that had emerged in the Soviet Union, those radicals who were more critical took inspiration from the life and work of Leon Trotsky, the Russian revolutionary exiled by the Stalinists in the late 1920s and then assassinated in 1940 at his home outside Mexico City.

At stake was the very definition of socialism. The Soviet Union had indeed abolished capitalism. Farms, factories, stores, and housing were now owned by the state. But was this socialism? *Democratic* socialism? In the Soviet Union any party, publication, or group other than that of the Communists was banned as "anti-Soviet." In the name of building socialism, millions were murdered, starved, or sent to the gulag during the 1930s. If this was socialism, Trotskyists in the United States and elsewhere felt, then human liberation was impossible and the left's most reactionary opponents had won a devilish vindication.

When the Soviet Union invaded Finland in 1939 and 1940, American Trotskyists debated anew the character of the twenty-year-old Communist regime. Orthodox Trotskyists, led by James Cannon, a veteran unionist and radical, argued that the Soviet Union was still a workers' state, "degenerated" under the Stalinist dictatorship, but nevertheless an ultimately progressive alternative to capitalist regimes, including that of the Finns, not to mention Nazi Germany or the United States for that matter. But this conception seemed at variance with social and political reality, leading many other Trotskyists to declare that there was nothing progressive about the new regime in Moscow. It was a "bureaucratic collectivist" autocracy, these critics held, in which all property and every other source of power was controlled by a new class of Communist Party officials, whose power and privilege was as pervasive and unjust as that of any Western capitalist.[2]

Those who held this latter view broke off from the Socialist Workers Party, led by Cannon, and formed a new group, called simply the Workers Party, whose leading personality was Max Shachtman, a brilliant, charismatic polemicist who would win the affection and loyalty of a coterie of intensely committed young radicals, including Irving Howe, Michael Harrington, and Hal Draper, the latter a mentor to Berkeley student activists in the 1960s. Adherents of the Workers Party called themselves "third camp socialists," opposed to both capitalism and Communism. They thought that World War II might well discredit rulers East and West, opening the door to a working-class upsurge in which radicals, socialists, and outright revolutionaries would find themselves in the leadership.

To such an end the Workers Party encouraged scores of members to take industrial jobs in the new defense industries. And, beginning in 1940, they published each week *Labor Action*, a lively agitational newspaper distributed at factory gates from coast to coast. Until he was drafted into the army, Irving Howe, a City College graduate, edited the paper, whose circulation would reach 40,000 by 1943. When he returned from his military posting—in Alaska, where he had plenty of time to read through the classics of American literature—Howe briefly edited *Labor Action* once again, but his interests were increasingly those of a modernist critic of the American novel. Still, Howe's commitment to an understanding and critique of the new unionism remained important, as indicated by his co-authorship with B.J. Widick, a Chrysler shop steward, of the *UAW and Walter Reuther* (1949), a book that celebrated the militancy and vision—as well as noting the limitations—of the millionmember auto union and its exciting new leader.[3]

The readership of *Labor Action* notwithstanding, the Workers

Party remained a political sect with a few hundred members. After the war, capitalism did not collapse and there was no mass radicalization. The WP did not grow or maintain a presence among the blue-collar working class, so its ambitions were properly constrained, as indicated by the new name it adopted in 1949, the Independent Socialist League. Howe and his friends soon found life in Shachtman's sect a "claustrophobic, depressing existence," but that did not mean that it was without influence.[4] Within its political and cultural orbit could be found some of the most imaginative writers, intellectuals, and academics of the early postwar era, including journalist cum sociologist Daniel Bell, novelists Norman Mailer and Harvey Swados, historian Richard Hofstadter, critic Clement Greenberg, and sociologists Philip Selznick and C. Wright Mills. Few paid dues to the Workers Party or ISL, but they were fellow travelers of a sort, many of whom would contribute to *Dissent* after its founding.[5]

Though Howe and a few other comrades left the ISL in 1952, they did not abandon the socialism that stood at the heart of their politics and persona. As Howe wrote a few years later, "We could not resign ourselves to a complete withdrawal from leftist politics, and so, like others before and after us, we decided to start a magazine."[6] And when they founded *Dissent* in 1954, they called it a magazine, not a journal, because the latter reeked of academe while the former sought to attract a larger and more variegated public. There would be no "line" or "program," but Howe and Lewis Coser, an émigré German sociologist who would serve as *Dissent*'s co-editor, remained committed to and nonapologetic about a dissident understanding of the world. "Socialism," the new editors wrote in an early issue, "is the name of our desire." *Dissent* would be introspective and sober in that quest, but hardly defeatist. "Starting a magazine is a way of thinking in common," wrote Howe, "and from thinking in common, who knows what may follow? There are some who say it can change the world."[7]

For decades *Dissent* was run on a shoestring, with no office other than the corner of a New York apartment and no paid editors. It helped that both Howe and Coser were Brandeis academics, a pattern that would continue when other professors at other schools took over the helm. By the 1960s *Dissent* had a modest 5,000 subscribers, so there was always an operating deficit, often filled by former ISL comrades whose jobs or inheritance gave them some extra funds.

Old comrades from the Shactmanite days provided much of the labor reportage in *Dissent* over its first decade and more: these were figures like Frank Marquart, B.J. Widick, Harvey Swados, and Sidney Lens, who had taken industrial jobs in the 1930s or assumed union leadership posts in the next decade, often in Detroit or Chicago. As evident from some of the articles we reprint in Part I of this collection, many of these writers were highly critical of the labor movement, but hardly because they thought, as many postwar intellectuals believed, that American workers had been seduced by mass consumption and a debased popular culture. As Harvey Swados observed, this "myth of the happy worker" was just that, an ideological construct that failed to grapple with the social reality of work, in the factory or elsewhere.

In 1959, *Dissent* published its first special issue on labor, in which Howe wrote, "If, a few decades ago, American intellectuals often deluded themselves by contriving an image of the American worker as a potential revolutionary, today they are inclined to accept an equally false image of him as someone whose socioeconomic problems have been solved and who is joining the universal scramble for material luxuries." *Dissent*'s correspondents in Detroit and elsewhere rejected that trope, but they laid a good share of the blame on a union movement they thought increasingly stolid and complacent. As Howe put it in the introduction to that special issue, "A major shift in attitude toward unions has occurred among American intellectuals, including many of liberal and left-wing opinion. Unions are no longer regarded with warmth, let alone a sense of identification. Like so many other institutions in our society, unions are looked upon as a distant, impersonal they—an attitude that is, apparently, often shared by union members themselves."[8] This critique struck home, with *Dissent*'s special labor issue selling out in record numbers and time.

By the time *Dissent* published another special issue on labor, "The World of the Worker" (1972), the rest of the country had come to realize that the United States was still very much a class society and that chronic discontent—the "blue-collar blues" it was then called—was the lot of many millions, even if populist demagogues like George Wallace sought to turn such class resentments toward a bigoted right. But if writers and editors at *Dissent* were ahead of the curve when it came to an understanding of white working-class mentality in the early 1970s, they had pretty much missed the boat when it came to the New Left generation of young radicals who did so much to transform American culture and politics in the 1960s and 1970s. Irving Howe and his cohort of *Dissent* editors and writers had enthusiastically endorsed the rise of civil rights militancy in the late 1950s and early 1960s and they welcomed the activism of the student radicals who took such inspiration from that democratization of American life. Meanwhile, a somewhat younger element began to write for *Dissent*. These included the political theorist Michael Waltzer, who had been Howe's student at Brandeis and who would become a co-editor in the mid-1970s; Michael Harrington, a gifted young Shachtmanite with a talent for popular writing, exemplified in *The Other America* (1962), his influential study of how and why millions remained in poverty within a society otherwise thought prosperous and affluent; and Mitchell Cohen, a self-described "social democrat" who would join Walzer as a magazine editor from 1991 to 2009.

But Howe and other Dissentniks, including Harrington, found even the earliest versions of the New Left politically and ideologically problematic. When the Students for a Democratic Society were writing their famous 1962 manifesto, "The Port Huron Statement," *Dissent* editors looked askance at the idea of "participatory democracy." In his memoir, Howe found off-putting and manipulative the "the early SDS style—a mixture of student bull session, Quaker meeting, and group therapy."[9] This was not the stuff of democracy, proletarian or bourgeois. And more pointedly, Harrington and other New York–based socialists famously clashed with SDS activists like Tom Hayden and Todd Gitlin, whom they considered to be too sympathetic to Castro's Cuba, infatuated with Third World revolutions, and both ignorant and contemptuous of the battles an older generation had waged on behalf of the labor movement, civil liberties, and the struggle for African American freedom. In a blistering 1965 critique, "New Styles in 'Leftism,' " Howe let a generation of New Leftists have it: "Do you suppose that the struggles of only a few decades ago to organize unions were any the less difficult, bloody and heroic than those in the South today? And if it's a revolution in the quality of American life that you want, then have not the industrial unions come closer to achieving that for millions of people than any other force in the country?" [10]

The breach between the *Dissent* brand of socialists and the New Left grew only wider in the latter half of the 1960s. When it came to the Vietnam War, most *Dissent* editors wanted the United States out of Southeast Asia, but they feared a Communist victory: for too long the magazine stuck with a call for "negotiations," which was not all that distant from Lyndon Johnson's determination to continue the war until stabilization of the South Vietnamese regime was assured. The presence of North Vietnamese flags and banners at antiwar demonstrations did not help matters. Meanwhile, *Dissent* found the rise in Black nationalism a retrograde gambit, even as the editors largely ignored the early stirrings of second-wave feminism. Howe later remembered himself as feeling "politically beleaguered, intellectually isolated" and so too was *Dissent*.[11] The editorial board in 1970 was largely identical to that of 1960, even as the magazine lost its stature as a lonely voice on the non-Communist left. By the 1970s a new set of publications were giving voice to such an analysis of American politics and society: *Studies on the Left, Radical America, Socialist Revolution, New Politics,* and *In These Times* offered young students and activists a Marxist interpretation of the world. And within academia itself emerged journals of a self-conscious radicalism, including *Feminist Studies, Radical History Review, Politics and Society,* and the pamphlets and periodicals put out by the Union of Radical Political Economists.

In the late 1970s and 1980s, *Dissent* renewed itself, even as the culture, the politics, and the shape of American capitalism shifted against the socialist idea. Three developments help to explain the changes at the magazine in this period. First, *Dissent* editors and writers linked themselves to a younger generation with the founding early in the 1970s of the Democratic Socialist Organizing Committee and then in 1982 of a successor organization, the Democratic Socialists of America, a product of the merger between DSOC and the New Left–influenced New American Movement. Michael Harrington, a prolific *Dissent* essayist who had replaced Norman Thomas as the best-known and most widely respected socialist tribune in the United States, played a key role in this reconciliation, which soon generated a source of readers, writers, and staff for the magazine in the decades to come. In short order, New Left veterans like Todd Gitlin, Michael Kazin, David Bensman, Mark Levinson, Joanne Barkan, Marshall Berman, Ellen Willis, Harold Meyerson, Frances Fox Piven, and Jo-Ann Mort joined the editorial board or took other active roles sustaining the publication.

Irving Howe was very much on board with the actual creation of an organization of socialists, a project he had eschewed thirty years before. Thus, when he interviewed a seventy-year-old Victor Reuther in 1983, he was delighted that this Reuther brother had joined the Democratic Socialists of America. But then Howe sharpened his query: "Look, you fellows in the Reuther tendency began in the socialist movement. Now you, Victor, and some of the others have rejoined it—but only after retirement. But if that's the pattern, we're never going to get anywhere—socialism only for the young and the retired? It ought to be possible for good trade unionists publicly to be socialists, as for many decades, from the time of Eugene Debs to the time of Norman Thomas, it was possible." [12]

Second, the social earthquakes leading to the fall of the Berlin Wall gave Dissenters young and old a cause that both could cheer. The rise of Polish Solidarity served as an inspiration to *Dissent*, contributors to which saw in it a demonstration of the enormous, world-transforming power of a working-class movement coming to power and embodying the anti-Stalinist politics that editors and writers at *Dissent* had been advocating all their adult lives. "Should We Call a General Strike?" That was the thrilling question *Dissent*

editors put on the magazine's cover, followed by an English trans-
lation of the debate on that topic held by Solidarity leaders in the
spring of 1981.[13] It did not happen, and by late fall of that same year
Poland's Communist regime suppressed the union and arrested its
leaders. But history was not to be denied: by 1989 Solidarity was
once again legalized and now holding actual state power, thus setting off the political and social dynamite that led to the implosion
of Eastern European Communism. "Nothing in our past thinking,"
Howe and Walzer confessed, "or in anyone else's, prepared us for
the remarkable turn of events in the Soviet Union. So much the
worse for theory, so much better for life!"[14]

Finally, and perhaps most important, the hard times that engulfed industrial America in the years after 1973 made journalistic analysis of what was wrong with American capitalism and how
the labor movement might respond of increasingly greater urgency
and importance. This was a terrain upon which both the founding
generation of *Dissent* editors and the men and women schooled by
the New Left might fight together. A $50,000 fund drive that ended
in 1985 came in a shade above $70,000, perhaps reflective of the
new harmony.[15]

Although there were plenty of issues that evoked controversy on
the editorial board and in the magazine's pages—Israel, affirmative
action, trade policy, and the wars in the Balkans and Iraq—*Dissent*
kept itself grounded and unified with timely investigative reports
from the labor front. *Dissent* was never a specialized publication
like *New Labor Forum* or one of the academic labor history or labor
studies journals. And this was a good thing when it came to following the travail of the union movement in the 1980s and 1990s,
because *Dissent* was always attentive to the way class issues were
embedded within the other conflicts, including tax and spending
policies, abortion politics, school choice, trade policy, and the dis-
covery that sexual harassment in the workplace was a huge issue
for women workers, both blue collar and professional.

Dissent coverage of the labor movement, in the United States and
worldwide, was punctuated by a series of special issues on the organized working class. In 1985 came a fifty-year retrospective on

the history of the Congress of Industrial Organizations and prospects for the return of such a dynamic movement. Seven years later, as the possibility of another Democratic administration beckoned, *Dissent* published several articles tracing out a variety of innovative organizing strategies. Five years later, in 1997, after John Sweeney and his New Voice team defeated the AFL-CIO's stolid old guard, *Dissent* was even more certain that a renewal of the union movement was in the offing. That was not to be, but the Cold War–built wall that had once divided the official labor movement from the activist left was largely shattered.

In the new century, opposition to the U.S. wars in Afghanistan and Iraq, the Wall Street collapse, and the rise of youthful organizing efforts against sweatshops and in favor of academic unions on campus energized labor-oriented activists, spurring *Dissent* to publish two additional issues of labor reportage. Of even greater note was the 2013 founding of the *Belabored* podcast by Michelle Chen and Sarah Jaffe, who for the next decade took listeners on a biweekly tour of the most current issues in the world of work. Chen and Jaffe stood as representative of the post–New Left generation of socialists, many of whom have been a part of the enormous increase in the size and influence of DSA and other activist groups in the years since the first Bernie Sanders campaign for president. Their work in the magazine and online documented the revival of labor activism and militancy in the years immediately before and after the pandemic.

A long-awaited changing of the editorial guard was signaled in 2009 when Michael Kazin, a Georgetown University historian, became co-editor of the journal, first with Michael Walzer and then with David Marcus, a millennial generation intellectual. Kazin had been an SDS leader at Harvard in the 1960s and a prolific, appreciative writer on New Left cultural politics and American liberalism cum radicalism more generally. His eleven-year editorship coincided with a generational turnover of the *Dissent* editorial board, a transformation that made the magazine highly attentive to the new currents animating the union movement and the Bernie Sanders wing of the Democratic Party. Marcus would depart for the *Nation* in 2016 where he became literary editor, but he was soon replaced by an even younger cohort that included Tim Shenk of George Washington University and, after 2020, Natasha Lewis, a British-born journalist and activist. In 2024, Patrick Iber, a University of Wisconsin historian, replaced Shenk as a co-editor.

Labor's Partisans is organized around five themes that recur throughout the seventy-year history of the magazine. Part I: "Socialists Look to the Postwar Labor Movement" features essays by the early *Dissent* crowd on the character of organized labor at the apogee of its twentieth-century power. Part II: "Democracy in American Trade Unions?" includes contributions that probe the character of labor's leadership over several decades and how those men and women can be held accountable to the union rank and file. Part III: "A Time of Troubles" reprints a series of pieces charting the decimation of organized labor that began in the 1980s and continued well into the new century. Part IV: "New Frontiers" shows the gradual shift within the magazine, both among its writers and in the subjects they explored, to document and explain the increasingly variegated character of the working class in a capitalist world that was itself in the process of a radical recomposition. Part V: "What Is to Be Done?" contains more recently published pieces that grapple with the pressing question of union renewal in an era of capitalist dysfunction. Finally, the book concludes with a round-table discussion in which three leading figures in, and analysts of, the labor movement—Luis Feliz Leon, Sara Nelson, and Daisy Pitkin—discuss the state of the unions in the 2020s and offer insights on the path forward.

Workers, organizers, and anyone else inspired by the new wave of union activity can find in this volume a window onto some of the critical events and debates surrounding the labor movement for the better part of a century. The essays collected here are, indeed, of much historical interest, but for today's readers they are also more than that. Together, they illustrate the evolution of a durable tradition on the U.S. labor-left, one that always remained committed to a socialist vision while also understanding the importance and peculiarities of the institutional labor movement, with whatever limitations it may have in the here and now. *Dissent* was not the only publication to wrestle with this tension, but in its venerable pages, an edited sample of which is here collected, readers can glimpse how labor partisans, from the era of the CIO onward, have reckoned with the challenges that confront those who seek to advance working-class power and transform our politics and society.

PART I

Socialists Look to the Postwar Labor Movement

When *Dissent* was founded in 1954, the American trade union movement stood at its organizational apogee. Never before or since had such a large proportion of wage-earning individuals been enrolled in a labor organization. Excluding those who owned a farm or worked in agriculture, just about one-third of all workers were unionists, with the merged labor federation—the AFL-CIO was created in 1955—claiming upwards of 16 million members. Another 2 million were members of unions unaffiliated with the AFL-CIO.

Sheer numbers, however, understate the strength of organized labor. The vast majority of all unionists worked in private industry, with many employed by the largest and most strategically influential corporations in the United States. In the 1950s industries like steel, auto, trucking, meatpacking, railroads, utilities, rubber, coal mining, and aircraft manufacture still constituted the "commanding heights" of American capitalism. They were all heavily unionized, with 80 and 90 percent of all nonsupervisory employees enrolled in one or more unions. Some, like the Teamsters, the United Auto Workers, the United Steelworkers, and the Machinists, had memberships approaching a million dues payers. In states like Michigan, New York, Pennsylvania, Illinois, California, and Ohio, union density stood close to 50 percent.

Although periodic recessions generated painful layoffs, working-class wages actually doubled between the end of World War II and the mid-1970s, thereby generating what some economists have called "the great compression," an era when income inequality was at its twentieth-century nadir. Untroubled by imports and competition from war-torn Europe or Japan, domestic corporations normally turned a healthy profit, thus insuring that no one thought to label cities like Detroit, Pittsburgh, Cleveland, Milwaukee, Toledo, and Flint part of a dismal "rust belt." During each contract renegotiation, the unions generally won higher wages and an increasingly elaborate set of "fringe benefits" that included pensions, health insurance, and supplemental unemployment benefits. There were many strikes in the 1950s and 1960s, far more than in the twenty-first century, but few ended in the defeat or destruction of a trade union.

However, for those who wrote on labor issues in *Dissent*, none of this generated anything resembling a sense of complacency or satisfaction. They measured labor's status and future prospects by a metric forged during the dramatic upheavals of the 1930s, in which many had been key participants or close observers. Contributors to *Dissent* no longer thought of themselves as revolutionaries, but they remained highly critical of the accommodation that so many union leaders seem to have made with the political and economic structures congealing in Cold War America. As Irving Howe put it in 1959 introducing a special issue devoted to the labor movement, "There is an uncertainty of purpose, a loss of vitality, a sapping of morale even in the best American unions." Nor were *Dissent* writers sanguine about labor's fate, if only because new technologies and new occupational configurations threatened to undermine the power organized labor had so recently achieved. Contributors to *Dissent* thought a class struggle was taking place every day in every workplace and they were worried that their side might not be winning it.

Thus Sidney Lens was hardly a celebrant of the 1955 merger between the old American Federation of Labor and the Depression-born Congress of Industrial Organizations. This unity at the very top did little to generate solidarity among the rank and file nor help democratize the actual structures of internal union power. And perhaps most ominous to Lens and his generation of old labor party advocates, the merger seemed unlikely to enhance labor's political clout. Rather, it deepened AFL-CIO dependence upon and subordination to a Democratic Party then drifting toward a decidedly more conservative posture.

Yet laborite political influence would be essential, writes Gabriel Kolko in a 1955 article considering the impact of automation on American work life, because collective bargaining alone seemed inadequate to the task. Thus, the UAW campaign for a guaranteed annual wage would indeed protect the income of auto workers from temporary layoff, but it could do nothing to assure that the inexorable march of factory automation would not destroy the livelihood of millions. Daniel Bell takes this critique even further in his consideration of the meaning of work. Not only have the unions failed to challenge management on the organization of the work process, but they have accepted the idea that efficiency is of value regardless of the degree of worker power exercised on the shop floor. Even the old socialist/syndicalist demand for "workers' control" of industry has been constrained by what Bell decries as "the cult of efficiency."

Such speculations confronted a hard reality when *Dissent* writers looked to the automobile industry and the role of the United Automobile Workers and Walter Reuther, its famous president. No union meant more to *Dissent* contributors than the UAW. Many, like B.J. Widick, Frank Marquart, Harvey Swados, Brendan Sexton, Patricia Sexton, Carl Shier, and Al Nash, worked in auto and aircraft factories, many as radical union organizers in the 1930s and 1940s. More important, top UAW leaders like Secretary-Treasurer Emil Mazey, Regional Directors Leonard Woodcock and Martin Gerber, and Reuther himself had come out of the socialist movement and still advanced a social democratic ethos. They were backstopped by staff intellectuals like Jack Conway, once a University of Chicago sociologist; Victor Reuther, who always stood a step to the left of his brother; Nat Weinberg, an alumnus of Brookwood Labor College; and Paul Schade, a Yale dropout who as a regional director in California played a key role in advancing the farmworker cause.

But none of this spared the union from a withering critique. B.J. Widick, a key leader at Chrysler Local 7, offered readers a granular, shop-floor account of the trench warfare between company and union that stymied UAW efforts to humanize and dignify auto work. That recession-era tale was followed in 1963 by a scorching indictment from novelist and onetime auto worker Harvey Swados. He recognized that the UAW was the most progressive of all the big American unions, but even so, its leadership had made a fatal accommodation to the industrial status quo, one which generated a manipulative mind-set among the leaders while cynicism and apathy flourished among the ranks.

Nine years after this Swados blast, Michael Harrington published a very different appraisal of the unions and their status in American life and politics. Against Daniel Bell, Clark Kerr, and others who foresaw a postindustrial society in which class antagonisms were being dissolved, Harrington defended the idea that a working class—blue collar or white, industrial or high-tech—continued to exist with interests sharply different from those who owned property or managed big bureaucracies, public or private. But Harrington gave the unions a political pass. Unlike Lens or Swados, who thought the labor movement was trapped within an alien party, Harrington endorsed trade union engagement with the Democrats, writing that organized labor represented a "class political force," a social democratic current, within a party, important elements of which were hardly sympathetic to working-class interests. Not unexpectedly, Irving Howe endorsed the main thrust of Harrington's perspective, offering in the early 1980s a far more sympathetic assessment of American trade unions, especially in an era when both the culture and the politics were turning against the very idea of solidarity. For good or ill, most *Dissent* writers would endorse this outlook in the years to come.

Problems of Labor Unity (1955)

Sid Lens

Sidney Lens (1912–1986) was born Sidney Okun in Newark, the son of working-class Russian Jews who reached the United States in 1907. He was a runner on Wall Street during the 1929 great crash, afterwards an organizer of retail workers in New York and Chicago. In the mid-1930s he became a Trotskyist but generally allied himself, inside the party and out, with A.J. Muste, the pacifist revolutionary and worker advocate. Lens was a militant and effective leader of Chicago retail unions from the late 1930s through the 1970s, even as he became a peace activist and prolific author on labor issues and Cold War politics. With Muste, Bayard Rustin, and other radical pacifists, he founded Liberation *magazine in 1956, after which Lens played an increasingly prominent role in movements against the arms race and the Vietnam War.*

The reunification of the CIO and AFL, after twenty long years, will send hopes soaring in the battered House of Labor. The word "unity" has a magic which deeply affects not only the man at the lathe but his intellectual friend as well. It conjures a picture of a strong, singleminded labor movement battering down the pillars of poverty and making its voice resound through the halls of Congress.

Much will undoubtedly be gained. CIO and AFL will no longer have to "consult," nor to bicker, for united action; the two groups will work through one executive committee and speak with one voice. In suggesting amendments to the Taft-Hartley law, for example, the united federation will not stumble about as at present, with the AFL proposing changes that help the building trades primarily, and the CIO proposing others of a contradictory kind. Multiply this by scores of lobbying activities, by the thousands of local actions, and it adds up to something of substance. The joining of research staffs, educational committees, political action forces, foreign affairs groups; the merging of newspapers and magazines; the elimination of overlaps in organizing staffs—these too are gains. Many people will be released for other activities; much *can* be done.

Reunification is a defensive measure, born of internal and external fears, essentially aimed at regaining some stature in the political arena. Internally Walter Reuther has his steelworker David J. McDonald, threatening to "take a walk"; George Meany has his teamster David Beck, still a big question mark. Externally there is the mounting pressure from Washington, the conversion of the National Labor Relations Board into a virtual management instrument, the prosecution of quite a few union officials (mostly bad, but a few good), the "right to work" laws in one-third of the states and threatening to spread further. These and other threats hastened the marriage, and if unity can change things somewhat it will be all to the good.

But we should not be mesmerized by the idea of unity. In its contemplated form it is rudimentary indeed. In fact, if more were attempted at this particular moment the schism would unquestionably remain. For what is being united is the two national federations, not the actual unions. AFL and CIO are essentially lobbying bodies, with no mandatory rights over their 144 national affiliates. Each of these latter is an autonomous body of its own, with the right to decide its own dues, call its own strikes, negotiate its own contracts, discipline its own members. AFL cannot instruct the AFL machinists on when or how or if to conduct a strike; the machinists international union is the true power center—along with 109 other such centers in the AFL and in the CIO. What is now being united is not these power centers. It is hoped that rival organizations come together at some time in the future—that AFL electrical workers and CIO electrical workers merge, that the rival chemical, retail, packinghouse unions amalgamate. It is hoped but this is far, far from certain.

The two lobbying bodies will now live under one name (though there will be a special department for industrial unions). They will weld together the staffs; they will federate the city and state central bodies. But these are distinctly secondary forces and distinctly secondary functions. The merging of the power centers may take years—perhaps it will never come.

The true test of "unity" is not whether the federations merge, but whether labor achieves what we have always called "solidarity." Will unity mean that no union member will cross the picket line of another union? That would be a gain for the labor movement revolutionary in scope. It would herald the organization of millions of white collar workers, retail employees, the whole South. It would strengthen weak union groups, would close the gap between the 75¢ an hour worker in the unorganized fields and the $3.50 rates in the building trades.

Such solidarity is truly a consummation devoutly to be wished. Even within the present AFL and CIO solidarity is practiced more in the breach than the observance. Solidarity is no longer a labor principle, it is a mere tactical arrangement between union leaders. When these leaders like (or need) each other they respect picket lines; otherwise they don't. There is no doubt, for instance, that the AFL teamsters would walk through a picket line of the AFL retail clerks in Los Angeles—and probably elsewhere. Mere "unity" within one federation has not in the recent past been a guarantee of solidarity, and there is no immediate hope that this will change in the unified federation.

Nor does unity promise more rank-and-file participation, higher social consciousness, the demise of business unionism and racketeering. Unity *can* be the beginning of these things; it can also merely pyramid the current sterile centralization of power. It is certainly no cure-all, no assurance of greater numbers or future victories.

As a matter of fact schism rather than unity has most frequently aided the labor movement. It was the break in the 1880s between the simple unionists around Samuel Gompers and the "uplift" Knights of Labor that ushered in the larger and more stable AFL. In our own time the birth of CIO within the AFL led not to the decimation but to a resounding growth of unionism. Minority movements have generally propped labor's principles, forced old line leaderships to put up a better battle. The Chicago syndicalists of 1886 stiffened the backbone of the simple unionists in the fight for an 8-hour day. Eugene Debs' American Railway Union and the Wobblies were pressures on the powers-that-be in the labor movement that resulted in benefits for the rank and file. And CIO's split from AFL *forced* the older federation to accept what it had so bitterly fought—industrial unionism. The AFL unions that have grown—outside of the building trades—are precisely those, like the teamsters and machinists, which have accepted industrial unionism.

The leaders who effectuated this merger want nothing but to attach themselves more firmly to the Democratic Party machine. Walter Reuther's famous CIO convention speech in which he renounced not only a third party today but even for the future, was a clear turn towards the right, an accommodation to his new partner. What is expected by the unifiers is more jobs in the Labor Department, a choice of Labor Department officials, personnel in the National Labor Relations Board and a dozen other plums. What is expected is a little political pressure to help at the bargaining table—as was the case under Roosevelt and Truman. All this adds up to greater *dependence on, a firmer alliance with,* the Democratic machine, and not political independence. Under such circumstances labor will not make the Democratic Party more radical; the Democrats will continue, as they have these past two decades, to make labor more conservative. The prospects are that unity in itself will not steer the ship of labor towards an independent party of its own but towards greater accommodation to machine politicians, Dixiecrats and those liberals like Hubert Humphrey-Paul Douglas-Adlai Stevenson who are in the process of deliberalization.

Such political action inhibits true labor solidarity, it subverts the interests of the rank-and-file worker to those of the leader and his machine allies. It pinpoints the basic danger of unity, that it may lead not to united action, but to greater centralized power, and thus inaction.

The disunity of these twenty years was not all harmful. It created useful competition between unions. When the CIO communications workers won a 10¢ raise from the Bell System, it put pressure on the AFL electrical workers to get a dime or more. And vice versa.

Even the claim that disunity meant ceaseless jurisdictional strikes and squabbles was an oversimplification. Of course, there were some useless jurisdictional disputes, particularly in the building trades. But too often what passes for a jurisdictional dispute is in reality an attempt by a militant group of unionists to get out of a bureaucratic or weak union. Thus, for instance, a group of tracklayers who tried for twenty-four years to democratize their union were able to achieve the result only when they could run to the other federation of labor—in this case the CIO. And a group of retail clerks in an impotent and disintegrating union were able to improve their bargaining power by going over to the rival federation. Many a group of workers has been able to escape from a bureaucratic conservative leadership precisely by this route. It hardly seems likely that with CIO-AFL unity such a safety valve will continue to be available—unless more basic changes follow on the heels of formal unity.

The unification of AFL and CIO can be a great thing for the rank and file worker—but only if it is the beginning of true solidarity, if it leads to the end of business unionism, if it results in a wave of new organization, and a rededication to old economic and political principles that have been forgotten. But such a task is herculean. For instance, if the unified federation tries to organize the 8 million unorganized employees in the white collar and retail fields it must first arrive at a *modus vivendi* with Beck, who insists that almost all department store employees up to the sales counter are in his jurisdiction. How will that square with CIO's concept of industrial unionism? And what guarantees are there—if this point is not ironed out—that the very vital help from the Teamsters will be forthcoming for such a drive? Each attempt at organization, at new collective bargaining techniques, at new and independent politics, will lead to the same dilemmas and conflicts. Unification creates a better mood for trying to resolve them. But if unity is born sterile, if it ends merely in strengthening the hand of top leadership, if it muffles the voice of the rank and file further, then it may lead not only to setbacks for labor but to future splits as well. We shall naturally hope for the best; but it would be folly to regard it as automatic.

The CIO Faces Automation (1955)

Gabriel Kolko

Gabriel Kolko (1932–2014), who became a noted historian of American capitalism and U.S. foreign policy, was born in Paterson, New Jersey, and took advanced degrees at the University of Wisconsin and Harvard. At the time he published this essay on the social impact of automation, he was active in the Student League for Industrial Democracy, a socialist group. Kolko spent his career at York University in Canada. There he became a leading figure among those New Left historians who thought twentieth-century liberalism, from the Progressive era through the New Deal and the Great Society, heavily influenced by elite business interests that sought to constrain both the free market and working-class radicalism. With the publication of The Roots of American Foreign Policy *(1969) and many follow-on books, Kolko also became a trenchant critic of U.S. diplomacy.*

The guaranteed annual wage is the most essential of the CIO's present answers to automation. In addition to preventing seasonal layoffs in such industries as auto which regularly suffer from the problem, discouraging mass layoffs of workers in old plants after constructing new ones, and guaranteeing forty hours' pay to a worker for each week he is called in, the GAW, as the UAW initially proposed it, is essentially an attempt to extend and enlarge unemployment compensation to 52 weeks. State payments are to be supplemented by the company to the extent of providing any workers with two or more years seniority the equivalent of a 40-hour-a-week pay check for a full year. The company would be liable to pay out a maximum of eight percent of its current payroll during unemployment, and the UAW wants a reserve fund of 20 percent of the base payrolls to be accumulated over a five-year period to cover any additional payments not provided for by the current tax on payrolls.

There are questionable elements in the plan, however, and the CIO has given no indication whether it is even quietly conscious of them. The GAW depends on the state unemployment compensation system, which in March, 1954, contained, after paying out generally low payments to a relatively small number of unemployed for a short time, a total national reserve of $8.6 billion, or a very small fraction of the income which would be lost if unemployment of any magnitude or length existed. The amount produced by an eight per cent tax on current payrolls has huge variable possibilities, and is very much dependent on the extent of unemployment. If a depression of the intensity of any period of the 1930s existed, the CIO realizes, as simple calculation dictates it must, that both the state and company systems would be hard pressed to maintain payments. And automation holds out, the CIO is willing to admit, the possibility of just such unemployment. If the unemployment lasts beyond a year (in early 1954 a fifth of the workers collecting compensation used up their benefits after 26 weeks) the worker is on his own. One CIO staff member has privately admitted that with automation all the GAW may turn out to be is a glorified severance pay scheme.

The CIO also knows the GAW has made it a distinct economic advantage for companies simply to introduce more automation rather than hire new workers to whom it might have to pay future GAW payments. In a sense, therefore, the GAW becomes a scheme to provide for workers already employed, and not those about to enter the labor market, shifting from other depressed industries, or out of unemployment payments. The classic role of labor increasing the nation's industrial productivity by pricing itself as highly as possible, and hence stimulating the innovation of labor saving devices, has proceeded on the assumption that machines create more jobs than they displace—and promise increasing prosperity for all. In the context of automation's ability to displace labor, the theory is ready for basic reappraisal along with many other traditional beliefs.

The idea of a shorter work week would also present several major problems under automation. First, it does not answer the problem of the displacement of traditional skills altogether, which will be discussed later. There is secondly the fact that a floor has to be placed on the extent to which a work week can be cut, since the trend in its decline has been geometric and not arithmetic, and to cut 25 hours off the work week within a generation or so, as we did from 1870 to 1950, leaves about a 15-hour work week. And thirdly, the experience of unions with the 36-hour week has been anything but happy. In Akron the rubber shops have been on a six-hour shift for nearly two decades, and a third of the rubber workers today hold two jobs, many in the rubber plants. Given general instability and insecurity in the economy, the shorter work week could conceivably mean the appropriation of many jobs by those anxious to earn more while they can.

But it is in the realm of demands it cannot negotiate at the bargaining table that the CIO has suggested its most far reaching, and probably relevant, program. As Walter Reuther has put it, it is a program that ". . . will help to assure a stabilized reservoir of purchasing power during the transition years that seem to lie ahead." An extensive public works program, improved social security and minimum wage laws, and, above all, the need for stronger progressive taxation and wage increases to distribute purchasing power so consumption can keep up with productivity increases, are the key CIO demands. Yet the CIO, besides giving this aspect of its answer to automation the least attention, has failed to describe the means by which it hopes to get this program implemented.

There has arisen a general consensus, both among business and labor economists, that workers under automation will pass from the direct production lines to maintenance functions, and will still be needed to keep automatic machinery in operating order. "The typical auto worker of the future may be a skilled maintenance man, engineer, or analyst," declares the UAW in its pamphlet on the topic. "The biggest single management job in the factory of the future will be the selection and coordination of the activities of highly trained specialists . . . ," writes industry's *Factory Management and Maintenance*. The underlying assumption in both cases is that the reallocation of manpower, and not unemployment, will present automation's most serious problem.

The general experience in highly automated plants until now has been that the over-all amounts of labor required has been radically reduced, but that the proportion of maintenance workers to whatever labor is needed is much higher than previously. The Dow Chemical Company's highly automatic Madison, Illinois, magnesium mill has about 400 production workers, of which an unusually large ratio of 35 percent is involved in maintenance functions. Yet the average amount of capital investment for each production worker in the Dow plant is still eleven times greater than the average in all U.S. industry. Ford, by a program of standardized tools, has reduced its maintenance problems to a minimum. Automatic control boards indicate when tools should be replaced, thereby cutting down labor needs and preventing serious repair problems. Inspection by automatic gauging and similar devices has cut down the need for labor in quality control.

Indeed, the speed of processes in automatic factories has simply tended to demand more machinery to meet the tempo in all phases of production. Rather than create more places for workers, the automatic factory seems simply to demand more machines. Steel magazine's projected profit and loss statement for an oil pump body factory found the setup and tool change in the automatic factory saving more than half the cost of a regular factory, supervision cost savings two-thirds regular costs, scrap savings one-half, machine repair two-thirds, while labor costs were less than one-third that of the ordinary plant.

The mere fact that a new machine is being introduced into a plant indicates a net diminution of labor employed, or else no economy would be affected. The only way original employment could be continued or enlarged is by the demand for products expanding enough to necessitate keeping on those not needed at old levels of production. If, as automation tends to suggest, labor is displaced at such a ratio and in such a volume as to make exceedingly difficult the possibility of a corresponding rise in production, the problems facing unions are far more indirect and subtle. Simple retraining and seniority agreements, while humanely vital, tend to become secondary to the central issues of income distribution, underconsumption on the part of lower income groups, and the premises on which the economy operates.

"An executive may know nothing about machine tools," said C.F. Hautau, chief engineer of a leading automation firm, last year. "But when we talk cost cutting, we talk his language." "We hope to be able to eliminate time-and-a-half overtime pay for Saturday and double-time for Sunday that we're now saddled with," frankly admitted one top Texas oil executive quoted in the *Wall Street Journal*. "Two significant changes are taking place in the battle of man and machine," wrote William Freeman in the *New York Times* in January, 1953. "The worker is coming to be regarded, partly as a result of union pressure, as having as much importance as the machine and requiring as much care in selection and maintenance. And efforts are being speeded to have the machine replace the worker so far as is possible."

Indeed, it is the very success of the union's position that has stimulated the movement behind automation. In addition to the power and resources built up by organized labor during the late 1930s, consolidated in the early 1940s and defended with success since that time, there is the logic of unionism's historic position on technological innovation. To oppose it would make labor seem reactionary, but to support it would have meant the elimination of jobs unless wage conditions were tied to increasing productivity. These stipulations only made labor more expensive, intensifying business' desire to install new labor-saving devices, and it may now be legitimately asserted that with automation the problem of expensive labor is fairly well solved. Automatic equipment does not strike, talk back to foremen, file grievances, or do any of the things presently obnoxious to management.

But most important of all, automation arrives at a time when American industry is particularly conscious of cost savings. During

the favorable market following World War II, labor in manufacturing industries was able to surpass slightly in earnings the increase
in man-hour productivity. As consumer markets closed with the
depletion of backlogged savings, and industry's expansion needs
were brought up to date, concern for increasing labor costs became
more pressing—and so did modernization. "The company with the
most room between costs and current prices is obviously in the best
shape" was one auto executive's solution to an increasingly tight
market, according to the *Wall Street Journal*.

Because of the tactical convenience of concentrating on immediate wage and working conditions, and because it has not
approached broader social and economic issues with the same seriousness, American unionism has historically been victimized by
those larger economic forces beyond the reach of routine union activity. Its disadvantages in negotiating during times of unemployment is only a reflection of the effect such an imbalance in its total
perspective can have.

It is in its demands for a more equitable distribution of consumers' purchasing power and extended governmental planning that
the CIO has raised its most significant answer to automation. And
it is in this realm that unionism has shown itself perplexed and unable to act with the decision it long ago discovered was necessary
on the bargaining table and picket line. For it cannot be said that
the CIO lacks those who can see the full implications of automation to unionism and society, or that it shares the common thesis
that the fear of technological unemployment is a perennial false
alarm. "The facts," declared the last CIO convention, "allow no
room for the illusion that expansion of employment in the manufacture of the revolutionary new machines will compensate to any
substantial degree for contraction of employment in the industries
using them."

The aim of the CIO for more equitable income distribution, a goal
which seems to be obtainable only through the decisive government action no major party has yet been willing to follow, raises
the entire question of what is now minimum union effectiveness.
Without some radical shifts towards a level of distribution which

would make it possible for mass consumption to keep up with the productivity increases of automation, there seems reasonable assurance that unemployment will follow.

The CIO, while it acknowledges the seriousness of the problem, is still primarily concerned with what it can do, here and now, to counteract automation's effects within the plant. The possibility that these means may be far from effective, or may create conditions for a new type of unionism based on a relatively few highly skilled workers with economic and social aspirations different from the mass of workers, has yet to be admitted publicly. Those in the CIO who understand these possibilities are confined to a relatively few staff members who illustrate the classic dilemma of how far hired hands can publicly deviate from official policy and still keep their tenure.

Nevertheless the CIO's declared goals of increased mass consumption, extension of educational opportunities to readjust the work force to the exigencies of automation, and more equitable income distribution remain. As automation's effects become more pressing and undermine the present position of organized labor, the inadequacy of its traditional methods for achieving these indispensable goals may have to be faced. Meanwhile, unionism's dilemma with automation is best epitomized by a statement made by James Petrillo of the Musicians Union a few years ago:

Unless something radical happens in the near future, it's a bad business for musicians. I advise youngsters to stay out of it—for the time being, anyway. The whole story about a musician's life is in the box. It starts and finishes right there. Gompers tried to fight the machine with the cigarmakers and the union went to hell. Lewis don't fight the machine and the miners are out like a light. We're playing at our own funeral.

Meaning in Work—A New Direction (1959)

Daniel Bell

Daniel Bell (1919–2011) was one of America's most influential sociologists and public intellectuals during the second half of the twentieth century. Born on Manhattan's Lower East Side in a family of Jewish immigrant garment workers, Bell became a socialist even before attending City College in the late 1930s. He edited the social democratic New Leader *during World War II, after which he spent a decade as* Fortune *magazine's editor on labor issues. While there he wrote most of the essays, including a version of this one, that would comprise chapters in his landmark classic,* The End of Ideology: On the Exhaustion of Political Ideas in the Fifties *(1960). Thereafter he taught sociology at Columbia and Harvard, publishing* The Coming of Post-Industrial Society *(1973) and* The Cultural Contradictions of Capitalism *(1976), both of which argued that transformations in the character of American capitalism had decentered class conflict and socialist ideology.*

In recent years there has arisen a sophistication which understands that the abolition of private property alone will not guarantee the end of exploitation. The problem has been posed as: how does one check bureaucracy. The problem is a real one. In socialist thought the "new" answer is to raise again the theme of "workers' control." This has shaped the demand for *comites d'enterprise* in France, for *mitsbestimmungsrecht* in Germany, and is emerging in Britain as the left-wing answer to the British Labor Party's plan, "Industry and

Society." It underlay, of course, the demand for workers' councils in Poland and Yugoslavia. I have no quarrel with the demand per se. But often it is difficult to know what the concept means.

In Communist theory (to the extent there has been one apart from the opportunistic absorption of syndicalist ideas), the slogan of "workers' control" was conceived of almost entirely in *political* terms, as one of the means of undercutting the economic power of the employer class under capitalism, as a means to power, but not as a technique of democratization or the administration of industry *in* a socialist society.

At the other extreme there were the detailed, imaginative, but unworkable blueprints pieced together by the medievalists, distributivists and syndicalists who formed the Guild Socialist movement in Britain before and after World War I. The movement has been insufficiently appreciated for the Guild Socialists wrestled, as did the earlier Fabians, with concrete problems of administration. Most of the questions which beset socialist and managerial societies today were anticipated and thrashed out in Guild Socialist debates. They were aware that nationalization of the means of production might result in the exploitation of the individual Guilds by the State (e.g., the building of unwanted new investment at the expense of consumption or leisure, the setting of high work norms, etc.). On the other hand, syndicalism, or the ownership of production by the individual Guilds, might lead to a separatism or "parochial imperialism" whereby a single Guild might seek to benefit at the expense of others.

As a compromise between statism and syndicalism, Guild Socialism has given us many useful guides. Its weakness is that it sought to grapple with too many problems and that it set forth too detailed a blueprint. It was, paradoxically, too rational. Human societies cannot be made over de nuovo. One has to begin, pragmatically, with existing structures and with the character, temperament, and traditions—and desires—of the people concerned.

If the slogan of "workers' control" is raised, the simple starting point, perhaps, is to ask: workers' control over what? Control over the entire economy? This is unfeasible. A syndicalist society is too much a single-interest affair, which, if extended with its own bureaucracy, would simply substitute one form of interest domination for another. In a single industry, or enterprise? One can question, further, whether this, too, is a meaningful—realistic—concept. The British Trade Union Congress report, in 1932, on *The Control of Industry*—which accepted the public corporation rather than Guild structure as the form of nationalized property, and joint consultation rather than syndicalist organization as the form of social control—was a hard-headed recognition of the limits of workers' control. And the new British Labor Party program on "Industry and Society," which extends the idea of social control, through State ownership of shares in enterprises, although increasing the risk of a new "managerial" class society, is, in principle, a large step forward in creating "social accountability" of corporations to society, which is the aim, too, of workers' control.

The major confusion in the idea of workers' control, as it has been put forward by socialists and syndicalists, is that the word control has always had a double meaning: as direction (e.g., to control the course of an automobile) and as a check (e.g., to control someone's rage). Usually, in the debates on workers' control, the proponents have rarely singled out the different meanings. Roughly speaking, socialists have talked of workers' control to mean direction, management of an enterprise by the workers themselves, or the participation in management. This latter sense is the meaning of workers' control as it is being tried in Yugoslavia. The difficulty inherent in worker participation in management is that it tends to minimize the separate interest of workers from management, and to rob the workers of an independent status in the plant. Historically, the trade union has been a restrictive and protective organization, acting to defend workers' interests. Where the union has become an instrument to "control" the workers, in the interests of national unity or for the state, workers have formed substitute bodies. This was the history of the shop stewards movement in Britain during World War I, of the workers' councils in Poland in October 1956. In Yugoslavia today, the Communist Party is in a dilemma. Because the workers have been brought into participation in management, there seems to be no functional role for the union; and some theorists have gone so far as to say that the trade unions ought to be eliminated. In Britain, on the other hand, the unions in nationalized industries have consistently refused to participate on the Boards of Management, or to take responsibility for production. The union continues to act as an independent, defensive institution vis-à-vis management.

Is there, then, no role at all for workers' control? If there is any meaning to the idea of workers' control, it is control—*in the shop*— over the things which directly affect his work-a-day life: the rhythms, pace, and demands of work; a voice in the setting of equitable standards of pay; a check on the demands of the hierarchy over him. These are perhaps "small" solutions to large problems, what Karl Popper has called "piecemeal technology," but look where the eschatological visions have led!

Let us separate out two things which are crucial, I believe, in affecting the worker in the plant: one is the question of equity in treatment; the other is the impact of technology and an engineering culture on the work process itself.

By *equity*, a worker wants a situation where no supervisor should have arbitrary or capricious power over him, and where some channel exists whereby his own grievances find an impartial adjudication. And secondly, by equity, a worker wants to be assured that his wage, *relative to others in the plant or area*, is fair. The question of differentials in wages is a difficult one. In the past these differentials have been set by custom, or by the supply-and-demand balances in the market. In recent years, engineers have sought, through job evaluation schemes, to set up "impartial" intervals between classes of jobs. Often these have failed because the "ornery" workers refuse to believe that mechanical criteria, mechanically applied, constitute equity; and sometimes because "power" groups in a plant refuse to recognize a scheme which disadvantages them. In the West, by and large, the functions of the unions (or of shop committees, since in Germany, for example, the unions deal with regional wage policies and have no roots in the shops) have been directed, with a large measure of success, to securing recognized standards of equity written into collective-bargaining contracts. The principles of

seniority, of arbitration and umpire procedures, of union determination of methods of sharing wage increases (e.g., through equal
or across-the-board allocations, or through percentage increases),
all attest to the victory of the workers' conception of equity, rather
than the employers', in the matter of fair treatment in the plant.

But in the second aspect of control, in the challenge to the work
process itself, the unions have failed. The most characteristic
fact about the American factory worker today—and probably the
worker in factories in other countries as well—is his lack of interest
in work. Few individuals think of "the job" as a place to seek any
fulfillment. There is quite often the camaraderie of the shop, the jok-
ing, gossip, and politicking of group life. But work itself, the daily
tasks which the individual is called upon to perform, lacks any real
challenge, and is seen only as an irksome chore to be shirked, or to
be finished as best as possible. Most workers, by and large, are not
articulate about work. Questionnaires and surveys provide merely
the muttered semi-approvals or disapprovals, the grudging assents,
or the grunted displeasures which mask the "to-hell-with-it-all" attitude of the individual who feels his life-space constricted. But the
behavior itself becomes a judgment. First and foremost, it appears
in the constant evasion of thought about work, the obsessive rever-
ies (often sexual) while on the job, the substitution of the glamour
of leisure for the drudgeries of work. Yet the harsher aspects are
present as well. It takes the form of crazy racings on the job or what
the workers call the "make-out" game, i.e., the break-neck effort to
fulfill one's quotas early in order to lounge for the rest of the hour
or day (and it is striking to see how this pattern is recapitulated
identically by the Soviet worker in his habit of "storming"), by the
sullen war against production standards, and, most spectacularly,
even if infrequently, by the eruption of "wildcat strikes."

Contemporary sociology has come to the melancholy, and defeatist conclusion, that technology as "progress" cannot be reversed.
In a rational order one would *reduce* to as little time as possible the
number of hours spent in irksome work, and then find respite in
leisure. But is this the case? Can we not do something about the
nature of the work process itself?

Actually, the root of alienation lies *not* in the *machine*—as romantics like William Morris or Friedrich Junger were prone to say—but in the concept of *efficiency* which underlies the organization of the work process. The idea of efficiency dictates a breakdown of work and a flow of work in accordance with engineering rationality. It seeks to increase output by erasing any "waste"; and waste is defined as those moments of time which are not subject to the impersonal control of the work process itself. Central to the idea of efficiency is a notion of measurement. Modern industry, in fact, began not with the factory—the factory has been known in ancient times—but with measurement. Through measurement we passed from the division of labor into the division of time. Through measurement, industry was able to establish a calculus of time and pay a worker on the basis of units of work performed. But the value of work itself could only be defined in terms of its cost to the user; and cost was—and is—conceived primarily in narrow market terms. Thus the psychological costs of indifference or neuroses, the social costs of road and transport, are charges all outside the interest and control of the enterprise. Thus such a consideration, for example, as the size of a factory is determined largely by the possibility of increasing output rather than by the costs involved in travel time for the worker, community crowding, etc. In these situations the human being is taken as one more variable in the process, and quite often a very subordinate one. Our emphasis has been on economic growth, increased output, but not on what kind of men are being molded by the work process. Even the recent vogue of "human relations" has been considered a justified cost to management not in terms of increasing satisfaction in work but of increasing output. The assumption has been made, of course, that if a worker is more satisfied he will increase his output. But what if the costs of satisfaction, involved in reorganizing the work process, mean a *decreased* output? What then? Which "variable" does one seek to maximize: the satisfaction of the work group, or the productivity of the enterprise?

The cult of efficiency has been an unanalyzed assumption in the "logics" of modern industry. Some of it is due to a utilitarian rationality; much to early technological necessity since the nature of early steam power required the bunching of work. Once the goal of efficiency was established, however, the rationalization of work began; so, in Taylorism, we have the detailed breakdown of time, and with Frank Gilbreth the economizing of motion.

In the United States apart from questions of production standards, the unions have failed to challenge the organization of work. To do so would require a radical challenge to society as a whole: to question the location of industry or size of plant is not only to challenge managerial prerogatives, it is to question the logic of a consumption economy whose prime consideration is lower costs and increasing output. Moreover, how could any single enterprise, in a competitive situation, increase its costs by reorganizing the flow of work, without falling behind its competitors?

But this is not only a failing of "capitalist" society. In the socialist societies, sadly, there has been almost no imaginative attempt to think through the meaning of the work process. In Britain, this has been, in part, the heritage of the Webbs, and their own concept of efficiency (capitalism for them was waste and anarchic; socialism would be a "tidy" society). But of equal weight is the fact that with outmoded machinery and in a falling world market, British society has been forced to think primarily of productivity in order to compete in the world markets. And who, today, would challenge the God of Productivity, if it might mean a lowered standard of living?

In Communist countries, where minority dictatorship has sought to speed rapid industrialization, the effects on the workers have been even harsher. Lenin's solution for the disorganization of production, for example, in a famous speech in June 1919, was to introduce piecework and Taylorism, in order to discipline the workers! In the West, at least, where dehumanized work results in increasing productivity, the fruits of that productivity are shared with the workers. In the Communist countries, not only is work dehumanized but the social surplus through "primitive accumulation" goes to enhance the power of the State.

For under-developed countries, where living standards are pitifully low, it is difficult to talk of sacrificing production in order to make work more meaningful to the worker. Yet these are not, nor should they be put in either/or terms. Engineers have learned that if efficiency considerations are pushed too far—if work is broken down into the most minute parts and made completely monotonous—it becomes self-defeating. The question is always one of "how much." But the question must be stated and placed in the forefront of considerations.

One need not accept the fatalism of the machine process—or create new utopias in automation—to see that changes are possible. These range from such large-scale changes as genuine decentralization, which brings work to the workers rather than transporting large masses of workers to the work place, to the relatively minute but important changes in the pace of work, such as extending job cycles, job enlargement, allowing natural rhythms of work.

The specifics are there: what is needed is a change of fundamental attitude. If one is to say, for example, that the worker is not a commodity, then one should take the step of abolishing piecework and eliminating the distinction whereby one man gets paid on a weekly or annual salary, and another man is paid by the piece or the hour. If one accepts again the heritage of the old socialist and humanist tradition of worker protest, then the work place itself and not the market should be the center of determination of pace and tempo of work. The "flow of demand," to employ the sociological jargon, must come from the worker himself rather than from the constraints imposed from above.

Even if costs were to rise, surely there is an important social gain in that the place where a man spends such a large part of his day becomes a place of meaning and satisfaction rather than of drudgery. Fifty years ago, few enterprises carried safety devices to protect workers' limbs and lives. Some protested that adoption of such devices would increase costs. Yet few firms today plead that they cannot "afford" to introduce safety devices. Is meaningfulness in work any less important?

The Limits of Unionism (1959)

B.J. Widick

Branko J. Widick (1910–2008) was born in Serbia, immigrating with his family to the United States just before World War I. In the 1930s he was an Akron journalist, and an organizer and writer for the Newspaper Guild, the United Rubber Workers, and the UAW. By the late 1930s he was a Trotskyist and after 1940 allied with Max Shachtman's Workers Party group. After service in World War II, Widick got a job at Chrysler's huge Jefferson Avenue plant where he was a key shop-floor leader for more than a decade. Although Widick supported the Reuther caucus in the UAW factional disputes of 1946 and 1947, the book he published with Irving Howe, The UAW and Walter Reuther *(1949), was not uncritical of the UAW president. In the 1960s and after, Widick taught at Wayne State and Columbia, publishing frequently on contemporary industrial relations and the racial tensions that gave rise to the great Detroit riot of 1967.*

One wet October morning the telephone at the foreman's desk rang. It was a call from the chairman of the shop committee. "I'm putting you in my place as committeeman," he said. "Why?" "Because," he answered, "I've been fired. I was escorted out of the plant. I'm calling from the Local." The technical grounds were insubordination.

As I kept trying to assess the impact of this event and waited for confirmation of my new status from the company's labor relations department, one thought stayed in my mind: How soon will the inevitable walk-out take place, and what will be its consequences? For in our Local it was traditional for the ranks to shut the plant whenever a union representative was fired. It was also a tradition for the company to crack down on wildcatters.

This new crisis would increase the turmoil of the past four months. We had been working without a contract because of the UAW strategy of "rock and roll" negotiations with the Big Three auto companies (that is, avoiding a major strike). The in-plant struggle had been fierce. The company, taking the offensive, had modified union representative rights, made grievance procedures stricter and pushed for higher work norms. The men had retaliated with a kind of passive resistance. Just two days ago the new contract had gone into effect, which meant—in theory—that the rules had been set down under which both sides would have to function in regard to wages, hours and conditions. But between theory and practice there was, as usual, a gap.

At a membership meeting of the Local the contract had been ratified almost unanimously. Yet the confusion among the workers was such that the very next day they had voted, under an old motion on the books, to go on strike. The contradictory character of these two decisions reflected ambivalent feelings among both the ranks and the secondary leaders of the Local in regard to the value of the new contract. Now that the committee man, a well-known union veteran, had been fired, explosive sentiments were certain to burst forth.

The next morning: Tension everywhere in the plant. "Why don't we walk out now?" everyone keeps asking. Discretion forbids any answer, since a hint by union leaders for direct action would quickly come to the notice of the company and enable it to fire them. By noon feelings have boiled over. The men pour out of the plant and into the Local hall, with an overflow crowd packing the street. Experienced unionists know that the mere size of the crowd says a great deal about the feelings of the men.

For the Local leadership a dilemma presents itself: should it recommend that the men stay out until the committeeman is rehired or go back the next morning and try negotiating? The leadership has to bear in mind the hard fact that the contract, recently signed, is binding; it has to remember that when another local had voted to stay out in a similar crisis last spring, the company involved had obtained an injunction, sued for damages unless the contract was immediately honored, and thus forced the leadership of that local to retreat.

There seems no alternative but to return to work. The company has already informed the Local that it expects the men back at the job the following day and that there will be no negotiations on the discharge of the committeeman unless work is resumed. The company has still another card up its sleeve. It can insist that the Local go through regular grievance procedure in this case and let the Umpire between union and management rule on the proper penalty. This does not strike us as a happy possibility, since in the past the Umpire has tended to favor the union on matters of wages and seniority but was harsh on matters affecting plant discipline.

Reluctantly, the men accept explanations along the above lines and agree to go back to work. Accepting an explanation and believing it, however, are two different things.

A few days later: Another, more serious explosion has just occurred. One of the major aggravating policies of the corporation—tested out in our plant—has been the introduction of a five-stage penalty system against any employee failing to meet work standards dictated by management. First a warning; then a day off; then three days off; and finally a ten-day suspension. "Come back anytime in the ten days you want to do the work. If not, you're automatically fired. If you come back and don't meet the standard, you're also fired."

Today the inevitable explosion followed. I was at the labor relations office arguing in behalf of the discharged committeeman when the phone rang. As soon as the labor relations man picked up the receiver, I could hear the angry noises. "You'd better get over to the trim shop," he said. "There's serious trouble there." Union representatives have the duty of getting to trouble spots to see if they can settle problems and keep the men on the job.

As I walked into the trim shop, I noticed three riot squad cars of city police near the plant. The plant protection men at the gates were all tensed up. The boos and roars grew louder and louder.

When the men saw the Local president and myself, they jeered still more. They felt that the union would simply tell them to go back to work while the problem was being negotiated; and they were sick of that. For a while I couldn't even find out what had happened: they were too mad, cursing the company, cursing the union.

Quietly I kept asking, "Tell me what happened. I can't do anything until I know what it's all about." Finally, they calmed down a little and told me: The company had ordered one man into the office to be penalized for not meeting the work standards, and the whole assembly line marched in behind him. As they reached the office, the new plant manager appeared, purely by coincidence. He was the man who was being blamed for the suddenly toughened company policies, and his appearance nearly provoked a riot.

This swift, violent and utterly spontaneous demonstration had thrown management off balance. Foremen stood helplessly on the side. No one knew what to do, no one expected the men to go back to work. Finally, a top company official said to me in front of the men, "Tell them to go home." This ludicrous suggestion snapped my own tension and I broke out laughing. "That's not my job," I said. "I'd be accused of leading a wildcat. How dumb do you think we are?"

As word of the exchange spread through the crowd, more people began to laugh. And unless someone made the mistake of calling in the city cops, I knew the situation was again under control. Another top official of the company stepped into the crowd and told the men, "We are asking you to go home, while we negotiate with your union." The Local president nodded in agreement, and soon the plant was cleared. All afternoon the union waited for the meeting, but company higher-ups decided not to negotiate because a wildcat was involved. The next day, one of the leaders of the demonstration in the trim shop was fired, others penalized.

Again the tension became unbearable. Unless we had positive assurance that the company penalties would be modified sooner or later, another eruption would obviously break out. Fortunately, the top company officials became convinced of this and indicated that if the plant continued work there would be redress of the penalties.

When this information was given to the men on the line, it was accepted and a sort of armed truce followed.

But the plant did not return to normal after these incidents, not even six months later. The near-riot in the trim shop was just the beginning of a grim struggle on the speedup issue, which in auto plants is never-ending. What exacerbated the struggle in our plant was the fact that the relatively easy work standards of the war years had been carried over into the postwar years, partly because of the militancy of our Local, partly because the international union "tolerated" the tactics we had used to maintain what were among the best working conditions in the industry. Now, however, that the corporation had suffered two bad years in 1957 and 1958, it began a major shake-up in its plant management, replacing the "softs," those officials whom the union had mellowed, with a new and tougher kind of organization man. The corporation now insisted that under no circumstances were wildcats to be tolerated in its plants.

Now, ordinarily, developments of this kind—guerrilla in-fighting followed by a truce of sorts—would tend to normalize relations in the plant. Emotions would have been discharged, small but galling problems settled, and the ordinary rhythm of plant life resumed. But these were unusual times in the life of both the plant and the union.

The ranks were irritated because the company was slow in returning the discharged committeeman to work. Even more troubling were the fears many men had of a lay-off. Once this plant had 14,000 workers. Production cut-backs, decentralization and automation had reduced the membership to less than 3,500. With a kind of obtuse willfulness, the company insisted on scheduling production according to the flow of orders. Sometimes this meant a four-day week, other times a six-day week. Particularly acute was the problem of Saturday overtime. When the company first announced there would be work on Saturdays, the unemployed members of the Local, as part of a city-wide movement, announced plans to picket the plant. Under a section of the contract which gives management the exclusive right to direct its work force, the company was legally entitled to schedule Saturday overtime. But many of us in the plant felt heartsick at the thought of being forced to come to work and finding our unemployed union brothers picketing the gates. All sections of the UAW protested the wisdom of such schedules; but to no avail.

The temptation to strike as an answer to the problems of the shop was overwhelming. Militant speeches were a dime a dozen. Memories of 1937—the heroic period of our Local, which functions in our folk-lore somewhat like the American Revolution—were passionately invoked. But the difficulty was that 1957 was not 1937. A strike now would have to take place within the framework of the contract, signed for three years, and adjustments would therefore be confined to the so-called strike issues such as speed-up, foremen working, relief time and the rehiring of the discharged committeeman.

A cold-blooded analysis showed that this time the company had a good many advantages. One of its major suppliers was itself closed by a strike, so that a shutdown now would have little adverse effect on our company—for that matter, it wouldn't mind closing for a while to avoid paying unemployment benefits. Sales were just fair. Short weeks were being scheduled. The company figured that if it gave some concessions—alleviation on relief time, elimination of foremen working, redress on a few wage classifications—it could afford to stand firm on work standards, perhaps the most important issue in dispute.

For the union the basic difficulty was that while it could get some concessions without a strike, this would not remove the resentments accumulated among the men during the past months, nor would it soften the work standards achieved by the corporation. But we also realized that, judging by settlements in other plants, it was unlikely that a strike could bring better results. So negotiations dragged on for weeks. Most of the union negotiators tried the tactics of the good old days, threatening strike, talking militant; but the extremely able company negotiators were not moved an inch.

In reality this was part of a very significant and, in some respects, ominous process of "educating" the Local negotiators that old-fashioned, tub-thumping bargaining was permanently out of the window. Hard facts and cold logic would carry more weight than vitriolic displays in the 1937 tradition. In this context, the Local negotiators began to feel frustrated. Their political positions in the Local became endangered, since the "outs" were exploiting the inability of the leadership to make quick and major progress.

Hard times usually signify a change in local union leadership unless it remains united, educates the membership on its problems, and offers a comprehensible and constructive program. But this time there were too many bitter feelings, too much anxiety over personal fates and prestige, and so the ranks voted the most vehement critic into the Local presidency. That such a change can solve problems which, by their nature, are beyond the control of the Local or even the UAW as a whole, may well be doubted. Meanwhile, a battered Local, with most of its membership lost and consumed by primitive factionalism, faces not only an uncertain future but an increasing skepticism within its membership.

For the men and women in the shop, the kind of brutal experience they have gone through during the past few years—suffering as they have from the effects of a changing industry, an anti-labor climate, the difficulty faced by the union in solving problems on a purely economic level—has led to a growing sense of insecurity and a kind of personal disorientation which will take a long time to overcome.

The UAW: Over the Top or Over the Hill? (1963)

Harvey Swados

Harvey Swados (1920–1972) was born in Buffalo to an upper-middle-class Jewish family. He attended the University of Michigan during the era of labor militancy in nearby Detroit. During World War II he was a member of the Workers Party while working in aircraft plants and as a merchant seaman in sometimes perilous waters. After the war Swados published novels and short stories, but when funds ran short, he briefly returned to industrial work in a New Jersey auto plant. Out of that experience came one of his most celebrated essays, "The Myth of the Happy Worker," as well as On the Line, *a collection of interconnected short stories evoking the pain, pathos, and intermittent joys of working-class life. Both were published in 1957. Thereafter Swados taught at Sarah Lawrence and the University of Massachusetts. In 1970 he published* Standing Fast, *a novel that recorded the exhilaration and despair of his generation as it moved from the radical hopes of the late 1930s to an acquiescent liberalism decades later.*

In the midst of the great organizing drive of the CIO, which was to culminate in the solid establishment of industrial unionism in the United States, John L. Lewis came to Detroit to address a mass meeting. Some ten thousand people crowded into Olympia Stadium to hear him promise them that they were not alone in their battle to build the United Auto Workers against the thugs and spies of the auto corporations.

A quarter of a century has passed since I sat among that throng of workers and their wives and watched them weeping unashamedly as Lewis exhorted them to stand fast against the corporations and to stand together for a better life. When I returned to Detroit recently with the aim of finding out what has happened to the powerful union built by those workers in the thirties and forties, I found first of all that it is impossible in the sixties to make the kind of generalization that used to come so easily. Even the memories of the participants can be faulty: An officer of the UAW described to me how the elderly come up to him at public functions honoring those who (in increasing thousands) are retiring from working life. "They try to remind me," he said, "of the good old days when we fought together to build the union. The fact is that most of those guys who are retiring now, and were middle-aged then, never lifted a finger to help us when we were young and reckless and had nothing to lose. Our union was built by young men. The middle-aged climbed aboard when it looked safe, but now that they're getting old they like to think that they participated in the early growth of the union."

As a rule, people are eager to associate themselves in memory with institutions which have grown to be not only acceptable but respectable. And respectable the UAW surely is. Any organization which strikes roots and acquires possessions will inevitably become as respectable in the community as any growing middle-class family. More to the point is that this organization, which was built by an alliance of radicals and disaffected workers, was characterized in 1947 by Walter Reuther himself as "the vanguard in America," as "the architects of the future." Is the characterization still valid? Such was the question that I posed to myself a few months ago.

Attempting to answer it is not too unlike attempting to find out what has happened to the American dream in the years since 1947. For if ever a union was typically American, that union is the UAW. Nurtured in the heartland of the United States, it has had to move with the decentralization of the auto industry, so that now well under a half million, or only about one-third of its members, are still in Michigan. Negroes make up perhaps 15 percent (no figures are kept) of its membership, as they do of the population at large. But while, thanks in part to an administration which is admirably free from racism, Negroes have been making excellent progress— Jack Stieber, in his *Governing the UAW,* quotes a forthcoming study on racial practices in unions to the effect that the UAW "probably has more Negroes in staff positions than all other major unions combined"—they are sorely dissatisfied, and have only recently succeeded in getting a Negro onto the Executive Board *as a Negro.*

In other ways too, the composition of this union parallels that of the United States. Not only is it a mixture of native stock (originally lured from southern and border states by promise of high wages) with immigrants and their children from central, southern, and eastern Europe; not only is it a mixture of urbanites and their country cousins, the latter displaced from the land by spreading suburbia or in search of an occupation more central than farming; but it is also made up increasingly of the very old and the very young. The retirees, who retain certain voting rights, are becoming so numerous that they now hold the balance of power in many local unions. What also makes the auto workers seem so typical is that they manufacture the product which more than any other—with the possible exception of the cowboy movie—has represented America to the rest of the world in the 20th century; which, except for a house, is the most expensive object that they themselves ever buy; and which is still enormously important to the American economy as a whole.

Which brings us to our final parallel, and one which should lead into the problems of these men and their union. Just because they are involved in the mass production of a product which is universally regarded almost with veneration, it does not follow that they derive unalloyed satisfaction from their involvement, or that they do not feel alienated from their tasks. And the fact that the auto industry is currently enjoying one of its best years, and that sales records are being broken month after month, does not mean that the vast majority of its workers are enjoying a real sense of security; they have learned from the bitter experience of recent years that seniority, far from guaranteeing employment, has come to serve as a roster for layoffs.

It is these twin specters—dissatisfaction with the job ranging from boredom in some cases to downright hatred in others, and the fear that one may be severed from the job and so severed from any possibility for gainful self-respecting employment—that remain characteristic of the auto worker as they do of millions of other Americans. What has their union done to vanquish these specters? What has it not done that it might have? And what is the relationship of the leaders to the led?

One thing must be made clear at the outset. The auto worker has made tremendous progress, thanks to the UAW and Walter Reuther. He earns a living that is well above the margin of poverty; he is not terrorized by ruthless bosses; he usually lives in a decent home in a decent neighborhood; his children can and often do go to college and leave the working class behind; and he can look forward to retirement not with trepidation but with honest expectation. For his pension is only one of the constantly-expanding fringe benefits which cushion him against the shocks of illness, hospitalization, and old age. What is more, his union has won him these benefits (many younger workers, probably thousands of them, really believe that the benefits have been "given" by the companies rather than wrested from them) without having to be corrupt, crooked, or collusive with the corporation with which it negotiates. Those who incline to excuse the behavior of other union leaders with the comfortable reflection, "at least they deliver," might try to remember that Walter Reuther and the UAW have been delivering, too, without having to deliver themselves or their dues-payers into the hands of goons or mobsters.

But when we say such things about the United Auto Workers and Walter Reuther we have only said letter A. There remains not just an alphabet, but an entire encyclopedia. If, however, we examine only B and C—job dissatisfaction and insecurity—a combination almost as peculiarly American and as unpredictable in its effects on the system as apple pie à la mode, we may learn more about the situation of these particular Americans than by psychoanalyzing their leader or pressing bouquets on the UAW for being what any union ought to be to start with: honest.

This is a problem which began with the industrial revolution and did not end with the Russian revolution—as we have been reminded by East Berlin, Poznan, and Budapest. It used to be known as the class struggle, and it provided part of the motor force for the original growth of the UAW. Now, under a different nomenclature— whether as work standards, speedup, production standards, or whatever lingo is used to indicate a difference of opinion between boss and worker as to how hard or how fast the latter ought to do what the former is paying him for—it continues to plague the UAW as a nagging endless irritation, a sore that will neither heal nor even respond to such medication as participation in profits.

For a while, the sociologists, the labor-management people, and even some labor leaders were assuring us that technological change would raise the workers' levels of skill, responsibility, and initiative. But as the rate of change increases, these assurances have become somewhat muted. "[A]utomation has not altered the fact that most production-line jobs do not produce the kind of occupational involvement or identification necessary to make work a satisfying experience," says Professor William A. Faunce of the Labor and Industrial Relations Center of Michigan State University.

What has happened over the years has been a codification of two basic articles in the endless struggle over the conditions of the job: 1) The inalienable right of the company to establish production standards. 2) The inalienable right of the workers to strike over those production standards (and over health and safety matters also), if the grievance procedures have been exhausted. The UAW-Ford Agreement states: "The right of the Company to establish and enforce production standards is recognized." The UAW–General Motors Agreement puts it this way: "Production standards shall be established on the basis of fairness and equity consistent with the quality of workmanship, efficiency of operations, and the reasonable working capacities of normal operators. The Local Management of each plant has full authority to settle such matters."

Seen from the outside, nothing could be more reasonable. In our economic system, production must supersede everything else. . . . Certainly even the most sophisticated observers concede this as a precondition for the efficient management of what A.A. Berle calls "the American economic republic." "This is the most successful economic system the world has ever seen," Mr. Berle told the *Herald Tribune* Book and Author Luncheon on 29 April, 1963. "We are some eons away from perfection, but—without being Pollyannish— we have an American system which we can call truly great." And indeed the grievance procedure, backed up ultimately by the right to strike, for which the union fought so hard, supposedly humanizes the work situation, and nicely countervails management's pressures for increased productivity, or for profits based on the exploitation of labor.

So it seems from the outside. Seen from the inside, the matter is somewhat different. Since the workers are no more privy to the production standards that will be set by engineers, time and motion study men, and plant supervisors, than they are to such other management prerogatives as product design or pricing, they are continually off balance. The difficulties posed by the fact that the union has no machinery to deal with production standards are simply insuperable. "You can strike one week over standards," a leader of the union said to me, "and next week they'll introduce new standards."

Put another way, the worker is ultimately powerless to protect himself, even when supposedly he has the union behind him, against a management which is determined to tighten the screws on him and his fellows, first in one operation, then in another, first in one department, then—as he reacts by going out on strike unselfishly, not for himself but to protest against even a handful of men being abused—in another. What good does it do to win a battle for yourself or for your fellow workers if you discover after victory not only that the war goes on but that the rules of war have been changed all over again, unilaterally, by your opponent?

But why on earth should the management representatives of the economic republic, who Mr. Berle and others assure us have developed social consciences unique in history, resort to such primitive methods of exploitation as stepping up the work pace, cutting back on lunch hour, cutting down on wash-up time?

The answer lies in the structure of the auto industry. For one thing, the parts supplier companies, which are still important to the UAW, are always being economically squeezed, and in order to stay in business must minimize their labor costs, with or without the cooperation of the union. By and large that cooperation has been forthcoming: the UAW is not an anti-capitalist organization and is committed to holding as many jobs as it can for its members.

If we are to understand fully the role of leaders and staffers in convincing the ranks of the necessity for sacrifice in order to keep their employers competitive, we must tear ourselves away from the cut-throat world of the parts suppliers, in which such euphonious public-relations labels as "Project Progress" are pasted onto sacrifices by the workers—who have no way of knowing the true position of their employers, or even whether their sacrifices will really prevent them from being driven out of business or simply closing down. For there is one other basic fact about the structure of the auto industry which cannot be overlooked, and that is the absolute dominance of General Motors.

If, in 1962, the total profits of the Big Three, after taxes, came to a little over two billion dollars, nearly one and a half billion of those dollars were earned by General Motors. The UAW newspaper, *Solidarity*, has expressed it with direct simplicity: "General Motors made more money in 1962 than any other corporation in the history of the world." This corporation is in fact not only more efficient and more powerful than just about any other corporation; it is also more efficient and more powerful than most states. Again according to *Solidarity*, which seems somewhat uncertain as to whether its readers should be horrified or awed, "the money General Motors took in from sales in 1962 was equivalent to the total expenditures of these major states put together: California, Illinois, Indiana, Michigan, Massachusetts, New York and Ohio."

It is not only that General Motors is so rich that, if all of its plants all over the United States were to be simultaneously destroyed by some national disaster, it could in a year rebuild them all with its own resources and not even have to borrow money.

Most important from the worker's point of view, GM has utilized its gigantic capital accumulation to install in its plants machinery

and equipment far more efficient than those of Ford and more particularly of Chrysler. As a result these weaker firms must—if they
are serious about staying in the race—increase output per worker
to keep their prices competitive, and to accumulate the capital with
which to buy more efficient equipment.

For an outsider, the immediate question arises: Why doesn't the
UAW attempt to challenge GM's production standards, not just for
the benefit of the GM workers, but to take the heat off the Chrysler
and Ford workers? The fact is that—whatever the reasons—it has
not. The consequences of this refusal to take on GM are what we
must now consider.

The UAW leadership functions with what might be called a social democratic outlook. It conceives the job of the union to be to
improve the lot of its members under the going social order, and
when the occasion demands, to shore up the more unstable elements of that order. As the years pass, it finds itself serving not
only its members, but the weaker firms in the auto industry as
well. Since it is precisely in these firms that the workers are apt
to be most squeezed and therefore most restless, it becomes the
self-imposed responsibility of the union to persuade those workers
that their very livelihoods depend on the yielding of concessions to
make their employer competitive.

What is curious, given leaders who once saw themselves as "the
vanguard" in America, is that the salesmanship is directed not so
much at the corporations as at the membership; and that the servicing is done not simply for the dues-payers but for the corporations
as well. In terms of servicing: The union has found it expedient to
cooperate with management to work out supposedly more reasonable production standards, particularly with the Chrysler Corporation, and more recently with parts suppliers. Thereupon it must
program into its transmission line, its Regional Directors and International Representatives, an understanding of the need to hold in
line those most directly responsive to the ranks—the stewards and
the activists—in order that production may continue uninterrupted.

In terms of salesmanship: The Regional Director and the International Rep move in on the workers, after having themselves

been presold at Solidarity House, whose front lawn is appropri-
ately graced by a larger-than-life auto worker sculpted in a style
which might be described as Stalinist Modern. Armed with all
the paraphernalia of entrenched bureaucracy—researchers, clerks,
writers, mimeographs, in addition to superior education, oratori-
cal persuasiveness and access to indirect means of suasion—they
take over local meetings ordinarily devoted to ordinary business,
and hammer away at the need for aiding the employer to become
competitive. The enemy, they explain, is not the employer—himself
a victim, like those in attendance, of circumstances. The enemy
is GM.

Obviously if the employer is determined to maintain those pressures which originally aggravated the workers, the situation is not
going to be resolved by the use of Madison Avenue techniques. And
indeed what often happens is that the workers, goaded beyond en-
durance, turn to their final resource, a strike vote. The strike, however, must be sanctioned by the International.

In such circumstances, one can hardly wonder at the prevalence
of cynicism and apathy among UAW members, or at the fact that
job dissatisfaction continues to be a running sore in the automotive
industry. There have been abortive attempts to attack the ailment
on an industry-wide basis . . . but it seems clear that unless and
until there's a determination to take on GM, in each of whose 135
separate bargaining units disputes on working conditions are settled separately, auto workers will continue to thrash about blindly,
often sacrificing job conditions they had earlier won in years of
militant struggle.

Now when we think of the distance between leaders and led, the
conclusion seems inescapable that the use of manipulative techniques has been widening the gulf that separates the two. If we
talk to the workers about the leaders, we find the latter referred to
as "they." If we talk to the leaders, and to the staffers at Solidarity House and in the various regions, we find the workers referred
to as "they." People who are being manipulated . . . can hardly
be expected to identify, in the old-fashioned fraternal sense, with
their manipulators.

As for the latter, it was inevitable that feelings which were orig-inally prideful and perhaps even boastful should have been grad-ually replaced by attitudes which can often be characterized as at best patronizing and at worst contemptuous.

I was struck by the near-unanimity with which the staffers in-sisted, wherever I encountered them, in Solidarity House, through-out Detroit, and in other areas as well, that the leadership was "ahead of the workers." A man would have to be a fool, or what amounts to the same thing, imbued with a mystic faith in the pu-rity as well as the progressive historical mission of the proletariat, to deny that auto workers, like other workers and like most other Americans in fact, are shot through with racism, jingoism, a per-vasive narrow-mindedness, and a conservative resistance to new ideas; or to deny that their officers and technical advisers are more sophisticated, more free from bigotry and flag-waving, more hospi-table to adventurous thinking. But to say this is hardly to exhaust the subject.

Surely it is precisely those who have led workers to victory in struggles that are now a part of history who should be the first to understand how the struggles themselves function as educational forces for the participants—and the leaders. It is when struggles are postponed or aborted that the fabric of democracy must de-teriorate. It is when people are in motion, and are led toward an ethical goal, that they are most receptive to challenges to received wisdom; more than that, they themselves become innovators, and discover that they are capable of an inventiveness and an intellec-tual audacity of which they themselves could scarcely conceive in less adventurous times.

It is the unofficial contention of the UAW officialdom that their very success in negotiations over the last ten or fifteen years has in a sense foreclosed the possibility of their being "the vanguard in America." That is, the substantial slice of the economic pie that they have gotten for the dues-payer, and the trimmings too, the health insurance, pensions, and the rest, have made him into a pretty satisfied fellow, a member (whether black or white) of an elite, the aristocracy of labor, more concerned with paying off on his home and getting a boat to go fishing than with "taking on GM" or otherwise rocking the boat. Not only is this a fact that can hardly be called into question, it is one that should always be kept in mind in any evaluation of the present situation and the future prospect of these typical Americans. But as I have already tried to indicate, it is very, very far from being a complete explanation for the malaise afflicting an organization which was in the very recent past so magnificently combative and so uncompromisingly democratic. If both of these aspects of the auto worker's position—his increasing well-being and his endless frustration and bitterness on the job— are taken into account, perhaps we shall approach somewhat more closely an understanding of what has become of his union.

But if job dissatisfaction remains as a practically insoluble grievance . . . job insecurity is a much more recent and terrifying phenomenon. This may seem like purposeful misstatement, in view of the facts: that employment in the auto industry has always been seasonal because of model changes and the need for retooling, that long hard-driving periods of overtime have inevitably been followed by long uncertain months of unemployment, and that the auto industry has always been quick to feel the backlash of recession and depression. Furthermore, one of Walter Reuther's finest negotiating achievements, SUB (supplemental unemployment benefits), which has been in effect since 1956, has made employers "think twice about mass hirings and layoffs" (the words are *Business Week's*), and the union's ongoing push toward the GAW (guaranteed annual wage) and an eventual white-collar status for its membership has succeeded so far in penalizing employers for short work weeks and is forcing them to stabilize employment and improve scheduling. When one learns of these substantial steps toward civilized working conditions made by an aggressive and sophisticated union leadership, one is entitled to wonder how the worker can be more insecure now than when he was nothing but a warm body, bought up by the day and dumped often before the day, to say nothing of the season, was over.

The answer is devastatingly simple. In former times, when a worker was laid off he took his gun and went hunting, or he drove back down home to the old folks' farm until word came that they were hiring again. If it got really tough, he went on relief and sweated it out until things picked up and he was called back. Now, a layoff may mean that he will *never* work again.

It is only within the past six or seven years that the impact of the second industrial revolution has begun to be felt in the auto industry (as it had somewhat earlier in the coal mining industry, and as it has yet to be, we are given to understand, in the vast white-collar, clerical, and technical areas of the economic republic). A few figures will indicate what technological innovation and automation are just *beginning* to do to the automotive industry: "In 1953," according to *Newsweek*, "917,000 auto workers turned out 7.3 million cars, trucks, and buses; in 1963, 723,000 workers produced 8.3 million vehicles." Briefly: One million *more* vehicles produced by 184,000 *fewer* workers.

Suppose we narrow this down somewhat. In February 1956, the all-time peak month of auto production, Buick Local 599 of the UAW had 27,635 dues-paying members. In December 1962, the best month since 1956, this local had 13,022 members. Briefly: The Buick plant in Flint, Michigan, is now turning out about the same number of cars that it did six years ago, with about half the number of workers.

Otis Bishop, President of Local 599, claims to be the best crankshaft lathe operator in Buick. He is also old enough to have felt the full force of the depression at first hand; during the worst of it he lived in a freight car for a year. Yet he feels that the prospect of the laidoff, or more accurately the displaced worker, is more frightening now than it was then, and he told me several stories to illustrate his feeling.

Clearly, it is both reasonable and ethical that the UAW work for the abolition of overtime, which is certainly unconscionable during a period when despite new records in auto production some 90,000 auto workers are jobless. But one is entitled to wonder whether this expedient too will result not in putting some of those 90,000 jobless onto the payrolls of the Big Three, but rather, in the long run, in accelerating the process of replacing workers with machines.

In short, the available evidence indicates that what is known in the auto industry as the "improvement factor" works to improve the lot of those fortunate enough to hang on to their jobs, but, far from creating new job opportunities, serves to insure that those whom it disemploys will never again be needed in the industry. The UAW is far from being a jobholders' protective association, like certain of the craft unions. But—despite a splendid program of activities ranging from summer encampments and UN Workshops to a brand new Labor Studies Center—the UAW remains, like the Longshoremen's Union, the Steelworkers' Union, or the Mine Workers', an organization of the employed, committed to its dues-payers and not to those who are steadily disappearing from the industry.

One searches in vain through the roster of staff members involved in research, planning, public relations, etc., etc., for a single man whose primary responsibility is for the unemployed. Nor can one find, in a union brimming over with schemes for getting people to register, moving in on this or that primary, supporting school bond issues, etc., etc., an unemployment program. This lack is, as one staffer frankly conceded to me, "a most shameful abdication of the radical conscience."

It may also explain why in 1956, when there were 200,000 men out of work in the Detroit area, the UAW could draw only (as a UAW leader told me) 2,000 people to a meeting on the West Side, and only 1,300 people to a meeting on the East Side.

The simple truth is that neither the UAW nor any other union, no matter how large its membership, how influential its representatives on Capitol Hill, or how many millions it has invested in gilt-edged securities, has the capacity or the power to resolve problems of this magnitude, even when they affect the lives of its own members. (This is a fact which ought to be borne in mind in all those tiresome discussions on "big labor" and its abuses of the privileges accorded it by a softheaded public.)

"We live in an epoch," B.J. Widick has written, "in which trade unionism increasingly cannot solve union problems." Given his socialist background and his quick intelligence, no labor leader is more aware of this than Walter Reuther. What one must be wary of is making too simple an equation between what a labor leader says and what he is able to do.

Labor leaders like to, often have to, talk big. Just so, one can read about Reuther's political impatience in *U.S. News & World Report*, which says darkly that he "is prepared to urge more forceful pressure on the part of President Kennedy to cure the unemployment problem. It's Mr. Reuther's contention that if the President can't get action from Congress on this problem Mr. Kennedy will be defeated for re-election in 1964." But nothing is arising from the impatience, disenchantment, or bitterness of a nature to trouble Mr. Kennedy's sleep. As Murray Kempton has observed, in connection with the 1962 UAW convention's resolution accepting President Kennedy's decision to resume nuclear testing (after Walter Reuther had earlier opposed test renewal), "it is the posture of the American labor movement to disagree with a decision of President Kennedy's only up to the point that it is made."

Mr. Kennedy, who has never been charged by anyone with being a poor politician, knows perfectly well that Walter Reuther has no place to go. And this is why, it seems to me, Kempton's judgment that Reuther has "fallen out of history" may be cruel—but it is not unjust. Just as Reuther knows that he cannot resolve basic problems of the work situation without taking on GM (a struggle that many observers honestly feel could not be won against the giant of an industry that is geared to make 20 percent profit in a 35-week year), so he knows that he cannot resolve basic economic problems without political action, and more political action than Mr. Kennedy is prepared to undertake. But just as no one can go around Reuther's left in the UAW, who wants to try going around Kennedy's left in the nation?

Whatever Reuther's earlier ambitions may have been—to enter national politics, to take over the AFL-CIO, to be appointed U.S. delegate to the United Nations—they do not now seem relevant to me. If he is deeply frustrated, as he gives every evidence of being, from his compulsive journeying to the fringes of the "Free World" to his wearisome speechifying, that is more significant, for it reflects the

impasse of a million-membered union without which he would be
another Adlai Stevenson or Henry Wallace—or Harold Stassen.

The head of an AFL-CIO union sympathetic to the UAW has described Walther Reuther to me as "ambitious without a specific ambition," and as eager to be at the center of a social movement, but
no longer having a social movement in which to function. If this
is so, it may be at least partly because Reuther has done little to
keep a social movement alive *within his own union*. Throughout that
union, one is continually being reminded of the great role played
by radicals—Wobblies, Socialists, Stalinists, Trotskyists of various
persuasions—not only in building the union but in maintaining
through the 40s and even the 50s the kind of democratic ferment
that raised the persistent notion not merely of trade unionism but
of a movement with goals. When one of Reuther's aides commented
sadly that the union and its leader sorely missed the spur of the
socialist group led by Max Shachtman, I could not but reflect that
not only had Reuther done a job on these political people, he had
also domesticated some of them to the point where they are now to
be found roaming the corridors of Solidarity House, on the payroll.

It is true that the various radical movements have, for the time,
all but disappeared. But radical thinking has not, even within the
precincts of the UAW, thanks to the presence in it of men educated
in the left but not yet ossified. One cannot complain, as one might
with almost any other union, of an absence of intellect, or of lack
of application of that intellect to the problems of our age. What one
can say, I think with justification, is that the UAW leadership no
longer takes its own demands seriously.

Old Working Class, New Working Class (1972)

Michael Harrington

Michael Harrington (1928–1989) was born in St. Louis to a Catholic family. Educated at the College of the Holy Cross and the University of Chicago, he was radicalized when he joined Dorothy Day's Catholic Worker Movement in the early 1950s. However, he soon described himself as but a Catholic "fellow traveler" after joining the Young People's Socialist League, a venerable group then dominated by those supporting Max Shachtman's brand of Trotskyist politics. Harrington became a nationally recognized figure with the publication, in 1962, of The Other America, *a moving, analytical study of poverty in the United States. Thereafter, Harrington proved a leading spokesman for American socialism, especially in the 1970s and 1980s, when he was a prominent figure within the Democratic Socialists of America, a group he had helped found in the late 1960s after the Socialist Party split over the Vietnam War.*

In recent years the American working class has been called conservative, militant, reactionary, progressive, authoritarian, social democratic and, the unkindest cut of all, nonexistent. Except for the last, all the labels fit. The labor movement—I sharpen the focus on the organized section of the working class—contains more blacks than any other institution in American society, as well as more young whites attracted by the populist racism of George Wallace. Notwithstanding its tendencies toward ethnocentrism and anti-intellectualism, the labor movement has provided a decisive political impetus for whatever democratic planning there is in America. The organized workers are, in short, no one thing; they are a varied, dynamic, contradictory mass whose position in society can drive its members toward a practical social idealism, an antisocial corporatism, or any one of the complicated variants between those extremes.

I believe that the American workers have been a crucial force behind every social gain of the past two generations, and in domestic politics their unions constitute an American kind of de facto social democracy. Perhaps the exigencies of the future will deepen the best impulses within the labor movement, and I am on the side of those within it who are fighting for such a development. But my partisanship does not make me an apologist. Precisely because I am concerned and involved, I cannot afford to gloss over tendencies that run counter to my hopes. I must try to understand the past and present of the working class with as much candor as possible if I am to help those struggling to create its future.

It is an extraordinary thing that those who argue there is no working class in the United States can be found at the most disparate points of the political spectrum. Herbert Marcuse, who had a notable influence on the New Left youth of the 1960s, writes that " 'the people,' previously the ferment of social change, have 'moved up' to become the ferment of social cohesion." Paul Sweezy and the late Paul Baran, sympathizers first with Russian, then with Chinese Communism, argued that the organized workers in the United States have been "integrated into the system as consumers and ideologically conditioned members of the society." Perhaps the most emphatic statement of the theme comes from Clark Kerr, a brilliant, pragmatic technocrat. He holds that "the working class not only tends to disappear as a class-conscious and recognizable element in society; it needs to disappear if modern industrial society is to operate with full effectiveness." High technology, he continues, requires consensus and cooperation and therefore cannot tolerate class conflict over basic principles. So even though there are obvious differences between industrialists and file clerks, there are not "any clear class lines to divide them—only infinite gradations."

I disagree with those, from the authoritarian Left to the democratic Center, who think that the American working class does not exist (the Right, which I will not consider here, tends to have a vulgar Marxist, or paranoid, version of the power of organized labor). To use Marx's famous distinction, the working class in this country is not simply a class "in itself"—a mass sharing "a common situation and common interests"— but it is a class "for itself" and the "interests which it defends . . . [are] class interests."

First of all, consider the "old" working classes: the primarily blue-collar workers who do physical labor in the industrial economy. It has renewed itself in the last quarter of a century and become a greater force in American politics than at any time in the nation's history.

The total nonagricultural labor force in 1969 numbered 77.902 million men and women. Of these, 48.993 million were "production and nonsupervisory workers on private payrolls," with the 14.647 million in manufacturing the largest single component. Another 12.591 million were employed by federal, state, and local government, and many of them held down such blue-collar and organizable jobs as sanitation man or postman. There were 20.210 million union members, mainly concentrated in machinery, transportation equipment, contract construction, and transportation services.

This working class, both organized and unorganized, has a "common situation and common interests," experienced first and foremost in the reality that it does not have enough money. In 1969 the Bureau of Labor Statistics computed a "modest" budget for an urban family of four at $9,076, an amount in excess of the income of well over half the families in the United States. The "modest" standard, it must be emphasized, lives up to its name: it allows for a two-year-old used car and a new suit every four years. In addition to this deficiency in income, most of the union members are employed in manufacturing, construction, and transportation, i.e., in jobs with little intrinsic interest and, in the case of an assembly line in an auto plant, a dehumanizing routine. They are paid not as individuals but as members of a class: after the age of 25, the worker's income does not normally vary with increasing experience, as does that of professional and managerial employees, but usually rises as part of a negotiated group settlement. Indeed, the very fact of being paid a wage by the hour emphasizes another determinant of working-class existence, the vulnerability of the job to the vagaries of the business cycle, the ever-present possibility of being laid off.

How is it that such a massive social phenomenon and such obvious trends have been ignored, or declared nonexistent, by many observers? In part, as Penn Kemble has argued, the vantage point of intellectual perception has changed radically during the past 30 years. The social critics of the 1960s and early '70s are relatively affluent compared to the marginality and even joblessness they had experienced during the Depression. This change in their own class position may have made them less sensitive to the daily struggles of less favored people.

Somewhat more subtly, there were those who acknowledged the existence of the traditional working class but argued that it had become co-opted by the society and therefore lost its distinctive character. But that, as we have just seen, is a misleading simplification. It may be that the workers, as Sweezy and Baran argue, want to be "integrated into the society as consumers," but it is surely of greater moment that the structure of injustice will not allow them, as a rule, even a "modest" income.

Still, the most sophisticated revision of the idea of the working class is based upon a very real, and momentous, shift in class structure (a shift that is also, as will be seen, the key to the emergence of a "new" working class). It is argued that economic classes defined by property relationships—entrepreneurs owning factories, shopkeepers their little businesses, farmers and peasants their plots of land, and workers possessing only their labor power to sell—have become obsolete. The joint stock company, Ralf Dahrendorf holds, separated ownership and control and thereby obviated a theory of class determined by property or the lack of it. He concludes that in the advanced economies authority, not ownership, is central to the formation of social class. And Alain Touraine writes, "It is anachronistic to depict social armies confronting each other. As we pass from societies of accumulation to programmed societies, relationships of power become increasingly more important than opposition between social groups."

These theories are usually developed with the comment that Marx, fixated as he was upon a primitive model of capitalism, was unaware of such changes. For even granting that there have been profound transformations in the structure of the advanced economies, some of them unforeseen by even so perspicacious a thinker as Marx, what is it that makes the workers I have just described more likely to join unions than any group in society? What predisposes them toward a certain political point of view? The answer, I believe, is embarrassingly old-fashioned. These workers derive their livelihoods almost exclusively from the sale of their labor power on an anonymous, and uncertain, labor market and it is quite easy to distinguish them from their "fellow employees" who are corporation presidents or managers. There is a social chasm between these groups, not the infinite gradations postulated by Clark Kerr.

To begin with, in the upper reaches of the society property is not quite so passe as the notion of a clear-cut "separation" of ownership and control suggests. A 1967 *Fortune* survey revealed that 30 percent of the 500 largest industrial concerns "are clearly controlled by identifiable individuals or by family groups." More generally, the nonowning managers at the top of the society accumulate wealth. They often enjoy special stock deals and other arrangements: in 1971 the *Wall Street Journal* reported that the biggest part of executive pay in the auto industry was a bonus based on the size of profits. So it is that these managers must be counted among the golden elite.

There is a distinct and identifiable universe of the working class even after one has taken into account the tremendous changes in class structure since Marx. The pay is better now, the boom-and-bust rhythm has been attenuated, the famous built-in stabilizers, such as unemployment insurance, are at work. Yet there are crucial elements of working-class life—relative deprivation, the impersonality of the work process, greater susceptibility to layoffs than experienced by other groups in the society, group wages—which remain and are the objective determinants of the class itself.

The theory that America has always been immune from the class struggle is the generalization of a profound half-truth. A country without a feudal past, possessing a vast continent to be settled once genocide had been committed against the Indians, and populated by successive waves of immigrants from the most varied European backgrounds, must differ in a number of crucial ways from the nation-states of the Old World where capitalism first emerged. Lenin wrote of America (and Britain) that there were "exceptionally favorable conditions, in comparison with other countries, for the deep-going and widespread development of capitalism."

Morris Hilquit, theorist of American socialism in the first third of the century, also talked of the "exceptional position" of America with its vast land mass, its prosperous agriculture, its tendency to make wage labor seem only a "temporary condition." But once we grant the apparent uniqueness of American capitalism, is it indeed true that class consciousness failed to play an important, much less a decisive, role in the nation's history? I think not. The conditions we describe as "American exceptionalism" slowed the emergence of that consciousness. It did not, however, stop social class from becoming the most important single determinant in our political life.

Moreover, the chief factor inhibiting and distorting working-class self-consciousness was not, as is widely thought, the wealth of the society. Werner Sombart's famous remark that socialism in America ran aground "on shoals of roast beef and apple pie" was made in 1906 and has survived as a myth until this day. Indeed, if one compares Germany and the United States between 1890 and 1914, the workers experienced steadily a relative rise in their living standards in the country that produced a mass social democratic movement rather than in the one that did not. But if it was not prosperity that prevented the development of a socialist class consciousness in America, what was? Selig Perlman provided part of the answer in his seminal *Theory of The Labor Movement*:

American labor remains the most heterogeneous laboring class in existence—ethnically, religiously and culturally. With a working class of such composition, to make socialism or communism the official "ism" of the movement would mean, even if other conditions permitted it, deliberately driving the Catholics, who are perhaps a majority in the American Federation of Labor, out of the labor movement, since with them an irreconcilable opposition to socialism is a matter of religious principle. Consequently, the only acceptable "consciousness" for American labor as a whole is "job consciousness" with a limited objective of "wage and job control.". . .

Perlman was right: heterogeneity made it impossible to organize the great mass of the newly arriving European workers until the 1930s and acted, in a thousand different ways, to impede consciousness of membership in a single and united class. Yet Perlman was wrong: even in the 1920s when he wrote, and much more so later on, the workers were constantly forced by the exigencies of their class situation to go beyond "wage and job control" and raise class issues about the organization of the entire society. Strangely enough, many scholars failed to take note of this significant phenomenon. For they had adopted, even when they were antisocialist, the criteria of the left wing of the Socialist party: that class consciousness must necessarily and exclusively take the form of allegiance to a socialist or worker's party. That party alliance did not come about; class consciousness did.

For all the dramatic struggles of the 1930s, it is clear in retrospect that the working class was not in a revolutionary mood. This point must be stressed because many scholarly critics of the notion of a class struggle in the U.S. have unwittingly adopted, not simply a Marxian definition of the concept, but a "romantic" Marxian definition. For Raymond Aron, a seminal theorist of the notion of "industrial society" (i.e., of consensus capitalism), the class struggle only exists where there is a "fight to the death" between workers and capitalists which eventuates in violence.

Such an idea can indeed be found in *The Communist Manifesto*, for it is a corollary of Marx's youthful error of supposing that society was fast polarizing into only two classes. But the mature Marx did not hold this view and defined the class struggle in a far more subtle and complex fashion which can also serve as an excellent guide to the reality of the American 1930s. In his famous Inaugural Address to the International Workingmen's Association, Marx spoke of a campaign to restrict the working day to ten hours in England as "a struggle between the blind rule of supply and demand, which is the political economy of the middle class, and the social control of production through intelligence and foresight, which is the political economy of the working class."

The kind of class struggle envisioned in *The Manifesto* did not emerge in the America of the 1930s or since; the kind analyzed in the Inaugural Address has. Given the obvious exigencies of the situation, the workers were committed as a class—and, with the elections of 1936, organized as a class—to win full-employment policies requiring that the government manage the economy. But if the American workers thus committed themselves to "the social control of production through intelligence and foresight, which is the political economy of the working class," they did not call this policy "socialist." It was not simply that the historic factors identified by Perlman were at work. Beyond that Americanism had become a kind of "substitutive socialism." In this country, as distinct from Europe, bourgeois ideology itself stressed equality, classlessness, and the opportunity to share in wealth.

So in the 1930s there emerged a mass political movement based upon class institutions (the unions) which demanded, not simply narrow legislation related to the needs of this or that trade or craft, but a mode of planned social organization that would give priority to the value of full employment. Since it involved significant modifications of capitalist society as it had existed until then in the United States, this idea met with violent resistance, both physical and ideological, from most employers. They recognized that, even though the worker insisted upon his loyalty to the American ideal, he was reading it in terms of his own class needs.

For all of its truly exceptional characteristics, American capitalism eventually forced its working class to become conscious of itself and to act as a major factor in political life. The labor movement [has moved] into politics in a much more profound way than in the

1930s. By the end of the 1960s, the AFL-CIO, the Auto Workers, and
the Teamsters all supported an ongoing political apparatus which,
in terms of money, lobbying, campaign workers, and the like, was a
major factor in the United States. As David Greenstone documents
in his book *Labor in American Politics*, "the emergence of organized
labor as a major, nationwide electoral organization of the national
Democratic Party was the most important change in the *structure*
of the American party system during the last quarter of a century."

The unions thus became a class political force, even if in a fairly
undramatic way. There was little rhetoric of class war. Yet the very
appearance of national health insurance as a political issue is primarily the result of a campaign waged for years by George Meany
and Walter Reuther. Even in the area of race, where so many observers tend to pit blacks against the unions, labor is the most integrated single institution in U.S. society and has done more to raise
the living standards of black Americans than any force, except the
federal government. In 1968, for instance, the polls indicated significant support for George Wallace among young white workers in
the North during the early fall. Yet when election day came, most of
those same workers voted for Hubert Humphrey. Most of them had
not changed their personal prejudices in the process, but they had
understood that the exigencies of their class situation demanded
they vote for a full-employment economy rather than against
blacks—i.e., for Humphrey, not Wallace.

This kind of collectivism is far from the romantic Marxian consciousness as defined by Aron, but it is distinctive and clearly goes
beyond narrow organizational interests. Moreover, there are a good
many indications that the unions will be forced to be even more political in the coming period. It is now apparent, even to its sophisticated devotees, that the free market is utterly incapable of allocating
the resources of a technological society in a rational fashion. In 1971
Daniel Bell, who only a decade earlier had talked of the end of ideology, wrote, "It seems clear to me that, today, we in America are
moving away from a society based on a private enterprise market
system toward one in which the most important economic decisions
will be made at the political level, in terms of consciously defined

"goals" and "priorities." It is on the basis of this analysis that Bell has been writing about a "post-industrial" society in which the decisive "new men" are the "scientists, the mathematicians, the economists and the engineers of the new computer technology. . . . The leadership of the new society will rest, not with business or corporations . . . but with the research corporation, the industrial laboratories, the experimental stations and the universities."

It is at this point that the politics of the American working class become crucial. For if it is indeed true that economic decisions will be increasingly made by a political rather than a market process; if the question is how to manage the economy rather than whether to do so, then what mass force is there in society to fight for social values? Some "new men" might join a progressive political coalition in their off-duty hours but, under present conditions, their working lives will be dominated by corporate values that oppose, or at least would severely limit, any restrictions on the company's freedom of action. Moreover, the corporations tend to favor reactionary Keynesianism, in which the economy is stimulated by incentives to capital rather than through the meeting of human needs, which is social Keynesianism. The largest and most effective force in the society with a commitment to that kind of progressive Keynesianism is the trade union movement.

This working class, very different from the one studied by Marx, is at the moment going through a new mutation—one that has given rise to theories about a "new" working class. There is no question that a momentous transformation of the American class structure is taking place. In 1980, according to the projections of the Department of Labor, there will be 15.5 million professional and technical workers and 15.4 million operatives (assemblers, truck drivers, bus drivers). That obviously describes a profound shift away from the industrial proletariat of semiskilled workers. In *Toward a Democratic Left* I spoke of these people as a "new class" rather than a "new working class" because I wanted to stress the discontinuities signaled by their appearance. In the present context my focus will be upon those factors which drive such professionals, technicians, and others in a trade union direction—toward collective bargaining on the job and political pressure for full-employment policies outside the job. So I speak of a new working class. The choice of terms is not crucial; the careful delineation of a new social reality is.

The new stratum on which we focus is not based upon property or employment in the private corporation. Its members work, for the most part, in public, or semipublic sectors—education, health, social services, defense and defense-related industries, aerospace—and they are therefore dependent on federal political decisions for their economic wellbeing. They also tend to be employed by large organizations and often, for all their educational attainments, they are subordinate participants in a hierarchical system.

And it is obvious that in many aspects of their life, above all in their education and income, most of these people more clearly resemble the salaried middle class than the working class. Yet there are important parallels between the new strata and the traditional working class; indeed, they permit one to speak of a "new working class" so long as it is understood that the phrase cannot be taken as a precise definition. Most of the new strata members occupy subordinate positions in large production units, and this is the basis for the unionism and "near unionism" which has already developed among them. Second, almost all of them are in jobs directly dependent upon the political process, and this means that their notion of collective bargaining includes political action from the very outset. At the top of the income scale, particularly among the scientists and the engineers, the new strata shade off into the upper reaches of management; at the bottom, among the scientific technicians without college degrees, they merge with the more skilled members of the traditional working class. But in between those limits there is a large new grouping, numbered in the millions, which, for all its middle-class education and income, is impelled by virtue of its position in society toward collective bargaining and politics.

All of this should not be taken as implying extreme optimism about a future in which a still dynamic old working class will join with the organized new working class to make the good society. There are status factors that can, and have, kept these groups far apart. There is a tendency toward corporatism in the new strata and in the old working class as well, with an emphasis on a very narrow and self-interested job protection. But there also is at least the possibility that the progressive tendencies in these two working classes, old and new, could provide the basis for a new political coalition in America dedicated to social and democratic—eventually perhaps social democratic—planning.

Images of Labor (1981)

Irving Howe

Irving Horenstein (1920–1993), the co-founder and first editor of Dissent, *was born in the Bronx to immigrant, working-class Jews from Bessarabia. Well before graduating from City College in 1940, Howe had become a Trotskyist, first in the Young People's Socialist League and then as a member of the Workers Party, where Max Shachtman was the guiding ideological figure. Howe edited the party's agitational newspaper,* Labor Action, *for nearly two years before being drafted into the army, where he served in Alaska. After the war, Howe's writing gravitated toward a politically inflected literary criticism, although his first published book, co-authored with B.J. Widick, was the* The UAW and Walter Reuther *(1949). While editing* Dissent *he taught for many years at Brandeis. Among his most important works were* Politics and the Novel *(1957),* World of Our Fathers: The Journey of the East European Jews to America and the Life They Found and Made *(1976), and* Socialism and America *(1985). With Michael Harrington he helped found in 1972 the Democratic Socialist Organizing Committee, later Democratic Socialists of America. The essay that follows is taken from Howe's introduction to* Images of Labor *(Pilgrim Press, 1981).*

That there has long been in the United States a working class numbering in the millions, with needs and interests of its own; that significant aspects of the experience and culture of these workers set them apart, even if not quite so sharply as in Europe, from other social classes; that many American workers have organized themselves into trade unions which together comprise a powerful labor movement, defending the rights of its members and often acting in behalf of social betterment throughout the nation—all of these may seem utterly self-evident statements, indeed, self-evident to the point of the commonplace. *But* they are not. For the truth is that the working class, both as actuality and idea, has never been wholly accepted in American society or adequately reflected in American culture. My own recollections from school and college are that trade unions or the workers as a distinct social group were rarely mentioned in classrooms or textbooks. If you look at our popular culture—from comic strips to movies, from novels to television—you will be struck by the extent to which this crucial segment of the American people is blocked out. A film like *Norma Rae* comes to seem notable simply because it is there.

Why should this be so? One reason, I think, is that a recognition of the working class as a major component of American society runs counter to the dominant American myth. That is a myth of a nation of independent craftsmen, small farmers, sturdy business-men, usually self-employed, sometimes hiring a few "hands," but mostly succeeding through their own industriousness and sobri-ety. It is a myth closer to the realities of the age of Jefferson, even Andrew Jackson, than the age of Nixon and Carter.

The persistence of this myth in American life is something to marvel at. It fails increasingly to describe our social reality, yet it hangs on. It is utterly inadequate to, indeed, glaringly in contradic-tion with the America of giant industries, massive plants, concen-trated wealth, and enormous, multinational corporations.

But people want it, need it.

That this myth once had great liberating power in our society and culture; that it still has some attractive moral elements, such as a stress on individual effort and a defense of private life—yes, of course. But in its decline from Ralph Waldo Emerson to Herbert Hoover (and all the mini-Hoovers of later years), it has often dis-abled us from seeing what is there in front of our collective nose.

And still, we cling to that myth. We cling to its picture of a small-town or pastoral nation, if only because it answers some deep need within us, some overpowering nostalgia. Perhaps it's a case of what historians call "cultural lag," sentiment and idea lagging behind reality. Sometimes this lagging can even serve a useful purpose: it may enable keen criticisms of our social arrangements. Sometimes, I would say more often, this myth is cynically exploited, as in political ballyhoo and corporate advertising. Anti-union corporations appeal to the tradition of "individualism"—as if a solitary worker, unlinked with the workers next to him, could ever be a match for the wealth and power of a giant company!

One reason for the reluctance to acknowledge the sheer idea of an American working class has been the claim—and it has some truth to it—that things in America are "different." American workers, it is said, are not so rigidly held into fixed or limited class positions as workers in Europe. That may also explain why the American labor movement has not been nearly so friendly to socialist ideas as the European labor movement. And as I say, there is some truth to these claims, though with the passage of time, less and less truth. Mainly, however, the idea of the working class as a distinct and major presence in American life has not been fully accepted because of our incorrigible nostalgia for an earlier, simpler America where there were few industrial laborers, few large corporations, few immense cities.

But there is no going back. Whatever else, for good or bad, we cannot go back to this earlier America. It no longer exists, except in isolated pockets here and there. We will either work our way to a more democratically humane and socially just society within the context of advanced industrialism, or we will drift further into a corporate-dominated, bureaucratically-managed society. In either case, however, advanced industrialism (or post-industrialism) will remain, and so too will a significant working class and strong labor movement.

What seems especially strange about these failures in national self-perception is that work as human activity finds a very important place in 19th century American literature. In Whitman's poems work is lyrically celebrated; in Mark Twain's *Life on the Mississippi* work is lovingly evoked; in Herman Melville's *Moby Dick* work is described with a passion for exact detail. For the most part, however, the work portrayed in 19th century American literature is that of the independent craftsman—the steam-boatman of Twain, the day printer of Whitman. And the same seems to be true for 19th century American painting.

The worker as we know him and her first appears in a strange, haunting story by Melville, "The Paradise of Bachelors and the Tartarus of Maids." Set in a 19th century factory, this story anticipates the work that we know in factories and shops: the dehumanized labor of men and women tending machines. "At rows of blank-looking counters sat rows of blank-looking girls, with blank, white folders in their blank hands, all blankly folding blank paper. . . . The human voice was banished from the spot. Machinery—that vaunted slave of humanity—here stood menially served by human beings, who served mutely and clingingly as the slave serves the Sultan."

This anticipation—eerie, moving—of modern factory life is notable for its rarity. Only with Theodore Dreiser's great novel, *Sister Carrie*, in which a young farm girl suddenly finds herself laboring in a Chicago shoe factory, do we fully confront the modern industrial world. Dreiser offers a grueling description of the tediousness and exhaustion of factory labor: "Her hands began to ache at the wrists and then in the fingers, and toward the last she seemed one mass of dull, complaining muscles, fixed in an eternal position, and performing a single mechanical movement. . . ."

Such recognitions are not the rule. It is easier to slip into the cliches of "individualist" nostalgia and bland denial, ignoring the reality of the American workers, pretending they have little or no shared existence. But to block out of our national consciousness the lives of millions upon millions of human beings is a form of snobbery. It is reactionary. It is inhumane.

Once American society entered the era of industrial urbanism in the last third of the 19th century, it underwent a major change in social structure. The dynamic of capitalist development brought a greater concentration of economic power. Now, most workers were employed by an impersonal company or corporation. Populations

were reshuffled. Millions left the small towns and farms. The craftsman faded from the scene. Lifestyles were adapted to the stringent
demands of the factory. No longer—except in a few "light" industries like those manufacturing women's garments—could work be
located in the home or done by the family. The lure of business profits led to large-scale manufacturing away from home, outside the
family, cut off from familiar community, beyond any previously-
known structure of work.

More and more, the factory came to be an institution antithetical
to humane values. No longer was "sweat" a metaphor for the satisfying reward of a day's toil. Instead it meant work in airless lofts
that were often incubators of disease, or on assembly lines with no
safety standards. Wages were often as close to subsistence as employers could get away with.

It's roughly at this historical moment, in the latter half of the 19th
century, that large-scale unionism was born. There had of course
been unions before then, heroic and combative ones earlier in the
century. But now, driven by need into the vast new complexes of
city and factory, and often consisting of immigrants still confused
by their new circumstances in America, the workers began to organize in self-defense.

It was hard. Blood was shed and repressive legislation enacted.
Brutal injunctions were issued by union-busting judges. The early
years of the American labor movement form a desperate time, not
nearly well-enough known. It is a time of violent struggle, of strikes
kept going through struggle and defeat, of a society still largely operating with the laws of the jungle, a crude notion of "survival of
the fittest."

Even in these early, difficult years, the labor movement stressed
more than hours and wages, desperately urgent as hours and wages
were to millions of people. This country could not have survived
as a democracy if its working people had not enforced the claims
and enlarged the scope of democracy by organizing in protection
of their rights. You can always measure the level of democracy in
any country by the freedom its workers have to organize unions of
their own choosing. But more: the unions struggled for some larger

vision of fraternity and decency. They were among the major social groups that campaigned for free, universal public education. They imbued their members with a sense of dignity, the persuasion that they were not just numbered cogs in someone else's machine.

There have been hundreds, thousands of union battles. It turned out that you had to keep fighting all the time, in defense of rights already won, on behalf of improvements long overdue. There was no resting. Unions that fell back on their haunches were soon unions without members, without achievements. Because no matter how much employers and their spokesmen sweet-talked, they were always ready to take the initiative, begin a counter-attack. Efforts were made to form a national federation of unions: some failed because the times were not yet ripe and the opposition was too fierce, but later, others succeeded. The Knights of Labor, which by the 1880s had close to a million members, was a mixture of lodge and union. The Knights practiced all sorts of secret rituals, partly for the fun of it, partly to protect themselves from informers. Flourishing for a time and then declining, the Knights were replaced in 1886 by the American Federation of Labor, the most stable grouping of American unions we've ever had. Even in its youthful fragility, the AFL made a mark by campaigning, under Samuel Gompers' shrewd pragmatic leadership, for the eight-hour day. In language more conservative than earlier unions, though in practice often fighting bitter battles, the AFL usually avoided political and ideological issues and concentrated on "bread and butter." Bread being expensive and butter scarce, this strategy often worked. The AFL became the umbrella group for a number of strong craft unions made up mostly of skilled workers; but millions of industrial workers, supposedly "unorganizable," were ignored. They had to wait till the early 1930s, when the CIO was formed under the colorful leadership of John L. Lewis, the head of the miners' union. Spurred by the wretched circumstances of the Depression years, enabled partly by New Deal legislation, and often staffed by idealistic young radicals, the CIO swept through the country organizing auto, steel, chemicals, rubber, and a bit later hospital and municipal employees. It was an exciting moment. I remember it from my own early adolescence when hundreds of thousands of workers poured into the unions, went out on sit-down strikes, suddenly showed remarkable gifts of organization and capacities for sacrifice. In 1955 the AFL and CIO came together in one federation.

Strong though it remains, the AFL-CIO still represents only about a fifth of the American working class. Major gains have been made since the days of Franklin Roosevelt and John L. Lewis—don't let anyone tell you otherwise! The "welfare state"—which means a society that doesn't trust to the magical "laws of the market" but intervenes actively in behalf of the poor and helpless—is still very far from what it should be. But the lives of millions of workers are now far better than they were several decades ago. We have old age pensions, social security, unemployment insurance, and above all, the right to organize. Even when some hard-bitten corporations tried, in the late 1970s, to bust unions, they had to go against the more-or-less established norms of the society; in the late 1920s, it was the exact opposite.

Let's be candid. Trade unions are led by men and women, not saints; their membership consists of fallible human beings, not ideal "proletarians." This is to say that trade unions have their faults. Some are very far from what they should be with regard to internal democracy; the record concerning treatment of opposition and dissident groups is spotty. Other unions are hidebound, rigid, and unconcerned with anything but the immediate needs of their members. (Not that there is anything wrong with being concerned with immediate needs!) Still other unions have until recently discriminated against blacks—I'm pretty sure that while there have been major improvements in this respect, there is still room for more. And only recently have unions begun to show an appropriate sensitivity to the demands and needs of women.

The prejudices of our society and the corruptions of our culture necessarily seep into the unions. It could hardly be otherwise, but this makes them a target for criticism. Some of that criticism is valid, some not.

I've already indicated the kinds of criticism that seem sensible, but here let me mention two kinds that do not. The first kind comes from sectarian "leftists" who complain that unions collaborate with employers (but they have to sign contracts, they have to work within the limits of the given situation, even if they are also trying to extend those limits). That unions don't take the lead in making revolutions is entirely understandable, since they aren't organized for that purpose; they are organized to protect the interests of all workers, both the vast majority who don't want revolutions and the tiny minority who say they do. The other kind of criticism comes from high-minded middle-class folk who, from some perch of rectitude, complain that unions aren't sufficiently concerned with "the general welfare." Let's acknowledge that sometimes this is true. But more often, it is nonsense. For when unions fight for minimum wage laws or regulations providing safety on the job, they are protecting millions upon millions of people, including many who are not even union members. There's a tendency in American discourse to talk about some abstract "public," but in fact the actual public contains a very large segment of working people. When I read an editorial or hear a speech counterposing the "public" to the unions, I grow suspicious.

I come from the generation that entered early adolescence just as this country was succumbing to the Great Depression. The desperation, the poverty, the sheer sense of helplessness of those days forms an experience almost impossible to communicate to younger people lucky enough not to have known it firsthand.

My parents had to find jobs in the garment industry once their little store went bankrupt in 1931. I remember my mother coming home exhausted each evening, and ending the week with a $12 paycheck. I remember my father, who stood all day over a steaming press-iron, coming home during the summer months with blisters all over his body. When the great strike of the garment workers was called by the International Ladies Garment Workers Union in 1933, my folks, who had had no experience with unions before, responded immediately. Like tens of thousands of others, they picketed, they borrowed money for food, they stood fast. The strike over, my mother brought home her first new paycheck: $27. It seemed like heaven: we felt freer, better, stronger. And there was meat on the table. After that, my folks were never active in the union, but they paid their dues faithfully, and if a strike was called, they were the first to go out. This was the ethic I grew up with, the ethic of solidarity. Almost half a century later, I still believe in it.

So when I hear snobs and reactionaries attack unions, I find myself going into a rage. Sure, I know the unions are open to criticism on many counts; but I continue to believe that without them our lives would be far worse than they are. I know for certain that mine would have been far worse. The unions form a backbone of social strength; they make life a little better for the underpaid, the oppressed; I want them to improve but I want them to grow stronger too.

It is time we recognized, in our social arrangements and our cultural experience, the centrality of the American working class. Much of what passes among us for immigrant history, as well as the history of minority groups, really has to do with the working class. If we don't within the working class of this country have as cohesive and visible a "common culture" as has existed in Europe, that is partly due to the diversity, the newness, the sheer size of America. But dig a little beneath the surface, brush aside the conventional myths and cliches of American middle-class life, and you will find plenty of evidence that workers and their unions ought to be far more prominent in our cultural expression than they are. Not in any crude propagandistic sense, but with sympathetic and critical honesty.

PART II

Democracy in American Trade Unions?

Are American trade unions democratic? If not, why not? And what can be done to make them so? Those questions vexed editors of and contributors to *Dissent* ever since the magazine's founding. Indeed, the 1950s were an era when the issue of democracy and corruption within U.S. trade unions attained great prominence, highlighted by the sensational hearings headed by Arkansas senator John McClellan, during which a youthful Robert Kennedy, then the committee's chief counsel, locked horns with Teamster leader Jimmy Hoffa. Focused upon union racketeering and corruption, the 1957–59 McClellan Committee hearings did much to tarnish the reputation of all unions regardless of how they were governed and led. Conservatives hostile to any sort of trade unionism led the charge, but leftists could hardly stand aside because socialists and radicals had long championed rank-and-file voice and democratic governance within the trade unions that claimed to represent working-class interests.

Undemocratic and corrupt practices within the trade unions came in many forms, but there were two categories that came under the scrutiny of *Dissent* writers. The first arose out of the Hobbesian economic conflicts that characterized an urban world far removed from the great steel mills, packinghouses, and auto assembly plants that the CIO would organize. Here were the construction sites, trucking firms, restaurants, hotels, laundries, bakeries, and service trades that craft and occupational unions fought to organize against intense employer hostility, especially in the era before the Wagner Act began to legalize and structure industrial relations. This was a lawless realm of petty entrepreneurship, police corruption, political payoffs, and gangland violence. Amid such social and economic chaos, craft unions like the Teamsters and the Building Service Employees International Union (forerunner of the SEIU), the plumbers, carpenters, and others in the building trades often used strong-arm tactics and backroom deals to regulate the labor market. In these highly decentralized organizations, many local union leaders came to see their operation as something close to a family enterprise, and if the Wagner Act and the New Deal made organizing all the easier, then it was an even larger and more valuable business, jealously guarded from any challenge, be it that of an employer or rank-and-file unionist.

Even more troublesome to most of the *Dissent* labor partisans was the issue of democratic governance—or its absence—in the great industrial unions that had exploded out of the 1930s. Here personal corruption was not normally the problem, nor were democratic formalities abridged: on the local level, contests for union leadership in the Steel Workers, the Mine Workers, the UAW, and many other big industrial unions were hard fought and frequent. But most of these institutions were centralized one-party regimes, where a challenge to the top leadership was something close to treason. In his 1948 study of labor leadership, *The New Men of Power*, C. Wright Mills, an early *Dissent* writer, analogized the industrial union leader to a general who recruits and commands an insurgent army. That role demanded the capacity to both mobilize and manipulate the membership because, as Mills put it, the labor leader "organizes discontent and then he sits on it, exploiting it in order to maintain a continuous organization; the labor leader is a manager of discontent."

Nearly a decade later United Steel Workers general counsel Arthur Goldberg used the same military metaphor to justify the union leadership's opposition to an insurgent challenge. The USW was engaged in a continual battle with a set of corporate adversaries who sought the union's defeat and destruction. Discipline in the ranks, not division, was essential to survival. That same mentality was apparent in the UAW, where Walter Reuther had come to power after a hyperdemocratic, decade-long faction fight. But once his caucus monopolized all the top officers, he made sure that no serious challenge arose to the leadership team he commanded. As Reuther told a 1951 UAW convention, "We are not fighting on top and there is no reason why there should be a single fight on the local union level. You are going to have contests for offices. . . . But let's have democratic contests without factionalism. Let's have democracy, but not factionalism." For the next half-century and more, Reuther and his successors would win election with close to 99 percent of the vote from UAW delegates at each union convention.

All who wrote for *Dissent* were labor partisans and most thought such autocratic leadership demobilized the membership, thereby opening the union to the kind of corporate assault those same high-handed union officials sought to forestall. Add an element of corruption to the mix, and public support for the trade unions would soon evaporate, enabling right-wing forces to fill the policy vacuum. And that is precisely what happened when Congress passed the Labor Management Reporting and Disclosure Act in 1959 (the Landrum-Griffin Act). While the new law did contain a "bill of rights" for rank-and-file unionists, Landrum-Griffin also tightened Taft-Hartley prohibitions against secondary boycotts—a once powerful weapon that facilitated interunion solidarity—and also enhanced federal government regulation of union finances far beyond that of any other voluntary association.

In the first article reprinted here, Paul Jacobs explains the sources of Jimmy Hoffa's genuine popularity within the Teamsters at a moment when a set of court-appointed monitors were supervising the internal affairs of a union notorious for both corruption and organizing effectiveness. In explaining his larger-than-life persona, Jacobs makes the point that Hoffa's methods and mentality were not in fact all that different from other union officials who also commanded a big union during an era of social and political conservatism.

A federal prosecution for jury tampering would eventually send Hoffa to prison, but there was no rank-and-file revolt against his leadership. Not so in the Mine Workers and the Steel Workers during the early 1970s, where Herman Benson and William Kornblum explain how and why union insurgents defeated an entrenched leadership. In the Mine Workers the murder of union dissident Joseph Yablonski, funded and orchestrated by UMW president Tony Boyle, touched off a successful movement to democratize the union and throw Boyle out—and into prison. Help came from the Labor Department, the courts, and an energetic cohort of labor-liberal lawyers. In the Steel Workers union there were no murders, but discontent with the machine that controlled USW District 31, the largest in the union, covering Gary (Indiana) and South Chicago, gave rise to a well-organized democracy movement led by Edward Sadlowski. And once again intervention by the Labor Department was required to give insurgents a fair shot. Sadlowski would run unsuccessfully for USW president in 1977.

Hard times are never good for trade union democrats, so the closure of so many steel mills, coal mines, and auto plants in the next couple of decades marginalized such insurgencies. But the rise of service trade unions like the SEIU, whose president, John Sweeney, became AFL-CIO president in a rare contested election in 1995, revived the question once again. In a 1998 intervention, Steve Fraser notes the propensity of virtually all union leaders, left or right, craft or industrial, to privilege organizational power over democratic self-governance. While left-wing union partisans still agitated for the empowerment of the rank and file, Reagan-era conservatives were even more outspoken and successful in their quest for mandates, from the government or the courts, that would use the rhetoric of union democracy to subvert actual union effectiveness. In seeming response, both the Carpenters and the SEIU sought to consolidate smaller, democratically run locals, into a larger set of potent organizations capable of confronting employers of even larger size and resources.

Melvyn Dubofsky's portrait of Andrew Stern, the SEIU president early in the twenty-first century, confirms many of Fraser's insights. Stern did increase the membership and political clout of SEIU, privileging leadership authority over rank-and-file participation. But Dubofsky takes Stern to task for his high-handedness, which created chaos and resentment in those SEIU locals he sought to combine and in the labor movement as a whole when he organized a rival labor federation—enlisting the Teamsters and the United Food and Commercial Workers, as well as SEIU—that split the labor movement to little apparent advantage.

This section ends on a positive note with an article by Alex Press detailing how the democratization of the UAW paved the way for a burst of worker engagement and militancy, essential to the success the auto union achieved in its historic 2023 strike.

Hoffa and the Underworld (1959)

Paul Jacobs

Paul Jacobs (1918–1978) never completed college but he wrote eight books as a radical journalist and activist. Oriented toward the Trotskyists in the 1930s, he worked as an organizer for the International Ladies' Garment Workers Union in the early 1940s and as a CIO staffer after the war. Unlike some other Dissent *writers, he was an enthusiastic supporter of the New Left and a critic of Israeli polices after 1967. He helped found* Mother Jones *magazine in 1974 and investigated nuclear fallout and environmental contamination thereafter. An award-winning film,* Paul Jacobs and the Nuclear Gang, *was finished shortly after his death.*

It was all very odd, even eerie, as if by some trick one of my youthful political fantasies had come true in a perverted form. There I sat, in a union hall jammed with cheering truck drivers, listening to their union president denounce the capitalist press, radio and TV as instruments of the bosses and shouting at the tough, burly teamsters that they could never expect anything from their employers and that without the union they were helpless.

The reality of that meeting was tinged with fantasy for me because it took place not during the hectic thirties, in Minneapolis, when the Dunne brothers, leaders of Teamster Local 544, were the heroes of the Trotskyist movement, but in 1959. This meeting was in Detroit and the speaker was Jimmy Hoffa, talking to his own local union while a CBS crew filmed him for TV.

Now, obviously Jimmy Hoffa is not committed to overthrowing the capitalist system. Indeed, quite the opposite is true—Hoffa is a staunch defender of American capitalism (after all, it's been very good to him) and his speech was a singular exercise in vulgar demagoguery. But at that union meeting Hoffa symbolized, as he does in general, some of the most crucial problems facing the American trade unions.

Hoffa is still pretty spontaneous, although growing more cautious in his public speech. He exudes cockiness and ebullience; he has a great sense of native wit; he can be absolutely charming as he smiles with a boyish, dimpled grin; he's exceedingly smart and he works very, very hard at his job of running the teamsters. Indeed, that's all he does. There is little overt hypocrisy about Hoffa and a great deal of apparent forthrightness.

But there is another side to him as well, a more frightening one. When Hoffa becomes really angry, his grey-green eyes get incredibly cold and menacing. It's then that his ruthlessness, his obvious belief in physical violence as an instrument of power shows through as an important element in his personality. Usually the quest for power is but one motivation in most leaders' lives, but in Hoffa's case, power, linked with a desire to be feared rather than loved, seems an obsession. He has great contempt for and distrust of most people. He is tied, by strange cords, to the brutal men of the underworld. Still, other union leaders grow angry when crossed; others are avaricious for power; others use violence. It is Hoffa's attitude to the underworld that sets him apart.

Whether or not Hoffa has alliances with the underworld, he is certainly very tolerant of it. It is not enough of an explanation for his attitude to say that from a moral viewpoint he does not really recognize the underworld's existence. To Hoffa almost all of society is peopled by businessmen looking to make a fast buck; police officers on the take; respected insurance companies willing, indeed anxious, to give kick-backs to union officials in exchange for welfare and pension fund accounts; lawyers willing to make payoffs to get "good deals" for their business clients and employers who try to cheat their workers while stealing from their customers.

But even this cynical view of the world does not totally explain Hoffa's ties to the underworld. For Hoffa must also know that this area is where he is most vulnerable, if not as yet to the law, at least to the blows of public and private opinion. Nevertheless, he has continually resisted purging the teamsters of those elements who, only with the greatest charity, can be described as being even on the fringes of decency.

And while the presence of criminal elements in the union may be explained by the fact that the trucking industry has always been the kind of marginal business which verges between irrespectability and crime, it does not explain Hoffa's willingness to permit the continued access of criminals to teamster locals. It is true that even when the Trotskyists controlled the Minneapolis teamsters, there were mysterious underworld relationships that occasionally rose from beneath the surface. A local teamster union president in Minneapolis was once murdered under strange conditions and gangster elements once attempted, unsuccessfully, to muscle into one of the locals. It was the revolutionary ideology of the Trotskyist leadership, their commitment to use the teamsters' union for a larger political purpose that most effectively prevented the underworld from getting a foothold, either through force or collaboration, during their tenure of office.

It is (as we would have said once upon an ancient time) by no means an accident that Hoffa's power base, his home local, is a drivers' local. These are men who generally have little formal education. These are men physically isolated from each other at work, frequently away when union meetings are held, dependent upon business agents rather than fellow-members for the protection of their rights, working in an industry to which respectability has been late in coming and where the police, on highways and in towns, are rarely thought of as friends.

The industry tradition of toughness, the isolated conditions of work and the special characteristics of the drivers help define the loose boundaries of the moral territory in which Hoffa roams without great complaints from his union membership. In a hostile and dangerous work world, where toughness for both employers and employees is essential to survival, where the union contract is necessarily complicated, where it is expected that an employer will try to cheat his employees and vice versa, it is only natural for the members gladly to abdicate responsibility to the toughest and smartest of them all—Jimmy, who may be a son of a bitch but is, after all, "our" son of a bitch. And if he makes deals with the underworld . . . well, that's the way of the world.

Hoffa's completely paternalistic attitude toward the teamsters is one common denominator he shares with other union leaders. The members of the teamsters' union are Hoffa's constituency: he takes care of them, and in Hoffa's case this is done personally, through direct contact. Hoffa is probably the only international president who still runs the affairs of his own local while carrying out his other work. He is on the phone every day from Washington to Detroit, conducting local business and he attends local meetings at least every six weeks, settling shop grievances, giving contract interpretations, speaking to new groups of workers as they are being organized and generally behaving as an extremely active local leader.

In return for his work on their behalf, Hoffa demands total loyalty from the union members and his staff. He is probably more accessible to them than the president of any other international union in the U.S. Since Hoffa's feeling that he is the key element in the success of the teamsters' union is also shared by his staff and followers, he rarely faces palace revolutions or even the threat of them; his staff and much of his membership share his belief that they are dependent upon him for survival.

But is any union leader more paternalistic than David Dubinsky? Does Walter Reuther permit any less personal loyalty than Hoffa? When for the first time David J. McDonald faced opposition from within the steelworkers' union, wasn't his administration's entire machinery put into high gear to smash the possible revolt? Paternalism, the leader's identification of the union with himself, and the demand for personal loyalty are hardly unique to Hoffa and the teamsters; all that is unique is that Hoffa has been more gauche about doing what other union leaders have learned to do with finesse. "I've had to do everything myself to make this union a success," he once told me, openly stating without modesty what many others believe true but do not say of themselves.

Like some other union leaders, Hoffa views the union as his personal property, a resource available to him for his disposal as he sees fit, restricted only by the bothersome limitations imposed upon him by law plus some vague and undefined attitudes of doing "good" for the membership. He always speaks of the teamsters as "my union" and the "my" here carries the connotation of personal property in addition to that of pride.

To Hoffa dues money is akin to the operating capital of a business. This view of the union as an institution whose resources can be *incidentally* used for the personal financial benefit of its leaders is reinforced by those institutions that seek business from unions. Certain insurance companies, for example, hot in pursuit of the vast sums of money now available in welfare and pension funds, have always sought to persuade union leaders that the choice of which insurance carrier got the union account was fundamentally a matter of the leader's personal preference, a preference which they then tried to affect in a variety of ways.

There is a wider range of attitudes among trade union leaders and members on this question than on the identification of the union with its leader, but I think that at least a few other union leaders secretly share Hoffa's attitude towards the union treasury. They feel restrained from acting out their beliefs by fear of exposure, the internal controls of the unions or by the carryover of attitudes formed when their organizations were struggling to survive.

When, however, one examines the far less important but curiously troublesome problem of expense accounts, the distinctions between union leaders grow less sharp even among those who reject Hoffa's view of the treasury as a vehicle of personal power. I am not here concerned so much with the possible financial rape of a union treasury through the exploitation of expense accounts (though this is possible in rare cases) as I am with the "legitimate" use of expense accounts while on union business or the practice, not at all restricted to unions, of manufacturing a reason to take a trip and then justifying it by the excuse of "business."

This is only one instance of practices now common in all of our society, practices which to union leaders like Hoffa are built into the very matrix of the world. One of the reasons for Hoffa's deep cynicism is that he continually contrasts the stated ideals of the society with the actions of its members and then concludes from the comparison that the only common denominator for all people is hypocrisy.

Let me make clear that what concerns me here is not whether other union leaders are more hypocritical than Hoffa. Some are, some are not. That is really no matter. What does seem important to me is that Hoffa does share with many other union leaders a common set of values and aspirations, based, naturally, on the predominant mores of American society.

"Don't give me that!" says Hoffa scornfully to me when I argue heatedly with him about the narrowness, in his perspective, of trade union purposes. "What do you think I am, the State Department? I don't want to get into world politics. I have enough trouble taking care of my own members."

"If I had a bunch of Detroit cops here, I'd clean out these joints in no time," he said disgustedly as we once strolled, loudly quarreling, along Grant Avenue, the Boulevard of the Beats in San Francisco. "All these people need is a bath," he sneered scornfully as he looked at the habitues of the Co-existence Bagel Shop, thus expressing the most primitive reactions to anything out of the ordinary, anything disturbing the status quo—reactions more quietly shared by most other union leaders.

"I don't want to change the world," says Hoffa and here again he only states openly what many other American union leaders actually believe, in spite of all the resolutions dutifully passed by them at all the conventions.

When Hoffa says he doesn't want to change the world, he is speaking for those union leaders who don't even want to change their own unions. Except for a few men, considered oddballs by their colleagues and, to a great extent, by their members, most American union officials are convinced that fundamentally the world in which they have achieved leadership is the best of all possible worlds and needs few changes, either externally or internally.

Let's now refer to the issue of democracy in the teamsters,

comparing Hoffa's union with others. During the CBS television show on the teamsters, several shop stewards were interviewed and discussed the low attendance at union meetings. To outsiders, especially liberal outsiders, the fact that only a small percentage of union members attend meetings is somehow taken as an indication that undemocratic practices prevail. Yet the teamster attendance record is probably neither better nor worse than that of any other union—throughout the unions attendance at normal meetings is poor. For many years, at union summer camps, and training schools there have been dreary sessions devoted to increasing membership participation at local meetings. But attendance still remains the same—low. Suppose, however, it didn't. Suppose it went sharply up and there was none of the intimidation of members which may, in fact, exist in some teamsters locals. What problems would be solved? Does anyone seriously believe that Hoffa would not be overwhelmingly reelected teamster president even if every teamster member voted in a secret ballot election? Would this fact make it right for Hoffa to be president?

Attempts to equate "democracy" in unions with membership participation conjure up sharp dilemmas within the teamsters. At the moment, Hoffa is engaged in a struggle with the board of government monitors over his right to hold the presidency of the union. For months, Hoffa has been attempting to hold a union convention and have his right to the presidency reaffirmed by the convention delegates. The monitors, however, have thus far refused and instead are preparing court actions to have Hoffa removed from his office.

But Hoffa's desire for a convention and the monitors' refusal to permit it are obviously based on his and their belief that such a convention would certainly elect Hoffa president, even without his having to stuff ballot boxes, illegally elect delegates or in any way attempt to influence improperly the choice of delegates to the convention.

In this situation the courts, through the monitors, are being asked to prevent the direct control of the union by its members— one form of that "union democracy" so glibly idealized by Congress and the press. I am not here suggesting that because Hoffa is the membership's choice, therefore the membership is right; I am only trying to point out that "union democracy" in the sense of a free membership choice of a union president is not really wanted by many who plump loudly for it if the results are known, in advance, to be contrary to the generally accepted standards of public good or particular private interests. In this case, the generally accepted standards mean keeping Hoffa from the presidency, if possible, even though the membership may want him there.

One rather interesting element in this situation is that the remainder of the trade union leadership has been silent on this attempted intrusion by the monitors and courts into the teamsters' internal life. If, as seems possible, Hoffa is prevented from holding an election and then deposed from the presidency, it could easily set a precedent for similar court action in other cases. Yet the possibility has not brought any public protest or comment from other union leaders in the AFL-CIO probably because no matter what their feelings, it would be considered impolitic for any union leader publicly to identify himself with Hoffa in this situation.

Yet there seems to be another consequence of the attempts of Congress and the monitors to remove Hoffa: sympathy with him appears to be building up within his own union and possibly among other union leaders. Just as the U.S. Government made a martyr out of Harry Bridges within the ILWU and outside it, so Hoffa is beginning to take on the air of a man who is being harassed. When Hoffa addressed a recent meeting in San Francisco of the Western Conference of Teamsters, he shared the platform with and was applauded by the president of the very large California AFL-CIO and by its secretary-treasurer, the single most powerful labor leader in the state. Somehow, these officials feel more comfortable with Hoffa than with other, more ideological, leaders. Hoffa, more than Reuther, is their kind of a guy.

The sometimes public and more frequently private attitude of friendliness maintained by other union leaders towards Hoffa is also accounted for by simple economic self-interest. Strategically, the teamsters are in an excellent position to assist or hurt other unions and it is the recognition of this power, for example, that lies behind Hoffa's attempts, for three years, to bring about an alliance between the teamsters and Harry Bridges' ILWU.

Neither the teamsters nor ILWU membership appear disturbed about an alliance, although a merger would be far more difficult to sell to the ILWU ranks. In the case of the teamster members, their expectations of Hoffa are of a simple order. Like most other union members, they are content, on the whole, with the wage increases he brings them and willing, indeed anxious, to abdicate to him all responsibility for making serious policy decisions. The great majority of them do not conceive of the union as either an instrument for the carrying out of any social ideals or as an arena in which they can seek leadership positions.

If a teamster member does desire to be a union leader, he rarely pursues his goal through challenging the existing administration. Rather, he seeks to become part of the administration and attach himself to the leader in power. Here, too, there is a great similarity between the teamsters and other unions. The special conditions of teamster members, their lack of education, isolated work, character of the industry, etc., only define the particular ways in which the union operates but do not fundamentally differentiate the members from those in other unions.

Is it possible to raise the membership expectations of Hoffa? Or must he be restrained from the outside? There are some who think neither of these alternatives is the answer but that the solution is in raising Hoffa's level of aspirations. I am dubious about this last possibility. Hoffa's only real interest is the economic role of the teamsters union and the power he derives from it. Never in any conversation has Hoffa displayed any concern except for the very narrowest of worlds. Within those worlds, he's enormously knowledgeable, outside them very ignorant, although obviously capable of learning quickly. But he evinces no real desire either to broaden his intellectual horizons or change many of his basic attitudes.

What does the future hold for Hoffa and the teamsters? Predictions are always dangerous but assuming that Hoffa retains his leadership of the union either overtly or covertly, the teamsters should continue to grow faster than many other unions. The

American industrial economy is changing rapidly. Automation is replacing large-scale worker production of goods while the work force in the service and distributive trades is increasing. Unions like steel, auto and rubber, dependent on mass production industries, will decline in membership while the teamsters, organized more on the pattern of the English general union, has the opportunity of growth.

While I was in Detroit with the CBS television crew, I heard Hoffa speak to a group of city employees from Dearborn, Michigan, who were attempting to organize a teamster local there. I sat in the rear of the room watching Hoffa assure them of his support and thinking how curious it was that a group of city employees, generally a conservative group, would come to Hoffa and the teamsters in the face of the violent public attacks upon the union. Then I realized that these city employees were mad, damn mad, at their employer and I remembered, from my own experience as a union organizer, that when workers are angry enough to voluntarily organize themselves, at some risk to their jobs, what they seek in a union leader is, above all, the quality of toughness, so important in the American tradition. They want a union leader who, they believe, can solve their particular problems with their employer now, not one concerned with world affairs. It is precisely because Hoffa reflects the narrow but very sharp demands of American workers that his thundering against employers sounds like the rumbles of the class war. However, like a summer storm, far off in the distance, the sound is an illusion—to Hoffa, and his members, the class war is only a short engagement, occasionally violent, fought with no weapons barred, no quarter asked or given but quickly ended by the signing of a new contract.

Thus workers come to Hoffa and they will probably continue coming to Hoffa, for Hoffa, without social concepts, is at least as much in the tradition of the successful American labor leader as is Reuther, with his deep concern for abstract ideas of justice.

Labor Leaders, Intellectuals, and Freedom in the Unions (1973)

H.W. Benson

Herman Benson (2015–2020) was born in the Bronx to a middle-class family. He joined the Young People's Socialist League in 1930, worked as a tool and die maker in New York and Detroit, and after 1940 became an organizer for the Workers Party and an editor of its weekly newspaper, Labor Action. *In the postwar decades Benson became a tireless advocate for internal union democracy, exposing corruption, racketeering, and other criminality within several trade unions. He helped frame the 1959 Labor-Management Reporting and Disclosure Act (Landrum-Griffin), after which he worked to defend dissidents and insurgents in numerous unions, including the Machinists, Painters, Teamsters, Steel Workers, and United Mine Workers. In 1969 he founded and for more than a quarter century led the Association for Union Democracy, a support network and advocacy group for those challenging entrenched union officials.*

Once the insurgent Miners for Democracy had triumphed and Arnold Miller had defeated Tony Boyle by 70,373 to 56,334 for United Mine Workers president, the grueling job began of restoring a union that, under an authoritarian regime, had sadly disintegrated.

For 50 years, democracy in the UMW had been suppressed and derided. The Auto Workers union, John L. Lewis delighted in saying, pumps its members full of "democracy," but "we" give miners "eating-money." Lewis wielded his powers of sarcasm to instill so deep a contempt for internal democracy that delegates would auto-matically snicker whenever some stiff-spined dissident (what hon-ors you deserve!) would speak up at a convention for the right to elect district officers and executive board members.

In those years, a cynical realism gripped many labor ana-lysts. Democracy, they discovered, was not necessary for effective unionism. For while rough-and-tumble labor leaders might tram-ple over malcontents, they got results for workers, and that's what the labor movement is all about, isn't it? The Mine Workers came to symbolize the triumph of "eating-money" unionism and proved that internal democracy was only an ideological fancy of fuzzy-minded intellectuals.

Now, that school of side-of-the-mouth-talking, tough-thinking, rough-dealing has collapsed with the victory of the UMW insur-gency. The miners' experience shows how debased a union official-dom can become in the absence of membership control. In recent years, the UMW ceased even to protect its members from death in the mines. While miners mined coal, the officials mined the min-ers. And at least part of that officialdom, according to confessions of participants, was ready for murder when its power was challenged. When Joseph Yablonski [who challenged Boyle for the UMW pres-idency] was killed, hardly anyone in the labor movement would believe that it could be an inner-union assassination; their minds simply ruled out such a possibility. Think again! It *is* possible. Lloyd Green and Dow Wilson *were* murdered for leading a Paint-ers reform movement in California against grafters. New York City building contractors *do* fear "a bullet in the back " if they talk about racketeering union officials. One painting contractor was almost killed. Seaman Jim Morrissey was beaten almost to death outside the National Maritime Union hall. In the absence of democracy, a horrible degeneration *is* possible, yes, even in our labor movement.

"So there is corruption in unions, so whereever you find people you'll find corruption of some kind. What else is new?" That kind of reaction misses the point. It is not just a matter of "exposing" union corruption, but of recognizing the nature of reform move-ments: the risks they run, what motivates them, what they signify.

When Yablonski first announced his candidacy against Boyle, AFL-CIO President George Meany shrugged it off as an attempt by a kitchen boy to move into the dining room. When Yablonski was shot, Meany was concerned only that the murder might be used to "smear labor." Yet Yablonski was leading a fight of workers for social justice. The insurgent miners' leaders, their local officers, their rank-and-file activists, those around the Miners for Democracy are the living heart of our labor movement, reared in it, infused with its ideals, men who were ready to face vilification, blacklisting, even possible death for those ideals. When the union was stolen from miners, they led the drive to take it back. Not the murderers or those who hired them, not the Boyle officials with their contempt for miners, but the insurgents—they represented what is admirable in the labor movement. Their victory reminds us of the democratic potential of the unionized working class.

Compare the Miners' union with the Steelworkers. As secretary-treasurer of the United Steelworkers of America, I.W. Abel watched from the heights as a rank-and-file rebellion spread throughout his union and then was defeated. When discontent continued to rumble, Abel estimated the chances, looked for support in the official-dom and, once he could count on half the executive board, made the plunge (in 1965). With some reluctance, he and his backers appealed to the membership against the then president, David McDonald. Sure of a majority on the executive board, Abel knew that at the worst he would at least be credited with the number of votes actually cast on his behalf. With a minority on the board, McDonald knew he needed help and proposed that the American Arbitration Association supervise the union's contested election. Abel's majority, feigning indignation at the suggestion that only outside intervention could assure a fair count, turned McDonald down.

By contrast Yablonski, who was a member of the UMW executive board, began his fight without the backing of even one other international official. He had to take his chances with the rank-and-file miners. In steel, there was a change in the guard; in coal mining, there was a revolution. In depth of feeling and readiness to act without awaiting official blessing, the rebel miners' movement resembled the early CIO. West Virginia mines were closed by rank-and file "wildcat" strikes for safety legislation; mass demonstrations took over the streets of Charleston, the West Virginia capital; hundreds of men came from the mines for mass lobbying in Washington. New organizations were improvised: the Black Lung Association, the Association of Disabled Miners and Widows, the Miners Project (a public-interest law project providing an independent legal staff).

But there was a difference. In the 1930s, a new workers' movement was stimulated and backed by a strong section of the established labor movement. From 1969 to 1972 the miners fought alone; the labor movement, in all its wings, remained aloof.

Inside the UMW, the officials in power handled big money as their collective private property: union treasury, insurance funds, union-owned bank, their own salaries and expenses. They manipulated these resources to stay in power, spreading cash around during elections and handling ballots like the cash. The oppositionists had to continue to earn their living digging coal—except toward the end when some took time off to campaign. They began with few resources, no power in the union, no support from established organizations. These insurgents set out to reform their union, not to desert or replace it.

The miners had help. Modest though it was, they would have been doomed without it: a few outside liberals, a few talented attorneys (Joseph Rauh, Chip Yablonski, Clarice Feldman), a few dedicated students, a solitary congressman, and one experienced labor staff man, Meyer Bernstein, who quit a secure job with the Steelworkers to take his chances with the miner rebels. These people deserve all the praise we can give them.

One kind of support the miners did not have at all. Labor leaders remained hostile, indifferent, or passive. At first, one might have dismissed the UMW battle as just another power contest between ins and outs. To sustain that view for long, you would have had to seal your mind tightly against the facts and busy yourself, like George Meany, with other urgent causes. If, however, you can recognize a crusade against corruption, or a gut battle for democracy, or a last ditch effort to save a union, or a "class struggle" operating within a union, or a desperate drive for protection against killing accidents, then the failure of even a single top labor leader to intervene points up a stark fact about the contemporary labor movement: it is incapable of supporting a progressive reform struggle within its own ranks.

Not that there aren't many union leaders who sympathized with the miner-reformers and rejoiced in their success. I assume that some may have privately donated modest sums to the insurgents. But not one spoke out, not even in the bleak days after the Yablonski murder when the opposition needed at least the consolation of moral support. (To be fair, there was one thin crack in this wall of conformity: Victor Reuther endorsed the Miners for Democracy, but he spoke for himself alone.) It would be easy to ascribe that failure to cowardice, or some other character weakness of this or that labor leader. But all of them? They are not really cowardly men. Then what was it?

I think they were concerned mainly with avoiding anything that might be considered stupid. There was an overwhelming consensus that it would be quixotic to act differently. A rigid, if unwritten, code governs relations among labor leaders, one that allows no legitimate place for rank-and-file reform movements and that outlaws support by the leader of one union for critics in any other. This implicit nonaggression pact comes to protect an assortment of malefactors in high places within the labor movement, even murderers. Even murderers? Otherwise, why no labor resolutions expressing horror at the Yablonski killing? Why no outcry, except locally, when Wilson and Green were shot in California? One of their murderers, then an official in the Painters union, is now serving a life sentence for the crime. When the Painters union held its convention in 1969, under tight control of its president, S. Frank Raftery, a motion to memorialize the two dead men was rejected, and the convention passed on to other business.

Those leaders who are dismayed by the labor movement's adaptation to corruptionists are on the defensive. Like a private citizen who watches impotently while thugs torment a victim, the decent labor leader feels helpless to assist the union reformer who is beaten to the ground. (Sometimes that's a figure of speech, sometimes it's a physical description.) It wasn't always so, nor meant to be. In the 1920s, when the AFL was dominated by know-nothings who opposed unemployment insurance and ignored mass-production manufacturing, progressive unions and militant groups fought inside and outside the AFL for other policies. In the late 1930s, the CIO, as a progressive wing, was half the labor movement. In the late 1940s, when he became UAW president, there was Walter Reuther. Those forces spoke out for democratization and demanded action against racketeers. There is no analogous progressive wing in the labor movement today; its absence, in my opinion, largely explains the widespread "disenchantment" of liberal intellectuals with the labor movement. And those unions which have adopted resolutions against the Vietnam War or endorsed George McGovern despite Meany's "neutrality"? Even they display small public interest in promoting union democracy or in taking the offensive against corruption in the labor movement.

Boyle's downfall began, to set an exact date, on November 20, 1968, when Consol Mine No. 9 in Farmington, West Va., exploded. Seventy-eight men died. While the smoke clouds still billowed, Boyle told a nationwide TV audience that the company had an excellent safety record. Later he called it "one of the better companies to work with." That explosion and that speech resounded in every mine pit in the country.

It was not money that aroused the miners but a suspicion that their union officials hardly cared whether they died or whether they could live when they got sick and old. From Yablonski's challenge in 1969 to Miller's victory in 1972, the insurgents said little about wage rates. They needed a union to stand up for modern safety measures; to watch out for gas accumulations, explosions, and rockfalls; to protest cheaply strung power lines and short circuits; to avoid careless welding flashes. They needed help to reduce the black dust that was choking them to early disability. They wanted to protect their pension money.

No grandiose aims were emblazoned on insurgent banners.

Nothing about Vietnam, no call to rally to McGovern, no radical slogans for social change. Their demands would be considered commonplace in any decent union, but miners had to wage an extraordinary fight to achieve them because they had lost their internal union democracy.

In this industry turned topsy-turvy by heavy machinery that rips away mountainsides and bores tunnels of huge diameter in the earth, throwing up storms of coal and rock dust, the companies count cave-ins, fires, broken bodies, death, silicosis, and black lung as normal conditions of doing business. They resist spending the sums necessary to make mines safer; they delay anything that might curb productivity. The new union leaders know they may soon have to confront the employers on these issues. To switch from sweetheart dealings to militant unionism means they may be forced to close down unsafe mines, to demand safety legislation and its enforcement, to be propelled deep into political action, to negotiate new deals. A revitalized UMW will need help from allies among Oil and Chemical Workers, from Steelworkers, from Transportation Workers.

The Miller team now has begun to fulfill a good part of its campaign platform. The new board cut top officers' salaries by 25 percent to 30 percent and abolished automatic expense accounts. It brought officers' pensions down from the stratosphere. The sum of about $2 million in assorted savings was returned to the union treasury, part of which will go to raise the wages of the union's custodial staff, some of whom were getting as little as $100 a week.

What, then, of reformers in other unions? The stolen elections, the corruption, the mishandling of pension money, the blacklisting, the initial failure of the Labor Department to enforce the law—that part of the miners' experience is still the plight of other unionists. We are reminded of these facts as Frank Schonfeld continues his fight in the New York Painters union for democracy and integrity. We will be nudged again when James Morrissey runs this year for president of the National Maritime Union.

In retrospect, we can see what combination of factors made possible the miners victory: There were courageous local leaders and rank-and-file activists without whom nothing would have been possible. There were prolabor professionals (liberals, intellectuals, civil libertarians, attorneys) who came forward to help. This collaboration made possible effective action within the union, access to the courts, and pressure on government agencies. At least this once, the law was enforced and a fair election assured. We saw in action the often-sought "alliance between intellectuals and labor." It worked.

Insurgency in the Steel Union (1975)

William Kornblum

William Kornblum (1939–) was a Peace Corps volunteer in Africa before taking his PhD from the University of Chicago in 1971. Thereafter he spent the bulk of his academic career teaching sociology at the City University of New York. Blue Collar Community (1974), his first book, was based on a three-year study conducted in the steel mill neighborhoods of South Chicago. There he analyzed the success and failure of the interracial, interethnic coalitions that sought to win power inside locals of the United Steelworkers. His later books focused on urban poverty and community in New York City.

"Freedom is a hard-won thing. You've got to work for it, fight for it, day and night for it, and every generation's got to win it again." The newest enactment of this political theme is unfolding in the United Steelworkers of America, where a young generation of leaders, up from the rank and file and gathered behind the banner of union democracy, has toppled an autocratic regional regime that had held power since 1937. And this may be only the beginning.

Freedom to vote for more than one candidate, freedom to vote without intimidation in a fair election, freedom to vote on the terms of the labor agreements, freedom to voice ideas that could take the union into new arenas of social action—these were the ideals that in November 1974 rallied almost 40,000 steelworkers in the Chicago region behind Ed Sadlowski, a steelworker and union organizer from South Chicago, who dared to challenge a union political machine that even the most astute labor analysts thought unbeatable.

Since his stunning upset in the Chicago-Gary-Joliet USWA

District 31—with its 130,000 members the largest and most powerful political subdivision of the union—Ed Sadlowski has been
raised from the obscurity of mill neighborhoods and union halls
to the status of an insurgent labor hero. Joseph Rauh Jr., the veteran labor attorney whose intervention with the U.S. Department
of Labor helped Sadlowski secure victory, calls him "a young
Walter Reuther."

This insurgent victory in the vast Calumet Steelworkers' region
stands with the Arnold Miller election in the United Mine Workers.
Both are examples that other young union leaders will follow. But
Sadlowski's victory in the Calumet District is still a far cry from
the capture of international steel leadership. Before one projects
this 36-year-old steelworker to the highest office in the United Steelworkers of America, as many outside the union are now doing, it
is important to take a close look at the conditions that made this
insurgency successful.

Sadlowski's prodigious political gifts have been apparent to
rank-and-file Steelworkers since 1961 when he won his first election as grievance man at U.S. Steel's South Works in Chicago. A
third-generation steelworker from a family of independent socialists and street-wise political activists, Sadlowski is articulate,
uncompromising with more cautious adversaries, and a brilliant
campaign strategist. But he is also quick to play down the role of
his own leadership.

"Our worst problem in organizing these campaigns is overcom-
ing the mystique that the labor boss is some kind of God. People
would say to us, 'You can't go against Joe Germano [the previous
incumbent] or his man. He's been there since the union was started.
They won't let you even get on the ballot.'

"So I get on the ballot. I win the first election but they steal it on
the count. The Labor Department comes in and I win the rerun by
two to one. Now all of a sudden I'm ballyhooed as the 'new man of
steel' in all the papers. This just leads to the same mythical bullshit
over again. If I start believing this I'm in trouble.

"When I went out for this thing most steelworkers outside
of South Chicago had never heard of me. The real game was in

pounding the pavement in front of the plants, getting to know the members, finding tough campaigners who wouldn't fold under pressure, and in knowing the issues in every part of this industry."

In the great basic steel-producing areas of the country, such as the lower basin of Lake Michigan or the Cleveland-Youngstown-Pittsburgh axis, steelmaking is a way of life; the mills are dominant institutions, shaping every facet of existence in the industrial neighborhoods that cluster in their shadows. Birth and death, time and money, songs and stories, all the comings and goings of people and machines, even the climate, the air and the water are tempered and stained by the making of steel. Certainly the national culture with its schools, television, and interstate highways brings mill people away from the world of steel more than was possible when the men worked a six-day week and a 12-hour day. But the national culture also leaves plenty of room for the ways of steelmaking people to persist. The interstate highways bypass South Chicago, Indiana Harbor, and Gary, in some ways leaving these mill towns more insular than they were in the 1940s.

Union politics in these big mills usually alternates between something that one year may approximate classical Athenian democracy and another year may be more like a banana-republic junta. All elections, from grievance man to local president, are hotly contested, in campaigns that may last for two or three months and involve the active passions of hundreds of campaign workers in the mill shops. The candidates must be union "citizens," members who have demonstrated their responsibility to the affairs of the local by attending a minimum number of meetings. More powerful criteria of friendship, political ideology, or ethnicity and race lead to intense jockeying among aspiring candidates who seek to form a caucus that can dominate the local's politics, often for 10 or more years.

Once in office a caucus does its best to remain there, and in some cases this may include flagrant subversion of the democratic process. The Sadlowski insurgents learned this the hard way when they lost their first district director's election in 1973 partly because the "loyalist" election committee at the big sheet-and-tin mill in

Gary forged approximately 700 ballots for Sam Evett, the machine candidate. But even in locals like this one there will always be groups of insurgents who refuse to stop organizing. Indeed it was through investigation by undiscouraged insurgents in the Gary local that evidence of the massive fraud against Sadlowski was first revealed. And it was this evidence that led the slow-moving Department of Labor to conduct its own investigation, and eventually to require a second district director election, which Sadlowski won by 39,737 to 20,158.

In big steel the discontent with the administration of USW President I.W. Abel runs deep. This is particularly true in the Chicago-Gary District, where big-mill workers have never shown much enthusiasm for the union president. The younger workers tend to blame the Abel administration for the erosion of steelworkers' wages, which have slipped from first among industrial workers in the early 1960s to about 14th presently. They also resent the recent increase in their dues, which was rammed through the 1974 Steelworkers' convention at the same time that union executives' salaries were increased by over 25 percent. Many older workers in Calumet's big steel plants, particularly those with 15 or 20 years in the mills, have resented I.W. Abel since his 1965 election, often for the very reason that District 31 boss Joseph Germano swung their district for him and made his election possible. Abel's genuine appeal to the ideals of union democracy in 1964 and 1965 never sold well in the big mills of Lake Michigan because they were being promoted by Germano, a director whose dictatorial rule often came into sharp conflict with the democratic traditions of the large locals.

Although he could never count on victory margins from the beginning for Abel or his other candidates, District 31 has remained Germano's fiefdom for 36 years. He could offset any losses in big steel by large margins in the smaller plants, particularly in the hundreds of factories on Chicago's West Side that are organized by the USWA. Here the situation was well expressed by a union staff representative who assessed Sadlowski's chances in 1972 as he campaigned against Germano's chosen successor:

In the smaller plants it's uphill for Sadlowski. There are over 500 shops in the District and most of 'em don't have more than 300 members. This means you've got to run all over hell to these small "bucket shops." The small fabrication factories and specialty shops are like machine precincts. Lots of the workers are new, and in a lot of 'em the local union officials are afraid to take a leak without running to their staff man. The staff man runs the local for them and gets them to bring out the vote he wants. If Sadlowski can cut into this vote he may win.

The insurgents did cut into the union machine's traditional strength in 1973, and they did so against overwhelming odds because in many instances they had no knowledge of how even to locate the shops. In many cases, workers in the small shops had little knowledge of what the job of district director is. Many were newly hired women, rural blacks, white Southerners, Latins, and a massive educational campaign was required to bring these workers into the mainstream of Steelworker affairs. These efforts were successful beyond anyone's imagining. In consequence the machine forces had to pressure some of the bigger mills to somehow come up with more votes against Sadlowski. This led to the chain of events that is still shaking the union's international leadership. Now a serious dues protest movement is accelerating throughout the union's rank and file.

The insurgents' victory in District 31 is convincing evidence that the union's current leadership is extremely vulnerable to challenge grounded on the most basic CIO ideals of better wages, freedom of representation, and respect to the individual worker. Sadlowski has also shown that the obstacles of dispersion and diversity in the membership can be overcome through the time-worn techniques of street organization. Even Elmer Chatak, chief organizer in the union's Pittsburgh office, must agree, because as the campaign manager for Sadlowski's opponent in 1974 he watched in disbelief as the insurgent landslide developed. "I've never seen a better run district campaign than Ed's," he said, "But it was really the dues issue that made his margin this big."

Chatak's qualifying remark may be true, but a steamrolling dues protest is only one symptom of more deeply felt discontents in the union's membership. In District 31 the insurgents tapped those discontents and turned them into a positive program, a simple set of goals that, applied throughout the Steelworkers union, could be this new generation's contribution to the labor movement in steel. Does this mean Sadlowski will be a candidate for the Steelworker presidency in 1976? The day after his final victory in District 31, while a crowd of well-wishers awaited him in his campaign office, he drove across the city to speak at a local union meeting in a small plant on Chicago's West Side. That election was over but the campaign to "open the union to the membership" had just begun.

Is Democracy Good for Unions? (1998)

Steve Fraser

Steve Fraser (1945–) is a New York–based editor and writer with an advanced degree in history from Rutgers. He is the biographer of Sidney Hillman, a CIO founder, and the author of several books and numerous articles on finance, politics, and social thought, both radical and reactionary. He was a principal organizer of the 1996 Columbia University "Teach-in with the Labor Movement," which helped bridge the gap between U.S. unions and left-wing academics and students. The next year he founded New Labor Forum, *remaining as editor for more than two decades.*

Ron Carey's recent downfall as head of the Teamsters Union carried with it genuine overtones of tragedy. His ascension to the presidency some years ago seemed just reward for his own incorruptible dedication to the rank and file and for the indefatigable efforts of the Teamsters for a Democratic Union (TDU), which contributed immeasurably to his rise. Then came the stirring victory over United Parcel Service last summer, an inspiration to all who look to a resurgent labor movement to help prevent the final "incorporation of America." A victory for democracy inside the country's most notoriously corrupt union had led, or so it seemed, to a victory for democracy for all. So when it turned out that Carey was going down, implicated in, of all things, a scam to manipulate his re-election through the misappropriation of union funds, it was dispiriting news indeed.

But this scandal is also a reminder that union democracy has been, for nearly a century, a quixotic crusade pursued, oddly enough, with comparable fervor and little success by both right and left. Today, Ron Carey's disgrace provokes as much lamentation in the columns of the *Wall Street Journal* as it does in the slimmer pages of *New Politics*, both journals saddened and outraged by yet another defeat for the cause of union democracy. This dirge has been heard before . . . and even before that. Already by the turn of the century, Daniel DeLeon, Socialist Labor Party and Industrial Workers of the World founder, had skewered the conventional trade union leader as a "hopelessly gangrened" appendage of the capitalist octopus. Such functionaries were in his eyes inherently corrupt, ruling their fiefdoms much like machine politicians, without any regard for the democratic desires of their constituents. They were, in a word, "traitors." This became an article of faith for assorted left-wing socialists, anarchists, and syndicalists. In some form it remains so to this day, encouraging among a diminished circle of left-wing trade union activists a sense of their own righteousness.

Echoing across the great social divide, the voices of business lobbyists, conservative politicians, and establishment journalists mimicked DeLeon's. Early in this century, anthracite coal barons took up the cause of union democracy, complaining that "the voice of the great majority of the rank and file of the miners . . . can only make itself felt through a more democratic management of the union." Union leaders were "autocratic" and "corrupt" "bosses" who needed to be unhorsed by the secret ballot and guarantees of freedom of expression and majority rule. During World War II, when the reputation and political weight of the trade union movement was in the ascendant, labor's congressional enemies mounted oblique attacks by citing union violations of democratic procedure. This salient became the dominant one in the managerial counterrevolution that immediately followed the war. Taft-Hartley began and Landrum-Griffin concluded, a decade later, a legislative effort whose ostensible purpose was to democratize trade unionism, but whose unspoken agenda was to reverse the balance of power between business and labor established during the New Deal. Today, Representative Peter Hoekstra of Michigan conducts hearings to ventilate the right wing's concern with the lack of democracy in the Teamsters and other unions, and to promote the Paycheck Protection Act. Worried that for the first time in a quarter century the labor movement might be recovering just a bit of its wasted political muscle, the act would require individual workers to agree to the political deployment of their dues money. Making it more difficult than it already is for unions to take decisive political action, it's a piece of pure legislative hypocrisy promoted as a democratic reform to "give workers a say."

So it's been: union democracy cherished by the left as the passway to social emancipation; discovered by the right as the passway to social counterrevolution. *On the Waterfront* was an ecumenical docudrama with enough meat on the bone to satisfy everyone: Catholic activists, trade union militants, good government bureaucrats, responsible business people, the whole family of upstanding citizens. This convergence should not obscure certain contrary elemental truths. First of all and most obviously, the motives of left and right crusaders for union democracy could not be more at odds. Clearly, in the case of the latter we are in the presence of a calculated cynicism. The clusters of Republican congresspeople and corporate flacks who staffed, testified before, and applauded the 1957 McClellan Senate committee hearings into union racketeering (five of the eight senators were from right-to-work states) and who muscled through the Landrum-Griffin Act (otherwise known as the Labor-Management Reporting and Disclosure Act of 1959) were about as interested in fostering "labor reform" and the democratic rights of the rank and file as King Leopold was in fostering humanitarian good works on the rubber and ivory plantations of the Belgian Congo. If union democracy appealed to them at all, it did so because they thought it might weaken the internal unity and resolve of trade unions. It is hardly a coincidence that Landrum-Griffin was passed during the 116-day steel strike—the longest industry shutdown ever.

Partisans of union democracy from the left, on the other hand, were and are motivated by a genuine commitment to one or another version of social democracy, a commitment that can be moral, strategic, or both. For the most zealous, union democracy can

become a consuming preoccupation, effacing all other considerations, assuming mythic stature. But even then its disciples redeem
themselves by a dedication to the disempowered that exposes the
sanctimonious cant of faux union democrats on the right.

So, too, the passions aroused by union democracy on the left and
right do not cancel each other out, rendering the issue moot. All
sorts of trade unions at various times and in a great variety of industries have been hopelessly corrupt and autocratically run, ready to
resort to everything from the quiet, if systematic, misappropriation
and looting of rank-and-file dues money to the most brutal repres-
sion of internal dissent. Nor, for that matter, are corruption and autocracy inevitably joined at the hip: Jimmy Hoffa (the disappeared
one) meticulously observed all the provisions of Landrum-Griffin;
Walter Reuther, who could rise to heights of imperial ruthlessness
in dealing with his opponents, was the soul of rectitude when it
came to conducting the business affairs of the United Auto Workers (UAW). No, union democracy, or rather its absence, is an all-
too chronic conundrum. Its persistence lends moral and political
legitimacy even to such legal remedies as Landrum-Griffin, whose
provenance is otherwise so transparently antilabor.

And yet it is also the case that there is no other voluntary, mass
organization in America subject to the same intense scrutiny of its
internal life, so regularly inspected, interrogated, and indicted with
regard to now closely it conforms to democratic norms of conduct.
Neck deep in its own failures and betrayals, corruptions and bad
faith, the American trade union nonetheless survives on the barren
landscape of civil society as a great, if battered, multicultural institution embracing the powerless and disenfranchised; one of a precious few actually capable of challenging the power and privilege
of the country's business and political elites. If there is no democracy within unions, there is no democracy without them.

Evolved to cohabit a modern world of complex, bureaucratic organization, the trade union is as far from the vanished and much
mythologized world of guild democracy as today's hollowed-out
mass political parties and administrative state agencies are
from the equally sentimentalized world of participatory village

democracy. To decry that leads nowhere. Moreover, unions, unlike other popular formations, are compelled to assume multiple and not always compatible roles: as vehicles of democratic expression and mobilization, as a kind of diplomatic corps engaged in closeted negotiation, as combat organizations imposing a solidaristic discipline with which to confront a centralized enemy utterly unconcerned with niceties of democratic procedure. Under such conditions, many union leaders secretly believe and practice what one of them openly confessed back in the 1920s: "As a democracy no union would last six months."

That inherent functional tension is heightened by the peculiarities of American political and industrial history. The labor movement's failure to form political institutions of its own (a labor or social democratic party of some description) and its inability or unwillingness to erect a system of industry-wide bargaining, have left trade unions to bear multiple burdens. They must function as private welfare states in lieu of government supports, which even at their most generous were hardly generous at all. Sitting atop a large stash of cash in the form of pension and other benefits is not only a temptation in the crudest sense. It is as well an alluring source of influence, opening up the back channels of power and high finance to people hardly accustomed to such access.

Unions must function as well like more or less autonomous political deal makers. Because no "labor party" consistently looks after its broader interests, each union is, in many instances, left to fend for itself, its leaders wheeling and dealing with local power brokers. Such political understandings may be necessary and fair—or they may not be. But in any event they can be dangerous intoxicants for the bureaucrats who negotiate them, especially because they know they're not accountable in the way they might be for more formal agreements entered into by a political party. Finally, because industry-wide or regional bargaining is such a rarity in the United States, unions too often find themselves competing against one another. Such internecine competition invites corrupt dealings with businesses always looking for an edge. All in all, union bureaucrats are presented with proliferating incentives to hold on to power and opportunities to enrich themselves well beyond what might be defined as "normal." This structural dynamic of American trade unionism accounts, in part at least, for why the crusade for union democracy seems interminable and interminably futile. The Association for Union Democracy, for example, has been waging the good fight for a half century; although there have been some highs, and especially some very grim lows, in the end it would be hard to argue much has changed over that span.

Even though American unions have consistently shied away from establishing a political existence of their own, critics have tended to treat unions as if they were incipient labor parties. They implicitly demand of the former beliefs, principles, and programmatic platforms only reasonable to expect of social democratic political formations. Since, however, they are trade unions, they consistently disappoint. So, for example, when it comes to the labor market, trade unions are natural monopolists prone to defend the interests and express the democratic will of their existing members by excluding others; in America that has meant (and in an alarming number of instances continues to mean) immigrants, blacks, and women. And the question of union democracy is made even murkier by the undeniable record of some union leaders' taking the initiative to end exclusionary practices only to be democratically repudiated by a rank and file jealous of its privileges. Similarly, what's often passed over in all the hand-wringing about the Teamster situation is that Jimmy Hoffa (the live one) enjoyed widespread support, nearly enough to win the election, even before it was known that Ron Carey had made his pact with the devil. Indeed, there would have been no devilish pact to begin with had not a worrying percentage of the rank and file displayed its pro-Hoffa sentiments. That, too, is a less attractive face of union democracy, which won't go away by demonizing Hoffa.

Allegorical depictions of the struggle for union democracy depend on a fanciful and ahistorical polarity between a virginal rank and file and a venal bureaucracy. If anything good happens, its source can always be found deep in the soil where the grass roots grow. And if things don't turn out as wished, if the ranks recede and fall silent, there's always a bureaucrat around to blame.

This simple tale of betrayal has been told over and over again, reaching a kind of tragic grandeur as an explanation for the rise and then the sad demise of the CIO as an insurgent force in American life. And it is undeniable that many unions degenerated in just this way, presided over by incompetents, crooks, petty tyrants, or just plain timeservers whose ties to the workaday world of their "clients" had gone extinct. But whatever truth this larger folklore may contain—and clearly there is some—it effaces a more complex historical logic. Whether in the case of the CIO or in other instances of genuine democratic labor insurgency, the hated bureaucracy emerges again and again as an outgrowth of the upheaval from below. The rank and file is complicit in the creation of the bureaucracy; the bureaucracy is its legitimate offspring, at least in the case of strong CIO-like upheavals. A powerful bureaucracy often signals the strength of its anonymous creators down below. The fact that they were able to fashion an institution capable of standing up to an enemy whose overlordship went unquestioned for so long is an accomplishment, not a mistake or failing.

Frequently formed under beleaguered conditions, it's hardly a surprise the union executive is vested with extraordinary powers, not dissimilar to a nation under siege and prone to the same suspension of full democratic liberties. (After all, the union shop is a kind of compulsory form of solidarity.) Except that in America there's hardly ever a truce, much less a lasting peace, in the war against unions. Union functionaries, certainly in the formative period and sometimes well beyond that, are themselves the most combat-hardened, articulate, politically alert, and devoted of democratic activists. In a word, especially when the bureaucracy arises amidst the Sturm and Drang of industrial warfare, it represents not the worst but the best the movement has to offer.

The Amalgamated Clothing Workers (ACW), a union about whose history I've written, pioneered in democratizing industrial relations in an industry notorious for its wild disregard for the needs and rights of its workforce. Before unemployment insurance and subsidized housing became public policy, the Amalgamated had established these democratic reforms in its own domain. And the internal life of the union, at the local level and sometimes beyond, was lively and contentious. Its bureaucracy was largely, although certainly not exclusively, peopled by veteran activists, a sizeable percentage committed social revolutionaries of one sort or another. Yet there is no question the union was often run without regard to formal democratic procedure. What was colloquially known as "the activity," an informal cluster of the most tested and trusted cadre, made key strategic and even lesser decisions. And they were not shy about thwarting the will of local majorities. So they might act to curb the appetites of powerful groups of skilled cutters or to censor factional opponents in ways not prescribed by the union's bylaws. When, to cite an admittedly extreme case, pro-fascist sentiment swelled inside certain Italian locals during the late 1920s and 1930s, the "activity" made sure this noxious voice was silenced. The UAW was a similar case. The fruit of mass upheaval, staffed by cadre with unimpeachable credentials, famous for its freewheeling internal debates, like the ACW an innovator in democratic social reform, and led by a man who might be characterized as a union ascetic, the UAW bureaucracy, under Reuther's command, could also be ruthless in pursuit of its own objectives. The UAW was a one-party state whose challengers, when they dared to raise their heads, might just as readily find themselves in trusteeship as campaigning for election.

From the time of DeLeon and continuing into the late 1960s with the eruption of the Dodge Revolutionary Union Movement and related movements of black workers, internal dissent against union leaders often carried with it a social charge, the explicit promise that the struggle for democracy inside the house of labor was part of the broader confrontation with capitalism and social injustice. Union democracy thereby became a cause attracting the attention of the wider progressive community. That is scarcely the case today. Red purges and Republican-instigated investigations into "labor racketeering" have left behind an unsavory aroma. Together they've made union democracy the official business of the government. Conservatives feel comfortable with that because they're always able to overcome their qualms about government interference so long as the state's punitive gaze is directed at the enemies of good business and good order. But across the aisle the role of the government in labor matters is viewed more suspiciously. Whatever the past machinations of Stalinists within the labor movement, it is hard to ignore the high hypocrisy that justified the government's intimidating campaign to excise them from the CIO; anticommunist affidavits and star-chamber excommunications were all about crippling the labor movement, not about saving the CIO for democracy. And whatever the truth about criminal infiltration of trade unions—and it was considerable—the image of "labor bossism" with which it was deliberately conflated was more a publicist's poison arrow than it was an antidote for union autocracy. Only the most dogged persistence by union oppositionists, as for example in the case of the long campaign in the sixties to unseat the David McDonald gang running the Steelworkers, succeeded; and it did so in spite of, as much as because of, the presence of Landrum-Griffin monitors from the Labor Department.

So, too, today the government's own views and personnel quickly take precedence over the putative interests of the rank and file it's supposed to be protecting. Standards applied by federal agents to the internal life of unions are tortuously more exacting than for any other arena of public life. Why should the government, after all, be deciding who can run for union office, how and when the elections are to be held, whether or not a union president ought to be elected directly by its members or, as is far more common, by convention delegates? Direct elections, for example, seem eminently democratic, but on closer inspection often turn out to replicate the devitalized practices of contemporary electoral politics, complete with high stakes fund-raising and sound-bite electioneering. Again, the byzantine intrigue that has engulfed officials assigned to monitor and adjudicate the Teamster case is a splendid demonstration of how union democracy under the auspices of the government easily turns into a beltway political brawl that has precious little, if anything, to do with the aspirations of the much-revered rank and file.

All these bedevilments of the crusade for union democracy have registered finally even among those most single-mindedly committed to it as an overriding axiom of their political lives. Once upon a time the direct (rather than convention-delegate) election of union presidents, the tethering of local business agents to their immediate constituents, and similar expressions of direct democracy were considered the elementary forms of the good union. But the all too evident ability of locally elected business agents, for example— even those without any taint of corruption—to frustrate the will and interests of larger majorities outside their local precincts has cultivated a greater respect for the specific contingencies of living unions and a more fluid, less fixed regard for the forms of procedural democracy. This new flexibility embraces the government's role as well; sometimes it's seen as good, sometimes not so good. Still, there is an abiding sense that whatever rises from below is genuine and progressive; whatever percolates down from above, even if it looks enticing, is to be dealt with, if at all, with kid gloves. Only movements led by rank-and-file militants, only organizers from within and not from the outside, can be trusted to push to the limit and beyond. The recent important victory of the Communications Workers of America at USAir is cited as evidence. There the conversion of workers into activists/organizers made all the difference.

In this compelling scenario democracy, meaning the active involvement and leadership of shop-floor workers, is merged with all hope of resuscitating the labor movement. Only the impure of heart could disagree. Arousing the energies and ideas of working people normally left inert by the tyrannies and indignities of everyday life on the job is not merely smart strategy, although it is that; intrinsically, it is an assault on the hierarchies of power and wealth and social position that root and reproduce in the dark world of production, a realm from which all talk of democracy is officially banished. Here, too, "union democracy" flies the flag of multiculturalism, overturning all the disabling divisions of race and ethnicity that poison the well of fellow feeling and collective action. And here as well "union democracy" breaches the fire walls protecting a favored skill or gender or nativity, daring to open up enclaves of union privilege to the more capacious embrace of working and poor people generally. It is here, finally, that "union democracy" blends seamlessly into social movement building, seeking to articulate desires extending far beyond the borders circumscribed by conventional trade unionism. The boundaries of the institution become plastic, allowing easy migrations back and forth between unions and community organizations as they mobilize jointly to confront the corporate order at and away from work. Down this road lies the permanent revolution, a state of perpetual industrial and social ferment, severing as well the umbilical cord to the Democratic Party, all of which sooner or later must undermine the ground beneath the existing order of things. Somewhere down this road the "union" in "union democracy" drops out, antiquated, as in no longer necessary or adequate.

Between here and there, however, the institution soldiers on, as does the intractable reality of contesting for power in the marketplace and in the political arena. In this intermediate zone, the relationship of power to democracy is complex, full of compromise and negotiation and even concession. There are some trade union leaders today—and they include people utterly devoted to organizing, tactically creative and militant, and who've achieved remarkable success against daunting odds in the South and elsewhere—who don't care a rat's ass for union democracy; indeed consider it an actual hindrance where a state of undeclared war against employers demands discipline, secrecy, and decisive action by small groups of outsiders less subject to daily intimidation. From afar it's all too easy to declaim against this preoccupation with institutional power while failing to take account of the precariousness with which these institutions cling to life.

Still others in positions of leadership have fashioned a more nuanced relationship between power and democracy. Recent developments in, of all places, the building trades, are suggestive. The reform regime presiding over the Carpenters Union in New

England warns against union democracy proceeding in a vacuum as a kind of narrowly focused procedural matter, all the while eliding the question of power and the active involvement of members in ongoing organizing from the equation. Traditionally, local fiefdoms in the Carpenters Union were simultaneously democratic and disempowering. They've remained hotbeds of a living culture of solidarity, a "brotherhood" of sentiment and skill—a phenomenon far rarer in the labor movement generally than it once was and therefore not to be sneezed at. Yet these locals and their leaders (not only in the Carpenters but throughout the building trades) jealously guarded their parochial (often racist and sexist) prerogatives and labor market monopolies even as the center of gravity of the industry regionalized. To stop the erosion of union power as well as to undermine the ability of local chieftains to frustrate the larger needs of the region's workers, reform meant centralization. Local leaders became accountable to a larger regional structure congruent with the industry's. Democracy in some sense suffered as locals lost some power and control over their own affairs.

But the process of regionalization and centralization was not accomplished by some ukase from above. Rather, encouraging activism at the grass roots was the most effective ally of democratic reform. COMET (Construction Organizing and Membership Education and Training) is a program aimed at enlisting the ranks in an ongoing campaign against the old forms of exclusivist democracy. It has of course bolstered the position of the new leadership, but at the same time seems a legitimate approach to inviting real membership participation in important union affairs. Similarly, the 1988 grassroots campaign in Massachusetts around the prevailing wage law mobilized twenty thousand people in all the building trades, which together led the way for the rest of the labor movement and established alliances between Massachusetts trade unionists and other community organizations in the state. Without exaggerating what was accomplished, the Carpenters' démarche is invigorating, breaking through the encrusted insularity of the old order, widening the sphere of democratic participation and social interaction. Like-minded efforts at democratic reform from above

and below that simultaneously wrestle with the shifting config-
uration of power in the "market" have marked recent developments in the Service Employees International Union (SEIU), in the
"Union Cities" strategy most conspicuously successful in Las Vegas
and elsewhere.

A labor movement far more inclusive, tactically daring, and politically independent than what we have today is a prerequisite of
serious democratic advance. Just how such a labor movement qua
social movement is apt to emerge, however, is not prescribed nor
neatly described by otherwise unobjectionable formulations about
mass organization and union democracy. The relationship between
power and democracy has never been a straightforward one. It may
be morally consoling, but nothing more, to cling to the illusion of
their easy reconciliation.

The Legacy of Andy Stern (2010)

Melvyn Dubofsky

Melvyn Dubofsky (1934–) was born in New York City, educated in the city's schools, and took a PhD from the University of Rochester in 1960. He helped pioneer and popularize the "new," "bottom-up" labor history inspired by British Marxists like E.P. Thompson and Eric Hobsbawm, but Dubofsky was also attentive to the legal and political context necessary for union formation and growth. He wrote books on early twentieth-century worker protest in New York City as well as a national study of the rise and fall of the Industrial Workers of the World. They were followed by a co-authored biography of John L. Lewis *(1977) and* The State and Labor in Modern America *(1994). Dubofsky taught at the State University of New York, Birmingham, for more than thirty years.*

For the past fifteen years, Andy Stern has been the nation's most ambitious trade unionist. No labor leader has curried favor with the media so assiduously or obtained more face time on television. Yet, a decade and a half after promising to implement policies that would rebuild the labor movement, a goal that remains for the most part unaccomplished, Stern has unexpectedly resigned as president of the nation's largest single union, the Service Employees International Union (SEIU).

Stern's counterparts in the past either died in office—Samuel Gompers, Bill Green, Phil Murray, Walter Reuther—or left office at a relatively old age—John L. Lewis, George Meany, Lane Kirkland, and even Stern's predecessor, the former president of the AFL-CIO, John Sweeney. Why Stern retired remains opaque, but we can evaluate the extent to which he delivered on promises first made when he assumed the presidency of the SEIU in 1996 and subsequently when he seceded from the AFL-CIO in 2005 and created a competing national union center, Change to Win (CTW).

Stern emerged on the national labor stage in the 1990s as one of several younger dissidents dissatisfied with Lane Kirkland's AFL-CIO, which failed to reverse unions' decades-long decline in members. By the 1990s, union density had fallen to levels not experienced since the first decade of the century and nearly to rock-bottom in the private sector. The strike as a weapon of worker power had been neutered and labor's political influence rendered ineffective.

Stern and his fellow dissidents, Bruce Raynor of the Amalgamated Clothing and Textile Workers and John Wilhelm of the Hotel and Restaurant Employees Union, allied with other union leaders to force Kirkland from the presidency of the AFL-CIO and to replace him with John Sweeney. The insurgents promised a different AFL-CIO, one that would bring "the movement" back to labor by devoting a greater share of union resources to organizing the unorganized, to creating effective forms of political education and mobilization, to minimizing labor's jurisdictional feuds, to integrating idealistic youths into unionism, and to building alliances with community-based social reform organizations.

At first, the Sweeney-led AFL-CIO implemented new policies. "Union Summer" recruited college students to a program that trained them to serve as organizers and future leaders. The AFL-CIO and its affiliated unions strengthened their ties with reformers outside labor in such movements as "Jobs with Justice," the campaign for living wage ordinances, and "Working America," an alternative organization for workers unable to join unions at their places of employment. The federation also allocated additional resources to the organization of workers, and it enhanced its political power by generating massive union funding and get-out-the-vote drives during the 1996 elections.

Stern, meanwhile, applied his ideas for revitalizing the labor movement to SEIU. When Stern took over, SEIU was situated to flourish. Sweeney had already set the course, using SEIU's traditional strength in such union cities as New York and Chicago to amass the resources necessary to promote an aggressive organizing campaign nationally. The jobs that SEIU sought to unionize could not be off-shored or undercut by cheaper labor abroad. Moreover, the workers Stern sought to organize were those most favorably inclined to unionism and most eager to gain its benefits: poorly paid workers in the secondary labor market, immigrants, racial minorities, and women.

Stern concentrated on unionizing laborers who worked in custodial occupations, cleaning urban office towers, and providing home health services. The organizing campaigns that he mobilized in Houston and Los Angeles under the rubric "Justice for Janitors" achieved notable success. While other national unions continued to shed members, SEIU grew. He chose another effective method to build his union, swallowing the memberships of heretofore independent unions in health services, another economic sector immune to off-shoring and cheaper labor abroad. That strategy gained the SEIU hundreds of thousands of members in two of the three most populous states, California and New York, and in the latter incorporated that state's most politically powerful union, Dennis Rivera's Hospital and Pharmacy Local 1199. Stern's SEIU grew into the largest single union in the nation, with more than a million members, and perhaps the most effective politically.

Stern drew his style of union leadership from two of the nation's most famous labor leaders, Sidney Hillman and John L. Lewis. Like Hillman, Stern sought employer cooperation rather than wage strikes or open class conflict. If gaining the voluntary assent of an employer to union recognition meant a less than perfect bargain, Stern took it, never subjecting such agreements to the vote of members. In an environment in which NLRB-mandated elections or strikes were rarely conducive to union success, Stern—like Hillman in the 1920s—preferred to take what he could get. Like Lewis, Stern believed that union power was more important than union democracy. Power came from mass membership and union density, realities that created labor market monopolies and political influence. Like Lewis, Stern preferred an organization controlled by capable administrators who knew how to bargain with employers and how to discipline members. If local unions proved independent of the national office and their members unruly, Stern—like Lewis— was ready to place them into trusteeship or to merge them into newly created locals with officers more loyal to the president. Like Lewis, Stern believed that unions and their leaders had a single overriding goal: to accumulate power and then use it to enhance workers' rights.

While Stern accumulated members and power in the SEIU, the Sweeney-led AFL-CIO had less success. The federation's leaders failed to convince its affiliates to devote adequate resources to organization, and union membership and density continued their decline. Politically, the AFL appeared inept and impotent, unable to deny national and state power to its enemies in the Republican party. So, borrowing another page from John L. Lewis's book on how to build labor power, Stern walked out of the AFL-CIO in 2005 along with Raynor and Wilhelm and several other unionists who chafed under Sweeney's leadership.

Stern's effort to build a competing national labor center, however, was quite unlike Lewis's creation of the CIO in 1935. For starters, Lewis created CIO with workers on the march and their friends in political power in Washington and many state capitals. Stern seceded when labor was in retreat and its enemies in political power. Lewis's insurgency allied unions and labor leaders who shared ideas and goals. Stern's brought together an ill-suited collection of allies, including two unions, the Carpenters and the Teamsters, who had long histories of autocratic leadership, corruption, and an inability to cooperate with their brothers and sisters in the labor movement.

The United Food and Commercial Workers, another of Stern's allies, found themselves in a strange new relationship. Now they were in bed with a union leader who was playing footsy with the executives of Wal-Mart, the aggressively anti-union enterprise and largest single employer of labor in the United States, which had already subverted the Food and Commercial Workers' presence in the retail food trades. The distinguished sociologist Daniel Bell

wrote this in 1995 about the alliance between intellectuals and organized labor that flourished in the aftermath of Sweeney's rise to
power: "For the intellectuals it's a lot of wishful thinking; I don't
mean that in an invidious way. The real test will be whether labor
has the ability to expand its numbers. Simply becoming more rhe-
torical and becoming more active politically is not in and of itself
enough." The same can be said about Andy Stern and his creation
of CTW. It was indeed a lot of wishful thinking.

CTW collapsed almost before it came to life. The Carpenters
and the Teamsters behaved no differently as part of Stern's coalition than they had as affiliates and frequent secessionists from the
AFL-CIO. Early on, the Laborers' International Union, another of
Stern's original allies, sought to reintegrate with the Building and
Construction Trades Department and remain in the good graces of
the AFL-CIO. The United Farm Workers, another ally, was a shell
of the union that had organized California's field workers in the
1960s and 1970s; by 2005, it was a minuscule, dictatorial union with
few members and few contracts. Saddest of all, Stern's closest allies
ideologically and culturally, fellow products of the 1960s student
rebellion, Raynor and Wilhelm, waged war against each other. That
conflict led to a bitter break-up with Wilhelm taking UNITE HERE
back into the AFL-CIO, Raynor joining hands with Stern, and the
two camps going to court to resolve a property settlement like parties to a bitter divorce.

What had Stern accomplished in his fifteen years of union power?
On the credit side, he built SEIU into the largest and most powerful union in the nation, used his union's political muscle to restore
the Democrats to national political power and to make Stern labor's
most effective voice in the White House, and, finally, he awakened
the AFL-CIO from its latest spell of lethargy by speeding Sweeney's
retirement and his replacement by Richard Trumka. His debits,
however, appear far weightier. Stern divided the labor movement
when it could least afford internal division and to no good effect.
His attempt to build mega-local unions engendered union splits in
California, resistance from many sectors of the membership, and
severe criticism from many of labor's most ardent friends. And he

aggravated relations between Raynor and Wilhelm, possibly to enhance his own personal power.

It is unlikely that Stern will be recognized as a labor statesman
comparable to Hillman or Lewis. He can claim none of their grand
accomplishments, having neither rebuilt a union from near extinction nor created a national labor center that precipitated the greatest upsurge in union membership in U.S. history.

Stern's accomplishments and failures remind me of an essay that
the labor movement intellectual J.B.S. Hardman wrote more than
eighty years ago. In the essay, a dream-like dialogue takes place between a powerful current labor leader and his former self, likely
based on Hardman's long relationship with Sidney Hillman. The
present and the past represent the passage of fifteen years, the
span of time between Stern's assumption of union power and his
retirement, and one can imagine Stern's younger self, like Hardman's, challenging his present self with these words: "We are not
to inherit a movement but to build it . . . you have abandoned democracy in the name of efficiency. Idealism you decry because that
upsets you . . . you hunt for the immediate and the tangible . . . you
have identified yourself with the organization which you are called
on to lead, to such a point that you cannot think of the movement
without you leading."

And Stern, circa 2010, responding: "The union is the queer-
est compound of contradictions. Its accepted vocabulary is that
of a militant venture. But, in point of fact and in terms of what its
members want it to be, it is a business enterprise all through . . . it
is [also] the most political of all things! It carries the gospel of rebellion, and it suppresses opposition within its own ranks with an
iron hand, ruthlessly."

That, it seems, has been a perpetual dilemma in labor history: the
evolution of labor leaders from rebels to union administrators.

How Union Democracy Builds Labor's Strike Power (2024)

Alex Press

Alex Press (1992–) was born in New York City and grew up in Pittsburgh, Pennsylvania. As an undergraduate in Boston, she was drawn into the Occupy movement and the movement against police violence. As a doctoral student at Northeastern University, Press became involved in the effort to unionize graduate workers, an experience that led her to labor journalism. As a staff writer for Jacobin, *Press has covered union drives in a range of industries across the country. She is the author of* What We Will: How American Labor Woke Up. *Press is a member of the NewsGuild of New York and the Democratic Socialists of America.*

Scott Houldieson had some questions. He had worked at Ford's Chicago assembly plant, United Auto Workers (UAW) Local 551, since 1989, but in the late 2000s, the company was in a financial hole following the Great Recession and the leaders of the UAW told him and his fellow coworkers that they were going to have to give up some of the benefits that had long made auto work a good blue-collar job.

Houldieson understood that times were hard; he'd seen the quarterly reports showing gigantic losses for the company even if it wasn't facing bankruptcy like its competitors, but something still didn't compute. The workers were conceding not only on wages and benefits like pensions, but on other issues too, which seemed to have devastating, long-range implications: namely, Ford wanted to introduce tiers into its contract with the union. Tiered pay schedules, in which workers receive unequal pay and/or benefits while doing identical labor, are anathema for a union, breeding resentment and mistrust in an institution reliant upon solidarity.

"To me, tiers are the dumbest concession you can make to try to save a company from bankruptcy because they're not hiring anybody," Houldieson told me. "They're laying people off!" It got him thinking: what, exactly, was the underlying reason the union's negotiators were giving up such a crucial bedrock for any union?

"They were just too tight with the company," Houldieson concluded. That realization was a result of extensive research, which led him to become the editor of his local's newspaper. He pinpointed the joint employer-union programs instituted in the 1980s as illustrative of the issue: they brought the union into a partnership with the bosses, and *that* was a problem.

Houldieson was speaking to me from the other side of victory, achieved shortly before we met in the Huntington Place Convention Center in Detroit, Michigan, in March 2023. The occasion was the union's special bargaining convention to determine its priorities for what were then upcoming contract negotiations with the Motor City's Big Three automakers—Ford, General Motors, and Stellantis (formerly Chrysler)—for whom some 150,000 members work.

In the years since the 2009 contract, Houldieson had become one of the most recognizable dissidents in what is still one of the largest industrial unions: from a peak of around 1.5 million members in 1979, the UAW now has 400,000 members and 600,000 retirees. In 2010, he met members of New Directions, a small but dogged reform effort within the one-party state that was the UAW, in which the Administration Caucus (first formed by the union's most famous president, Walter Reuther) monopolized control of the union and its resources through a system of delegate elections for the union's leadership.

From there, Houldieson joined the ranks of dissidents, scattered across not only the country's auto plants, but in other sectors represented by the UAW, too: most prominently, higher education, which now comprises some 100,000 of the union's active members. These reformers wanted a more democratic union, one which would not, as Houldieson saw it, be so friendly with the bosses. In late 2020, these members formed Unite All Workers for Democracy (UAWD), a reform caucus that sought to challenge the old guard in the name of uprooting what they considered to be a "corporate culture" that had infected their ranks. Houldieson was chosen to be the caucus's chairperson. Their first goal: direct elections for international leadership.

Unions are not only about improving members' pay and benefits. At their best, they're schools of democracy. Whereas the U.S. political system is stubbornly unresponsive to workers' desires and policy preferences thanks to its capture by the rich and powerful, in a union, every worker's voice matters. It is here that people denied the opportunity to lead in so many realms of society are given that chance: contribute and you will earn the respect of your brothers and sisters, persuade your fellow worker to your position and you can start winning what's most important to you and maybe even help change the course of history.

But the UAW in which Houldieson came up was far from this ideal, woefully lacking in democratic processes. The union had become a top-down affair, and as is often the case, that went hand in hand with misconduct. When members founded UAWD, the union was reeling from a far-reaching corruption scandal that had landed twelve UAW officials, including two former presidents, in prison. A federal monitor appointed to oversee reform suggested the union hold a referendum on direct elections; in 2021, that referendum passed with 63 percent of ballots in favor. The next year, the UAWD backed a reform slate which challenged for seven of the fifteen seats on the international executive board, including the presidency. It won all seven, but the presidential contest—between Shawn Fain, an electrician turned union staffer from Kokomo, Indiana, and UAWD member, and Ray Curry, the incumbent president and an Administration Caucus member—was so close that it had to be rerun. Fain was only declared victor and sworn in the day before the convention kicked off in Detroit.

But democratizing a union doesn't just mean reforming the means by which top leadership is elected; changing a union's culture is a lot harder than swapping in a new president. As I made my way through the long days and nights in Detroit that week, evidence of entrenched resistance accumulated: an old guard supporter trying to fight one of my interviewees as we chatted in the convention center; rumors of property theft and other tampering; whispered discussion as to whether old-guard staff would cooperate or sabotage new leaders; an animosity that was potent enough that Fain addressed it when speaking with me, admitting to a "divide in the room" on the convention floor, one he diagnosed as a difference in "philosophies."

Yet there were encouraging signs. It was clear that Fain was a genuine member of the UAWD, stopping by the caucus's makeshift headquarters inside a convention room (at one point, he teared up while professing pride in his membership). The convention itself set goals that signaled a sea change might really be underway: the union would prepare to come to the Big Three bargaining tables with ambitious proposals, immediately beginning a contract campaign to bring the union's membership—many of them checked out and demoralized by the UAW's prior approach—back into the fold, harnessing their energy and forging it into a weapon that could force the companies to fold, even if that would take a strike.

Everyone knows what happened next: the union struck all of the Big Three at once, though not by simultaneously calling out all 150,000 members covered by the contracts. Instead, the union engaged in what it called a "stand up strike," in which specific plants walked out in waves, escalating every few days to turn the screws on the executives when they failed to make what the union considered sufficient progress at the table. The approach, reminiscent of guerrilla warfare, rested upon trust in the membership to "stand up" when called upon to do so. Quite literally: insufficient progress at the table would lead Fain to call a local's leadership, directing them to walk their members off the shop floor, sometimes with hardly an hour's notice. They couldn't have pulled this off were channels not open for information and pressure to flow both ways, with leadership confident in not only members' *willingness* to fight, but in the contract priorities for which they were eager to do so.

It worked: after six weeks on strike, the UAW secured historic contracts at all three automakers. Before anyone (myself included) could catch their breath, the union announced its next gambit. The majority of America's autoworkers are now nonunion, so the UAW would try to organize much of the rest of the sector, roughly 150,000 autoworkers at thirteen non-union automakers across the country, the same number as are covered by the Big Three contracts. Presiding over an ever-shrinking membership, tending to the union's private welfare state without ever looking beyond its borders to the great mass of unorganized workers? No longer.

The UAW's success in the 2023 strike was not entirely a result of reformers' efforts: a tight labor market and a multiyear pandemic generated a highly favorable environment. As Fain once told me, workers came to reevaluate what's important in life: "being able to live; not scraping to get by."

Within just a few months the UAW has become far more open to debate and dissent. And Fain seems comfortable with that. When I asked him about the narrow 54.7 percent contract ratification vote at General Motors last fall, he said, "It sends a great message from the membership to the corporate class that, hey, they just got a record contract and they're still not happy with it." One gets the sense of a leader disciplined by an abiding faith in union democracy, an understanding that the well-worn labor assertion that a union leader's power comes from the membership is, in fact, true.

Of course, union reform efforts didn't start with UAWD. Fain himself traveled to last year's convention of the Teamsters for a Democratic Union (TDU), a reform caucus in the International Brotherhood of Teamsters which has been the pole of rank-and-file reformers across the US labor movement since its founding in 1976. There, he told the room of union militants that neither his presidency nor UAWD nor the Big Three strike would exist without TDU (as well as *Labor Notes*, an intertwined organizing and publishing project).

But the UAW's transformation has resonated. In 2023 a reform caucus has launched in the historically staid International Alliance of Theatrical Stage Employees (IATSE), where members nearly struck nationwide during their 2021 contract negotiations with the Alliance of Motion Picture and Television Producers (AMPTP). Reform initiatives have gained traction, too, in the United Food and Commercial Workers (UFCW) and among rail machinists, efforts bolstered by those workers' grueling experience during the pandemic. Fain's use of his bully pulpit to speak not only to his members, but to the entire working class, is helping fuel pro-union sentiment, and organizing drives in an enormous range of industries, fitful though they may be in the face of dysfunctional labor laws and still lacking in the coordination and resources so desperately needed and desired by much of the U.S. public.

The newfound push for democratization isn't only coming from outside inspiration either. Adam Conover, a television writer and member of the Writers' Guild of America–West executive board who was on its negotiating committee during last year's 148-day nationwide strike, told me that he believes it was precisely the WGA leadership's responsiveness to democratic pressure from members that allowed them to hold out for so long and win so much of what they proposed to the AMPTP.

"We turned our democracy into power and by doing so, we were able to force the companies to do what we wanted," Conover said. "Most unions don't use member power in that way but they should because having been a part of that process as a neophyte, it was enormously powerful. It was a life-changing revelation for me to experience and now, I'm a proselytizer of it."

"All we really want is union democracy so we can make decisions on behalf of the membership that the *membership* sent us to make," the UAW's Houldieson told me in Detroit back in March 2023. "We don't want any more top-down strategy because look where it got us. The membership doesn't want to go there again."

PART III

A Time of Troubles

Hard times came for the American labor movement during the last quarter of the twentieth century and the first years of the twenty-first. Periodic recessions slashed employment and union membership rolls, but no upswing in the business cycle restored union bargaining power or political influence. As a proportion of the entire nonfarm workforce, union membership fell from 29 percent in 1973 to just above 16 percent in 1991 and then, declining a bit more slowly, on down to 10 percent in 2020. At the same time, real wages stagnated both for union and nonunion workers alike even as wealth inequality became far more pronounced in the decades just before and after the turn of the millennium.

At first labor's losses were concentrated in the old, heavily unionized core of the economy—what used to be called "basic" industry—where rust-belt factory shutdowns devastated several of the great industrial unions founded in the 1930s. Union membership fell by more than half a million in the auto industry, by 300,000 in companies where workers were represented by the Machinists, and by more than 400,000 in telecommunications after the breakup of AT&T and the rise of wireless communications. The venerable construction trades dropped nearly a million dues payers, while the Teamsters, whose truck drivers, warehousemen, and food-processing workers were largely immune to pressure from either technological change or foreign product imports, lost almost as many members. In the textile and garment industry a series of mergers and amalgamations could not prevent foreign competition and employer resistance from the virtual elimination of a unionized workforce that had once numbered more than a million. And throughout Appalachia, tens of thousands of coal miners still put millions of tons of coal on railcars, but few of them were members of the legendary United Mine Workers of America.

Change is constant in a capitalist economy, so the decline of some industries and occupations might not have been so harmful had the labor movement organized new industry sectors that were now generating millions of new jobs. U.S. unions held their own in education, in public employment, among the talents of Hollywood and Broadway, and on the waterfront and among airline and railroad crews. And they kept a foothold in hospitals, clinics, nursing homes, grocery stores, and urban hotels. But the rapid growth of retail trade, whether at big-box stores or online, along with the rise of a franchise-based fast food and hospitality industry, created tens of millions of new jobs that the unions hardly tried to organize. Nor did organized labor make inroads along the new commanding heights of the twenty-first-century American economy: Silicon Valley and its many outposts, finance and insurance, wireless telecommunications, warehousing, residential construction, export agriculture, and the new automobile factories owned by foreign firms.

Conservatives blamed the competitive difficulties of so many American corporations on unionism's high wages, inflexible work rules, and periodic strikes that prevented U.S. industry from successfully competing against the technologically sophisticated yet low-wage competitors from abroad and the nimble "union-free" firms at home. Liberals were not so willing to slash the American standard of living, but they also thought that global trade and new technology signaled the demise of a "Fordist" industrial economy characterized by mass production, strong unions, and a New Deal state that regulated capital and encouraged the growth of organized labor. In this new world, the "adversarial" labor relations born during the era of capitalist industrial relations had become outmoded.

The radicals who wrote for *Dissent* were not persuaded that either globalization or technology was responsible for labor's hard times. In America's internationally competitive, labor-intensive industries, including textiles, apparel, consumer electronics, and light manufacturing of all sorts, imports from Mexico, South Korea, and both Chinas did slash blue-collar jobs in many older industrial regions. But in recent years manufacturing has employed fewer than 20 percent of all U.S. workers, and international trade, high-tech or low, has accounted for an even lower proportion of those workers displaced by low-wage competition. Indeed, the impact of free trade has always been far more of an ideological construct than a description of a single, integrated market leading to a new, unregulated international division of labor.

Instead, leftist writers saw the demise of the unions and the industries that had sustained them as a fundamentally political phenomenon, a capitalist counterrevolution against the social democratic structures that for two generations had sustained an era of New Deal economic regulation and trade union strength. The Congress and the courts had become increasingly hostile to the kind of labor action that had built the unions in the 1930s, but the turning point came in the late 1970s and early 1980s. Then, in the midst of the "Volcker shock" that sent interest rates soaring, the near bankruptcy of Chrysler Corporation was forestalled by a species of government-mandated "concession bargaining" that rapidly spread throughout unionized America. In turn, that corporate offensive was greatly aided by the Reagan administration's destruction of the Professional Air Traffic Controllers Organization, whose 1981 walkout was countered by the wholesale firing of some 11,000 strikers. From that point on corporate managers were greatly emboldened, and the strike, labor's ultimate weapon, almost vanished from the industrial relations world because so many of them ended in outright defeat.

But *Dissent* writers did not let the unions or the Democrats, their erstwhile allies, off the hook. Union timidity and their stolid, self-imposed isolation from the other progressive social movements often rendered them impotent when they faced an aggressive corporate adversary. Meanwhile Democratic presidential administrations, from Jimmy Carter and Bill Clinton to Barack Obama, largely saw the unions as a troublesome interest group, hostile to an increasingly neoliberal trade program and otherwise marginal to their larger political or policy initiatives. When it came to American labor's ideological or economic influence, this era constituted a generation-long nadir.

In our first article, Jack Metzgar, a steelworker's son, offers a poignant account of how deindustrialization devastated his hometown, Johnstown, Pennsylvania. Next, journalist David Moberg surveys labor's fate in the 1980s, an era of both plant shutdowns and managerial efforts to undermine working-class solidarity. David Brody, the noted labor historian, contextualizes the fate of the old industrial unions, including the Steelworkers, in a survey of how a new generation of scholars has evaluated the fortunes and failure of the Congress of Industrial Organizations, a half-century old in the mid-1980s. Dorothy Sue Cobble, also an historian, sees the firm-centered focus of the New Deal labor law as inadequate to a contemporary service economy, especially in a world where men as well as women workers shift jobs with increasing frequency.

Unions are still essential to a defense of working-class welfare, but the old industrial form may no longer be most efficacious. That perspective is exemplified by the work-a-day experience and organizational efforts of hundreds of thousands of home health care workers as described by historians Jennifer Klein and Eileen Boris. Their wages are funded by the state, although they are usually not government employees; and while their labor is often long and arduous, they work alone in homes and houses that seem at an imaginative distance from the steel mills and auto plants where the CIO was born.

Antiunionism took many forms at the turn of the millennium, a couple of which journalist Lisa Featherstone and historian Joe McCartin delineate. Featherstone explains how otherwise progressive employers, including Vermont's Ben & Jerry's ice cream and Oregon's Powell's bookstore, deploy an ethos of social responsibility to counter employee efforts to organize their own union. That appeal to what had once been a hallmark of liberalism was also central to a twenty-first-century Supreme Court decision that sought to weaken public employee unionism on a nationwide basis. By defining as "free speech" any degree of public sector bargaining and lobbying, a 5 to 4 majority on the court eviscerated agency-fee membership payments—and therefore much union financial strength—on the grounds that the speech of any individual opposed to the policy of a union majority required absolute protection.

Johnstown: Ordeal of a Union Town (1985)

Jack Metzgar

Jack Metzgar (1944–) came of age in Johnstown during an era of vibrant union-centered activism and prosperity. His father's U.S. Steel wages helped give Metzgar the education that enabled him to spend his career as a professor of humanities at Chicago's Roosevelt University, where he taught working adults in general education seminars. A founder of the Midwest Center for Labor Research, founding editor of Labor Research Review, *and founder and past president of the Working-Class Studies Association, Metzgar is also the author of the classic memoir* Striking Steel: Solidarity Remembered *(2000) and, more recently,* Bridging the Divide: Working-Class Culture in a Middle-Class Society *(2021).*

They had a merry Christmas in Johnstown, Pennsylvania. For the first time in three years, the holiday passed without a steel mill being shut down. The unemployment rate was about 14 percent, nearly double the national average but well below the 25 percent Johnstown suffered into the spring of 1983. Many people think the worst is over, and some are optimistic about the town's economic prospects.

Johnstown has attracted a lot of media attention since 1982, when it led the nation in unemployment. This mill town 60 miles southeast of Pittsburgh has become a regular stop on the rust-bowl circuit. Most reporters, while noting the sufferings of the unemployed, have been more impressed with Johnstown's positive qualities. It doesn't look like postwar Dresden or the South Bronx. It has one of the lowest crime rates in the country and a high savings rate. Even in its depression, delinquency rates for bank loans remained substantially below the national average.

Before too long an enterprising reporter is also going to notice that the "retraining" program set up in Johnstown by Mainstream Access is now being touted as a "national model" and that the new "Johnstown Corp." is one of the few examples of a shuttered mill being reopened by new ownership. With a look at the new Main Street and at long-term employment increases in the banks, retail outlets, hospitals, and at the University of Pittsburgh's Johnstown branch, you could argue that this town, a backward place for most of the 20th century, probably arrived at the future a little earlier than most of the scores of factory towns that are dying throughout the Northeast and Midwest. Whether it truly works is a more complicated question.

Because it was a classic company town for nearly 100 years, Johnstown has always been a place with class relations particularly visible. Even into the 1970s, the essential reality of Johnstown has been a conflict between labor and capital—not in the abstract sense of *Das Kapital*, but in concrete daily struggles waged by you and your friends against "the company."

In large measure, the United Steelworkers of America won their fight with Bethlehem and U.S. Steel in the 1950s and 1960s. It also organized dozens of machine shops, and everything from dairy workers to bank tellers. USWA and other union workers fought hard for wages, benefits, and workplace protections that until a few years ago were among the best in the world. By 1977, when the steel shutdowns began, Johnstown was a strong union town.

As the Steelworkers gradually put limits on the giant steel companies' control at the workplace, the town's social and political life began to develop autonomously as well. The local business class freed itself from Bethlehem Steel's dominance and, with bipartisan political (and union) support, it initiated extensive urban redevelopment plans.

With the decline of steel employment, the power of both the steel

companies and the Steelworkers plummeted, and the local business class acquired undisputed leadership. Since 1977 steel jobs in
Johnstown—and USWA membership in steel—have dropped from
13,200 to about 2,500. Similar drops in employment (from 10,000
to 6,000) have occurred at the dozens of coal mines surrounding
Johnstown. Meanwhile supermarkets shut down dozens of stores,
extracted concessions from the United Food & Commercial Workers, and in one instance busted the union entirely. Teacher, fire
fighter, police, and municipal unions were taken to the wall for job
cuts and contract concessions.

During the depths of Johnstown's depression in 1982 and 1983, a
ferocious antiunion sentiment emerged in this formerly solid union
town. Though the steel companies started it, the antiunion campaign had a popular base among unorganized workers (in retail
outlets, banks, insurance companies) and above all in the professional middle class, which had long resented Steelworkers' wages
and power. And even many other union workers joined in. Teachers
complained that Steelworker wages were too high for jobs requiring little education or skill. Steelworkers wondered how teaching
could be compared to "real" work in the mills.

Through it all, the local business leadership maintained a calm
distance. The local media fueled antiunion sentiment, not by rabid
attacks, but by a studied "neutrality" that "naturally" gravitated
toward company information (often in the absence of effective
union publicity). When the dust settled, the local business class was
there to pick up the pieces. Schooled through years of playing both
ends against the middle, this class has exhibited a resourcefulness
not typical of an urban area of scarcely 100,000 people.

The new Main Street is their monument, 20 years in the making, a token of their independence from steel and of their hope
for a service-based economy suitable for Yuppies. The new Main
Street is a substantial accomplishment. I've seen Homestead and
Youngstown and formerly thriving commercial strips in Chicago
and Detroit, where vacant buildings and boarded-up storefronts,
broken windows, and trash give everyone a feeling that things are
out of control, that the living will soon be broken or dead. A good

part of Johnstown's downtown was like that for most of the past five years; some of it still is.

Anchored by an expanded hospital, a bank, a new Holiday Inn, and City Hall, Main Street also includes two high-rise office buildings and a series of spilled-up exteriors of small shops and stores. Still, this new Main Street is not universally acclaimed. A lot of working-class people resent it. Main Street used to be theirs, a place where men in steel-toed shoes and women in work jeans felt at home. No longer.

There used to be 17 bars in that five-block area—everything from the seedy to the merely tawdry to the comfortably clean; now there are three, the best comfortably clean, the other two better than that. A half-dozen greasy-spoon restaurants have been eliminated. Gone, too, are the three old Main Street pool halls, each with its distinct level, or lack, of respectability.

There are now fewer places for people to gather, fewer places for hanging out to see who you might bump into. And the street suggests that a narrower range of behavior and dress than before is now acceptable.

The new Main Street is a shot in the arm for Johnstown, a sign that things are moving ahead. But it's not the Main Street of a steel town anymore, or of a union town. A lot of people are being left behind, and still more will be.

The mood in Johnstown is good right now. "We're coming back," a lot of people told me. Others said, more modestly, "There's going to be a Johnstown."

Ask somebody who lived through 1932 and 1933, when unemployment was nearly 25 percent here, what 1936 and 1937 were like, as unemployment dipped to a mere 15 percent. Many old-timers will tell you that those were very good years. When you've been face-down in the mud, to rise to your knees can feel better than standing up used to. Five thousand more people were working in Cambria and Somerset counties in late 1984 than had worked in 1983. In a labor force of scarcely 100,000, that's nothing to sneeze at. But the worst is not yet over. Though there's going to be a Johnstown of some sort, working-class Johnstown is all but dead.

The area has sustained a net loss of 13,000 jobs since 1977 and 6,500 people have left the labor force since 1980; if they hadn't, the unemployment rate would be over 20 percent. Fifteen thousand remain unemployed. Few of the remaining jobs pay enough to sustain the working-class way of life that had been established through a century of struggle with "the company." Much of the apparent prosperity—the well-kept homes, the healthy savings accounts, the consumer spending—is based on union pensions. As retirees die off, that money will be lost to the local economy and fewer and fewer retirees will have the kind of pensions that sustain life, let alone savings accounts. Nor has Johnstown heard its last shutdown announcement from Bethlehem Steel—though, it's true, there's not a helluva lot left to shut down.

The 11,000 steel and 4,000 coal-mining jobs that have been lost were some of the best-paying in the world. Steelworkers had top-of-the-line pensions and health coverage. Many of those who were 55 years old or older and with 20 or more years' service got special shutdown pensions, which provide a bridge until they're 62 and get Social Security. Retirees' health insurance is paid for by the company, as negotiated by the union. And many of the permanently laid-off got union-negotiated severance payments estimated to average nearly $3,000 after taxes. Indeed, a good part of the union-negotiated way of life goes on even after the company is gone. Even one of Johnstown's growth industries, health care, is based on the continuing health insurance extracted from the companies decades ago by union struggle.

Many of the jobs that have been created in the last few years are in retail trade. The largest downtown department store pays the minimum wage ($3.35 an hour) or just above, even for women who have worked there for decades. One of the local banks is USWA-organized, so the banks pay somewhat better—about $5 an hour for a starting teller. The United Food & Commercial Workers' Union has fought valiantly against contract concessions, in one instance allowing A&P to close a dozen stores rather than accept a drastically substandard contract. But last year another supermarket chain, Riverside Markets, shut down its stores, met its obligations to union workers, then sold buildings and inventory to a new owner, who hired back many of the same workers without a union contract. Riverside workers who used to earn $11 an hour now make $6.

In working-class Johnstown the wage trend is clear. The best-paying job is retirement. What's left of the steel mills exhibits the same trend. In 1977 the Johnstown plant of Bethlehem Steel employed 12,000 people. Since then it has permanently closed facilities where more than 8,000 people worked. Actual employment at Bethlehem has been around 2,000. Though it's hard to say for sure, if Bethlehem were working at full capacity (which it hasn't for quite a while) as many as 3,600 might be employed. Of those, about 1,500 would be in the car shop, manufacturing railroad cars; having granted concessions in order to keep the facility open, these workers are no longer covered by the Basic Steel Contract. People who once made $13 an hour now make about $7. In January 1985, Bethlehem asked its Johnstown workers for more wage concessions. Given the climate in Johnstown, it will most likely get them.

Besides Main Street, the newly formed Johnstown Corp. is the proudest symbol of "the Johnstown recovery." During the last week of 1983, U.S. Steel announced the closing of its Johnstown Works, permanently eliminating 1,200 jobs. Even before the closing took place, local business leaders went into action. They found a buyer who, with the help of a $4 million Urban Development Action Grant (UDAG) from the federal government, reopened the place as "Johnstown Corporation." Though Johnstown Corp. employed only 200 people by the end of 1984, it hopes to build up to 800 over the next few years. The new company reported a profit in the final quarter of '84, and just before Christmas paid out a small profit-sharing bonus to its workers.

The key to the deal facilitating Johnstown Corp. was that U.S. Steel (USS) absorbed the costs of the shutdown before selling the plant. USS assumed the obligations of its union contract—pensions and health benefits for retirees and severance pay for those who were eligible. Then United Steelworkers Local 1288 was disbanded.

This left the new owners free of union requirements. They can hire whom they want and pay a lot less. The plant is a combination foundry and machine shop, so it had a large number of skilled workers. In most instances, it makes sense to hire those who had worked for U.S. Steel, but the new owners are free to choose. Union activists and other "trouble-makers" are being by-passed, even where they're acknowledged as the best on their machine. In many instances management is hiring pensioners who worked there before the shutdown and whose health insurance is covered by their pension. Some workers claim that Johnstown Corp. is getting federal money to "train" former USS workers for work they've been doing for 20 and 30 years.

In order to get its UDAG money, Johnstown Corp. had to form a new USWA local. The new local, with an office inside the plant, negotiated a five-year contract when it had only 33 members. This contract calls for several of the fancy new sorts of provisions recommended by labor-relations experts—stock purchases, profit-sharing, and two seats on the company's board of directors. But there is no pension. Men who made $15 an hour now get $9, those who made $12 get $6, and those who made $10 get $4.50—which qualifies some for Food Stamps.

So few plants that shut down are ever reopened that Johnstown Corp. is a national story in the business press—an example of what entrepreneurial initiative can do to salvage rust-bowl communities. I've observed too many plant-closing situations not to appreciate the activism of the Johnstown business class. Part of me agrees with the Johnstown Corp. worker who said, "It's better than nothing." All of me agrees with another who replied, "That's about all it's better than."

I grew up in Johnstown during a period when life was getting better. The wages USWA Local 1288 extracted from U.S. Steel financed a good part of my college education. My father, a machinist there and a shop steward for 1288, retired at 57 and lived 12 of the best years of his life off his Steelworkers' pension. When he was young in the 1930s and had risked his job by doing a little organizing for the Steelworkers' Organizing Committee, had he ever expected to live so well? Without hesitation, he said "no," he had never dreamed such a thing. And that's not what had been important to him at first. "The big thing was the fear, you can't imagine the fear," he said. "They had your job and they owned you, you couldn't look at them cross-eyed. All I wanted was a 'mouth,' some protection for saying what I thought."

The fear is back in Johnstown. Steven Smedlak (a pseudonym) is 46 years old. He put in 18 years at U.S. Steel as a machinist and was a minor officer in USWA 1288. He and his wife have four kids still living at home. The family lives on $310 a month from Public Assistance and another $203 in Food Stamps. Steve has had six weeks of work since Thanksgiving 1981. Because of his former union activism, he doesn't expect to be hired back at Johnstown Corp.

The Smedlaks' home is paid for—"In that respect, we're lucky." Their old frame house, purchased years ago for $6,000, might sell for $12,000 now in Johnstown's depressed market. But if they sell their home, they'll have to pay back everything they've received from welfare. There's no national job market for the kinds of machines Steven knows how to operate and, anyway, it's impossible to imagine leaving their network of family and friends and moving away.

Steven Smedlak is the kind of man the Johnstown Chamber of Commerce likes to brag about—a hard-working, second-generation Slovak, a man slow to anger and quick to apologize. He doesn't frighten easily and never panics, the type of guy who digs in, holds his ground, and gets the job done. This is called the "Johnstown spirit."

Shortly before Christmas the Smedlaks' youngest daughter was arrested for shoplifting. The fine was $77, which the justice of the peace is allowing them to pay in installments. Thank God, their 14-year-old son Bryan got his buck last hunting season and the freezer is full of deer meat—none of which, so far as they know, has to be deducted from the welfare check. In a quiet moment Steven told me, "I've never been so scared."

Hard Times for Labor (1989)

David Moberg

David Moberg (1943–2022) was born on an Illinois farm, got his start as a journalist working on Carleton College's student newspaper, and then reported for Newsweek *in Los Angeles. He took an anthropology PhD from the University of Chicago with a dissertation on working-class activism at the General Motors Lordstown auto assembly plant. In 1976, Moberg joined the staff of Chicago-based* In These Times, *then a newly established socialist weekly. As the publication's chief labor reporter, he remained there for over forty years, offering readers not merely an account of the travails faced by the labor movement, but an analysis of how to overcome them.*

In the 1920s critics of the American Federation of Labor (AFL) "pointed repeatedly to the same weaknesses: the emphasis on a craft structure, the ignoring of industrial unionism, jurisdictional disputes, inertia in organizing the unorganized, weak or tyrannical or corrupt leadership, philosophic individualism, fraternization with businessmen, and political impotence," observed the historian Irving Bernstein in *The Lean Years.*

Union membership declined sharply during that decade. Unions were unable, often unwilling, to organize the growing new industries and were losing in their old strongholds. There was a succession of hostile, anti-union Republican presidents, including one who had made his fame breaking a public-employee strike. It was a time of rampant individualistic materialism and wild financial speculation. The economic boom was uneven, with agriculture and many industries, like coal and textiles, "sick" from overproduction and low prices long before the Crash.

Many of the biggest employers adopted an "American plan" to crush unions, create the open shop, and break strikes. Others pursued a form of "welfare capitalism," a paternalistic scheme designed to block unions by providing some combination of higher wages, limited employee stock ownership, a measure of job security, discounted basic necessities (housing, medical care), and a personnel system that was more orderly (if still very authoritarian) than the erratic shopfloor autocracy of the foreman. Some unions, under pressure, signed cooperative agreements with companies to improve business efficiency, although Bernstein concluded the effort was a "failure" largely due to weakness. Many labor leaders were more preoccupied with fighting radicals in their ranks than in saving a declining labor movement.

This story has, of course, a happy, if turbulent, sequel as the labor movement surged forward with the CIO (Congress of Industrial Organizations) organizing drive of the thirties. That surge was aided by new labor legislation and, even more, in the 1940s by wartime government encouragement of union recognition to keep war production flowing.

Clearly, there are sharp differences between U.S. unions today and those of the 1920s. Unlike most unions of the twenties, today's unions strongly believe government should help protect workers and regulate the economy. And labor leaders are more united as Democrats, although often divided on Democratic strategy. Still, parallels with the twenties are eerily compelling: membership decline and wage cuts, business attacks, corporate paternalistic alternatives to unions, desperate offers of cooperation from unions, governmental hostility, labor political impotence, and union leadership that too often is a dead weight dragging down any initiative.

Those who take comfort that organized labor somehow managed to bounce back must remember it was far from easy and involved a great upheaval within labor itself. Those who seek recent villains to blame for labor's troubles must come to terms with the deeper roots of the problems. And those who think that the strategies of the thirties will work again are probably half-right at best.

Unions in all industrial capitalist countries have faced hard times during the eighties, but no labor movement has suffered as dramatic a loss of numbers, power and influence as U.S. unions have. Yet it is important to remember that the decline started much earlier: In terms of union density (the percentage of the workforce in unions), U.S. labor has been losing ground for the past thirty-five years.

A small academic industry has emerged evaluating the reasons for this decline. Its basic conclusion is that the balance of power has steadily shifted toward business executives who, never happy with unions, increasingly acted to tame, avoid, and, where necessary, crush unions. The balance of power has also shifted as New Deal ideology lost ground even in the Democratic party; the tilt of the law toward unionization was undermined by common-law traditions of the superiority of private property rights; and decades of prosperity and U.S. economic superiority nurtured a revival of the always strong culture of competitive individualism. On top of persisting divisions of race, ethnic-religious heritages, gender, and region, American workers were also increasingly separated by subcultures of occupation, education, and styles of consumption. And by narrowing themselves to a mildly liberal business unionism that rarely challenged assumptions about American economic life, unions have helped dig their own grave.

Labor's predominant focus on negotiating and administering contracts for organized workers delivered well, for a while. But the unions were becoming a smaller island in a larger, increasingly hostile—or indifferent—sea. Labor joined big business in an aggressive foreign policy that was both anticommunist and, by extension, hostile to all Third World efforts at serious economic reform. "Military Keynesianism," indirectly using cold war military spending as an economic pump primer, replaced the left-wing Keynesian strategy of planning for full employment. Labor joined in the extirpation of the left, wiping out not only the Communists, who were frequently discredited by their own actions and even more so by their Soviet model, but also the shreds of socialist thought. Organized labor ceased to be a labor *movement*, in the sense of providing a challenge to the "overall system of social control of economic resources," as French sociologist Alain Touraine defines it.

The relative absence of the left from American life was nothing new, but it is one powerful explanation for the weakness of U.S. unions. Comparing several other industrialized countries, especially Canada, with the United States, sociologist Seymour Martin Lipset has concluded that the weakness of socialism and of trade unionism are associated. The "divergence in the trajectories of union density across the border [of Canada and the United States] reflects the undermining of the social democratic forces unleashed by the Great Depression in the south [the U.S.] and their maintenance in the north [Canada]."

But strong as the values of possessive individualism are, there has always been a countervailing, if weaker, tendency toward community and collective action. The current supremacy of conservatives and business over unions is simply one chapter in an ongoing struggle.

Once the postwar economic boom began running out of steam in the late sixties and early seventies, the isolation of the labor movement caught up with it. Profit rates began to decline; business started seeking scapegoats. As unions tried to protect their members with cost-of-living adjustments, the difference between union and nonunion wages and benefits grew. Especially in the context of a profit squeeze and harsher international competition, that growing wage differential meant more businesses calculated that it paid to avoid or break unions.

By the late seventies and early eighties, with Paul Volcker in command at the Federal Reserve and then Ronald Reagan in the White House, the business cycle was allowed to play itself out with full force. Unions reeled before high unemployment, threatened bankruptcies, and pressures of international competition (worsened by Federal Reserve monetary policies used to break both inflation and the institutional protection of workers' incomes). First, United Auto Worker (UAW) concessions imposed in the Carter administration's

Chrysler bailout, then Reagan's breaking of the Professional Air Traffic Controllers (PATCO) strike, set the tone for the decade.

In 1987 only 17 percent of all wage and salaried workers belonged to unions, virtually halved from the high point of 1953. The loss of union members during the early eighties recession was predictable, but unions continued to lose ground at nearly the same rate during the long recovery of the mid-eighties.

Was it because of a shift from manufacturing to services? Obviously that change undermined traditional union strongholds, but other countries, such as Canada, have gone through comparable or greater shifts, and their labor movements have grown or held their own. U.S. unions win a higher proportion of representation elections among service than manufacturing workers, but they have simply not made an effort in service industries commensurate with their growth. Was it because of a shift in jobs to the South, to women workers, or to smaller plants? Success rates in union elections are higher in many parts of the South than in old midwestern strongholds; women are at least as willing to join unions as men; and small plants are easier to organize than large ones (although more costly per worker organized), as sociologist Michael Goldfield's studies show.

Overwhelmingly, recent studies conclude that growing employer power and resistance to unions is the major reason for the decline in union membership, accounting for one-fourth to half of the drop, according to economists Richard Freeman and James Medoff. But Freeman and Medoff also estimate in *What Do Unions Do?* that one-third of the decline results from the unions' failure to commit enough resources to organizing. Also, in *The Decline of Organized Labor in the United States*, Goldfield concluded that unions with a strong tradition of rank-and-file combativeness generally have fared better in their organizing than more conservative or autocratic unions.

Management ploys to beat unions have become notorious: illegally firing pro-union workers (at least one pro-union worker in twenty among those being organized was fired in 1980 for union activity, according to one study), hiring anti-union consultants, barely veiled threats of plant closings, captive audience talks, one-to-one supervisory antiunion campaigns, lengthy delays in holding elections. The overwhelming majority of studies shows that such tactics are very effective. Even when they win elections, a third of the time unions typically do not get a first contract.

But over the past couple of decades many large corporations have also developed a new, nonunion style of "human resource management" that includes such features as an "open door" complaint system, teamwork, quality-of-worklife programs, encouragement of individual initiative, and flexible work rules. Management has often tried to pay enough and attend enough to complaints to minimize the appeal of unions. Thomas A. Kochan, Harry C. Katz, and Robert McKersie, MIT industrial relations specialists, argue in *The Transformation of American Industrial Relations* that many companies in recent decades fled from or failed to invest in unionized locations, attempting to shift production to new sites where they would head off unionization with this new system. Others, like IBM, succeeded in keeping out unions altogether. Increasingly, in the crisis-ridden eighties, employers have also used the "human resources" model and their own narrow readings of Japanese management style to transform relations with workers at unionized workplaces, usually in the name of meeting competition in the market.

It is easier for workers to confront the boss, say a Henry Ford, or even a big corporation, like GM, or "Giant Mother," than to argue with the dictates of the market. The market appears to render impersonal judgments beyond appeal. But the market is also a proxy for corporate power, and in any case its judgments are made according to certain value-laden assumptions. By their very nature, unions attempt to challenge some of these market assumptions, but the U.S. labor movement rarely made explicit intellectual assaults on these principles. Typically, unions attempt to "take wages out of competition" by enforcing a standard pay rate for an industry. They also attempt to temper the hardships imposed by market fluctuations, redistribute income (for example, between current wages and pensions), guarantee at least a minimal standard of living, and provide a measure of security.

But the rule of the market has hit labor with a vengeance. A once-stable corporate world has been broken up by international competition, deregulation, greater mobility of capital, and a new approach to corporate organization (constant reshuffling of assets, outsourcing and subcontracting of work, increased use of temporary and part-time workers). Add to all this the recent "market for corporate control," otherwise known as the Wall Street roulette of takeovers and divestitures.

The net social benefits of this market blitz are probably negative. Managers have had a field day for attacks on workers. Predictably this restructuring through the force of the market is leading to greater economic inequality. But restoring corporate profits through the exercise of power and redistribution of national income away from workers was the name of the game all along.

Unions had often taken advantage of imperfect markets, pushing up wages more easily in oligopolistic or regulated industries. They benefited from dominance of their largely unionized industries in the international market or a domestic market partly insulated from competition by, for example, the cost of shipping heavy products like steel and the American taste for gas-guzzler cars. Once competition rushed through these industries, workers found it hard to defend their past gains. Many people, including lower paid, nonunion workers, had come to blame unions for high prices, even though a stronger case could be made against management. But the losses of union workers were not always the customers' gains, even by the narrowest calculation.

In its most benign strategy, management has tried to recruit workers to cooperate in increasing efficiency through innovations like quality-of-worklife (QWL) programs and work teams. Despite some improvements, these new concepts usually are so restricted that they never deliver on the promise of a dramatically better worklife or tap the productivity gains that seem possible when workers have a real stake in their jobs. On balance, they have served management far better than workers.

The flexibility and sociability of the team naturally appeal to many workers, but the team—like many other new joint programs—

is often used as a way of getting workers to supervise each other on behalf of management goals. The flexibility of the teams can increase pressures through what Mike Parker and Jane Slaughter call "management by stress." For example, workers are allowed to stop an auto assembly line when they have problems. But that signal of stress can alert management to the need to fine-tune assignments for the maximum tolerable workloads. For the cost of occasional disruptions, management ultimately can squeeze more out of its workforce.

Unions have been tempted—or pressured—to join in cooperative efforts with management in order to meet competition or to save jobs. In a few cases, such as the Bricklayers and the Clothing and Textile Workers, unions have taken or shared initiative to modernize an industry. But more often, management calls the tune, and unions respond from weakness. The biggest problem with most QWL and work reorganization schemes is that workers as an organized force lose control: Most often it is management that initiates the program, defines the goals, and sets the limits. Often unions find that QWL emerges as a challenge to the union for worker allegiances. The teams or QWL can offer workers a new voice, especially since most unions do not enable workers very much to express their views. Many unions handle complaints in a bureaucratic fashion, often not involving the average worker, who typically does not file many grievances.

Even when the United Auto Workers accepted employee involvement and team approaches, the leadership could never completely agree on strategy and was unwilling to put the issue up for debate and decision by the membership. Instead, the auto companies were able to use market pressures to play local unions against each other to gain concessions. The union still bargained over the terms, but management was in the driver's seat.

One top UAW advocate of QWL reportedly lamented, "We started out trying to be like Sweden, and we ended up like Japan." In Sweden unions have real political and industrial power and have long espoused a socialist philosophy. They also have a clearer conception of what they want to change that would benefit both workers and, secondarily, the company. By contrast, Japanese unions are weak, fragmented, and company-oriented.

Unions lost power in the United States in part because they lost ground with the general public, their potential allies, and the Democratic party. Public approval of unions began to fall steadily in the sixties, but after hitting a low point in 1979 began to climb back a bit in the eighties, according to a recent Gallup poll. Perhaps people no longer blame unions for economic problems and increasingly see the need for unions. Yet the public is of at least two minds, liking the general idea of unionism and feeling sympathy for workers but viewing less sympathetically the actuality of unionism and greatly distrusting union leaders. The public has long associated union leaders with crime, corruption, and undemocratic practices.

Increasingly unions have come to seem irrelevant to most people's lives, more ignored than vilified. In the 1984 presidential campaign labor was derided as a special interest; in 1988 it was barely noticeable, although within its own narrowed ranks it ran a far better campaign for Dukakis than the Duke ran for himself.

Ironically, the most forceful public voice on behalf of labor interests comes from outside organized labor: Jesse Jackson, who discovered the working class after his 1984 race. In the 1988 contest he took up the cause of strikers and plant closing victims and campaigned on an innovative "worker bill of rights." Several top union leaders worked closely with Jackson, and others privately cheered his willingness to speak out for workers, even if some loathed his foreign policy ideas.

Despite labor's support for civil rights, with greatly varying degrees of fervor, the black movement since the sixties has largely displaced labor as the central social movement in America. Why labor and the black movement could not have been more closely linked is a monumental question in its own right. But clearly labor lost the intellectual and moral position of liberal-left leadership it had during the New Deal epoch, as students, blacks, antiwar activists, women, and environmentalists captured the day. All those movements, and labor too, would have benefited from closer ties with the unions; the lack of such ties hurt both. As a result, there was no broad, cohesive opposition to the corporate power that devastated labor in the late seventies and eighties.

Is there anything the labor movement can do to stop its downward slide? Is there anything it is doing?

Fundamentally, labor needs two things: (1) a broader, more cohesive base of members and allies and (2) a clearer, more ambitious strategic vision. It's easy to say yet also true that labor must become a *movement* again, challenging the overall social control of economic resources. But those who want such a movement must recognize that inevitably unions are also organizations: They have members who want services, existing interests to protect, and bureaucracies that are necessary and need not be evil.

Above all, this means organizing new members. But it also means "unionizing" existing pro forma members and developing greater solidarity among unions and their members. Labor unions need to broaden their conceptions of membership, but they also need to see themselves as one part, albeit large and important, of a broader movement that they rightfully may try to influence but should not try to control.

Strategically, labor must redefine as its goal the old ideal of industrial democracy, expanding it to mean economic democracy and not just workplace issues. An economic democracy recognizes that there are numerous stakeholders beyond the stockholders in business enterprises, especially large ones. These other interests, mainly from the community and the workforce, must have a substantial voice in major economic decisions. In the past union leaders often argued that collective bargaining produces industrial democracy. But what they must recognize is that collective bargaining is only one part of it, and economic democracy must be guaranteed to workers whether they're in unions or not. The more they advocate a comprehensive economic democracy, the more they appear to be speaking on behalf of all workers and all community interests, not simply their own. It is a strategic vision that can help broaden the base and increase the power of labor.

Labor's strategic vision must go beyond the issues of voice and power and lay out the kind of economy it wants. It is in labor's interests to support but also to redirect the competitive forces in the economy. Labor should lay out its vision of an economy that relies on increasing both the skill and wages of its workers through constant innovation in products and production processes. Government, labor, universities, and businesses can all be part of more cooperative endeavors to make such innovation continuous, but in order for that to succeed there must be security for workers and limits to the range of competition (focusing on ingenuity, quality, product price, satisfying customer needs, and reducing costs through technological innovation and worker creativity). Borrowing a page from the environmentalists, since cuddly mammals and sparkling lakes evoke more empathy than economically bludgeoned workers, labor strategist Tony Mazzocchi has argued for the creation of a Worker Superfund to provide university education and income support for displaced workers.

There is obviously some overlap of this strategy with contemporary management emphasis on increasing flexibility and innovation. The crucial difference is that labor needs to engage that debate at a strategic level—for individual firms, industries, and the nation as a whole—in order to redefine the "restructuring" of the American economy in a way that maximizes benefits for workers and consumers.

In the long run, unions should shift from their traditional orientation of protecting property rights in jobs toward guaranteed employment for all workers without loss of pay when losing previous jobs. Although some contracts, such as in auto, have shifted toward general employment security, they are usually too weak to provide protection. Only a government labor-market policy, such as exists in Sweden, can provide workers with the security and retraining to be able to accept change. As defender of the public, unions must be seen not only as advocates of innovation, increasing productivity, and improved quality but also as the guarantors that workers and consumers will be the primary beneficiaries.

Some of the most hopeful trends include the mobilization of rank and filers to organize, links with other community organizers, the use of comprehensive corporate attacks to broaden support, emphasis on building a union through organizing before a representation strike or election rather than just signing up dues payers, and tailoring campaigns and activities to the diverse needs of varied workers.

Although little has been done so far, the AFL-CIO has recommended extending some form of membership to former union members or other interested workers at nonunion workplaces—the beginnings of a needed break between having a contract and union membership. But the labor movement could make great progress by making full membership available to anyone who wanted to join and by organizing to represent workers at workplaces even where there isn't a pro-union majority (ideally with new legal recognition). Likewise, just as professional associations of public employees, teachers, and nurses have evolved into unions, new professional associations of technical, engineering, computer, and other highly skilled workers could also evolve toward a form of unionism.

Charles Heckscher, formerly with the Communications Workers, argues in *The New Unionism: Employee Involvement in the Changing Corporation* that unions should resemble associations so as to adapt to the new, participatory corporate style he calls "managerialism." These "associational unions" would involve varied employee groupings in multilateral, continuing negotiation about the full range of issues from work life to corporate strategy.

As a prescription for labor as a whole, Heckscher's ideas seem inappropriate—more a capitulation to management power than a way to create a distinctive, worker-oriented participation. But unions must move away from their traditional bureaucracy and put more decision making directly into the hands of workers. For many workers, especially the better educated, unions are valuable mainly as a way of providing a voice at work, not just letting some official do the talking.

And workers often don't have much of a voice within their own unions, let alone within the workplace. The AFL-CIO report on "The Changing Situation of Workers and Their Unions" called for improved communication between unions and their members. But it said nothing about the desperate need to expand union democracy, end the tradition of union "one-party government," guarantee open debate, and make it easier for dissident groups to organize. Without greater internal democratization, unions cannot credibly claim to be champions of economic democracy, and many otherwise organizable workers will shun them.

Unions obviously also need drastic labor law changes. First, unions, as in Canada, should be able to win recognition after simply showing membership cards for a majority. (Union membership in Canada has doubled, while it has halved in the United States.) Likewise, employers should be barred from interfering in union organizing drives and required to negotiate contracts after a union is recognized. But without regaining members, power, and allies, labor is not likely to win this legislative battle, and it must first figure out how to organize successfully in a very hostile climate.

Labor's complete dependence on the Democratic party, which has drifted away from even a fuzzy, mild social democratic alternative to unrestrained corporate capitalism, obviously has hurt immensely. Rather than fantasize about a labor party or simply accept whatever comes down the party pike, the most productive action would be for labor and allies to form a bloc within the party to push a coherent strategy of economic democracy. At times a few liberal unions have joined groups like the Progressive Alliance and the Democratic Agenda as left pressure groups within the Democratic party, but they have never taken such actions seriously enough and certainly never organized a systematic base within the Democrats. Where labor and groups like environmentalists or community plant-closing organizers now work together, labor was often hostile at first and slow to join. (For example, Steelworkers top officials first fought plant-closing opponents in steelworking communities, only later joining with them. They had no strategy for their industry except to follow the companies' lead and fight for trade protection.) Even now most union efforts to reach out for allies involve the same few, important unions, often against the wishes of the top AFL-CIO leadership.

For every story of hopeful beginnings, there are many more stories of union leaders asleep at the switch, uninspired bureaucrats

hunkering down and watching their unions decline, wholesale capitulation to management demands, attempts at backroom deals
with business executives, abuse of union resources to fight dissidents, lackluster or nonexistent organizing efforts, suppression of
creativity from below, and simple-minded business as usual. Above
all, most union leaders still devote more attention to controlling
members than to inspiring and mobilizing them. On balance organized labor is at least in as bad shape as it was in the 1920s.

If it cannot once again become part of a movement that challenges the overall control of society's basic resources, it is likely to
continue its ghostly slide toward the margins of American life.

The CIO After 50 Years: A Historical Reckoning (1985)

David Brody

David Brody (1930–) was born in Elizabeth, New Jersey, to working-class immigrants. After working his way through Harvard, he published in 1960 a pioneering social history, Steelworkers in America: The Nonunion Era. *Along with David Montgomery and Herbert Gutman, Brody was a founder of the "new labor history," an academic project that deployed studies of working-class culture and social organization to explain the trajectory of class conflict and accommodation in the United States. Brody taught for many years at the University of California, Davis.*

In his on-the-spot history of the industrial union movement in the 1930s, journalist Edward Levinson concluded triumphantly: "Labor was on the march as it had never been before in the history of the Republic." Fifty years of history have passed since John L. Lewis launched the Committee on Industrial Organization, and so have nearly 50 years of historical writing about those events that Levinson first chronicled in *Labor on the March* (1937). New directions in the discipline, especially the rise of social history, have prompted labor historians to explore well beyond the political/institutional boundaries that first defined the events of the 1930s. More important yet has been the impact of a new generation of historians whose ideological roots go back to the New Left. And, finally, historical judgments have been tempered by the unfolding history of the industrial-union movement, as it consolidated itself within the trade-union mainstream and then, in our own day, fell increasingly on hard times. If the CIO has not proved to be the transforming event that Edward Levinson anticipated, neither can later historians cast that history in the heroic terms of Edward Levinson's *Labor on the March.*

With all this by way of preface, let us proceed to some reckoning of where we stand today on what *Fortune* in 1937 called "one of the greatest mass movements in our history." Current scholarship, in fact, hinges very largely on the treatment of the CIO as a "mass movement." This is a subject by no means ignored by such leading CIO scholars of the older generation as Walter Galenson, Sidney Fine, and Irving Bernstein. No one, indeed, has written—or is likely to write—a more complete account of industrial struggle than Fine's *Sit Down* (1969) on the great General Motors strike of 1936–37. And Bernstein's *Turbulent Years* (1970) contains the best narrative history we have of the labor battles of the 1930s.

But consider the scene with which Bernstein concludes his book. President Roosevelt is meeting with a group of worried publishers in April 1937 at the height of the sit-down wave. He reassures them that the new unions are going through "growing pains." Collective bargaining, a difficult process in the best of times, can be learned "only by experience." Ultimately, "we are going to get a workable system." In Bernstein's schema, perfectly captured in the book's ending, the central history of *Turbulent Years* is about the institutionalization of the CIO. This also is Sidney Fine's view. He quotes approvingly Jay Lovestone's remark after the GM sit-down strike that "rarely does a single event of and by itself mean so much"—but with this qualification: "insofar as it applies to the growth of unionism in the automobile and other mass-production industries."

A rival generation of younger historians would have struck out Fine's qualification. "Recent historians associated with the Left," Staughton Lynd wrote in 1972,

... have declined to join in the liberal celebration of [the] results [of] industrial union organizing in the 1930s.... We have dwelt on happenings which for liberal historians are merely preliminary or transitory, such as the mass strikes in Toledo, Minneapolis, and San Francisco in 1934, the improvisation from below of local industrial unions and rank-and-file action committees. . . .

In Lynd's formulation, the rank and file becomes the true subject of New Deal labor history, and the logic of that history resides not—as Fine or Bernstein would have it—in how militancy progressed to stable collective bargaining but rather in how that process killed the rank-and-file character of industrial-union organization.

History does not readily shift in its moorings. This was one of those moments. Lynd's conception of industrial-union history drew its inspiration from the syndicalist streak in New Left thinking. The mainspring of revolution, as George Rawick had seen it in 1969, was "working-class self-activity," by which, as Rawick said of the sit-down strikes of the 1930s, "the genuine advances of the working class were made by the struggle from below, by the natural organization of the working class, rather than by the bureaucratic elaboration of the administration of the working class from above."

Rawick thought he was witnessing in 1969 the next phase in that struggle from below. He and others of the New Left glimpsed revolution in the factory unrest of the Vietnam era and, on a grander scale, in the Paris spring of 1968. That heady moment passed. But it implanted a syndicalist enthusiasm that, transmuted and refined, has to a considerable degree redefined the terms on which the historical study of industrial unionism has proceeded ever since.

That history turns on the theme of *containment*—of rank-and-file radical potential held in check and ultimately defeated. But who did the containing? A logical question, of course, and one that instantly established a fresh reference point for thinking about the institutional history of industrial unionism. No agency could claim exemption from this question and, given its syndicalist presuppositions, none passed muster—not the CIO, not the New Deal, not even the left.

Communist trade-union work, wrote Martin Glaberman, was best described as "'bureaucratic'—the tendency to substitute the power of officials and institutions for the direct power of the rank and file." For an anti-Stalinist like Glaberman, this tendency was fundamental in nature, stemming from a conception of "the motive power of historical development as being the Party rather than the class."

Even writers basically sympathetic to the CP role, once they fell within the containment mode, defined party history in terms of "mistakes" in the relation to the rank-and-file struggle. On this basis, James R. Prickett constructed a reperiodization of party history no longer pegged to the swings in Comintern policy. For Prickett, the decisive moment came when the CP shifted from the United Front from Below—from the rank-and-file work of the early 1930s—to the Popular Front—to integration into the industrial-union structure, a period lasting until the expulsions of the Cold War era.

As for the CIO, listen to how Staughton Lynd concludes his case study of the steelworkers' movements of the early 1930s:

> The rank and file dream passed into the hands of [John L.] Lewis in the bastardized form of an organizing committee [SWOC] none of whose national or regional officers were steelworkers, an organizing committee so centralized that it paid even local phone calls from a national office. . . .

The New Deal itself, however, has been designated the key agency of containment. Its potency here derived not so much from FDR's broad political appeal to the working class—a familiar complaint of the Old Left—as from the specific impact of the organizing and bargaining protections granted by the Wagner Act (1935) on the self-activity of industrial workers. Thus, in a characteristic statement, Rick Hurd writes:

> The tendency was to eschew direct action and to opt instead for NLRB elections, or where capital was obstinate to file unfair labor practice complaints with the NLRB. As a result the working class was taught to rely on the protection of the law rather than on their own strength. Although the New Deal

contributed only marginally to the unionization of the working class, it did help shape the movement which evolved. It
furthered the expansion of unions which worked within the
economic system. . . .

The events leading to the Wagner Act were circuitous and contradictory, heavily affected by the unexpected struggles over
Section 7a during the NRA period. What seems clear is that the
Roosevelt administration never had a blueprint for such legislation
and indeed mostly resisted it until its imminent passage. The legal
scholar Karl Klare, for example, saw the Wagner Act at its birth as
"indeterminate," and "susceptible to an overtly anticapitalist interpretation." That the outcome was otherwise Klare put down to
deep-rooted judicial reasoning processes that rested on "assumptions of liberal capitalism and foreclosed those potential paths of
development most threatening to the established order."

The difficulties in the New Left assault on liberal institutional
history should not blind us to the very real benefits likely to result
from breaking out of a unilinear approach to the labor movement,
the New Deal, and industry. One sees this, for example, in Steve
Fraser's work on Sidney Hillman, who best fits the model of the
labor leader well-connected to government and industry and actively pursuing a reconstructed labor-relations system. The connec-
tions do not, however, run to the old corporate liberals but rather to
early advocates in business and professional circles of the Keynesian state. Fraser has assimilated the New Left perspective, but the
outcome is both more sophisticated and less pejorative than, say,
Ronald Radosh's earlier work on Hillman. Nor should one under-
estimate the extent to which that perspective has taken hold among
historians. Thus a seasoned practitioner such as David Montgomery speaks of a "New Deal formula" that was "simultaneously liberating and co-optive for the workers." Governmental intervention
freed them from employer control, yes, but "also opened a new
avenue through which the rank and file could in time be tamed
and the newly powerful unions be subjected to tight legal and
political control."

As institutional analysis, the New Left approach redefined the terms, but not the terrain of industrial-union history. But if the rank-and-file upsurge was the core event in this history—the event that gave it a logic of containment—then historical inquiry had to proceed on an entirely different plane as well. Lynd's call to arms demanded nothing less than a rank-and-file history of industrial unionism.

It happened (not entirely by chance) at roughly the same time that larger changes within the historical discipline strongly reinforced the hand of the radical historians. Social history began to preoccupy the profession. For labor historians, this meant a shift in attention from union institutions to the workers themselves. Some students, strongly influenced by Edward P. Thompson and Herbert Gutman, explored working-class culture. Others, following the lead of Harry Braverman and David Montgomery, concerned themselves with the shop-floor experience of American workers. And much other social-history scholarship led by a variety of avenues— ethnicity, race, family, urbanism, and so on—into the study of working-class life. Little of this activity dealt with the modern period; 19th-century materials lent themselves much more readily to what social historians were trying to do. But once radical historians placed the rank and file at the center of New Deal labor history, it followed that social history would be enlisted in the effort to understand the mobilization of industrial workers during the 1930s.

Thus Peter Friedlander subtitled his book *The Emergence of a UAW Local, 1936–1939* (1975), *A Study in Class and Culture*. His point of departure was primarily the conception put forward in Thompson's *The Making of the English Working Class* (1963), and adopted by his American disciples, that working-class consciousness was the product of preindustrial worker cultures transformed in the crucible of industrial capitalism. "The crux of the problem of labor history in the thirties," so it seemed to Friedlander, was "the historic emergence of specific structures of personality and culture out of the collapse and/or transformation of a complex and variegated collection of prebourgeois cultures. . . ."

Friedlander undertook, in effect, a labor ethnography—arranging the workers partly by occupational categories but mainly by ethnic and generational groupings—of an auto-parts plant located in the Polish Hamtranck district of Detroit. Friedlander's methodology also was drawn from the social-history scholarship that aimed at capturing concretely and in depth the experience of 19th-century workers. The unit of study remained local but was defined by a single factory rather than by a 19th-century industrial town, and the local evidence came not from census records, town directories, and newspapers but almost entirely from the intensive interviewing of surviving participants.

Friedlander wrote social history, but in service to Lynd's conception of the labor history of the 1930s as the self-mobilization of workers for collective action. His story was about how UAW Local 229 became organized. What has proved notable, even remarkable, about his pioneering little book on a minor auto-parts plant is that its findings very largely prefigured an entire decade of further research on the rank-and-file history of the 1930s.

From the time union activity began in December 1936, triggered by the wave of sit-down strikes in the area, three years passed before the auto-parts plant became fully organized. Only step by step, as the union demonstrated its growing power in a series of confrontations with management, did the body of workers sign on. There was nothing random about this slow process. On the contrary, Friedlander was able to map quite precisely how the social groupings he had identified—the second-generation Poles, the low-skilled first-generation immigrants, the Appalachians and, last of all, the Yankee toolmakers and inspectors—joined the union and the kinds of union men they became. The social-history analysis Friedlander had undertaken suggested that their sociocultural characteristics inhibited the class development of his auto workers.

Not all subsequent research of this kind fits Friedlander's findings. The ethnic identity of French-Canadian workers, for example, was forged into a notably militant industrial unionism in the carpet industry of Woonsocket, Rhode Island. In a particularly keen analysis, Bruce Nelson has linked the militancy of West Coast maritime unionism—for which the San Francisco general strike of 1934 was the exemplary event—to the subcultures of the seamen and longshoremen. But, on balance, the ethnocultural influences seem to have run counter to rank-and-file militancy. The leading historian of Slavic-American workers during the Great Depression, John Bodnar, has stressed their "realism," the high value they placed on job security, the insulating effect of their familial and community ties. They became loyal union men (as did the immigrant workers in Friedlander's study), but they were not on the barricades in the great industrial battles of the 1930s.

The search for the rank-and-file activists that Staughton Lynd had in mind narrows down to a small band of industrial workers. Friedlander identified the four key men who launched the union struggle at his plant: the most important (and Friedlander's main informant) was Edmund Kord, an anticlerical Polish-American Socialist and night student at Wayne University; his ally in the torch-welding department had been a union miner; of the two leaders in front-welding, one was self-educated and probably of radical background, the other a devout Catholic active in church affairs. Around these four, a handful of activists coalesced to undertake the uphill mobilization of the other workers. What impressed Friedlander was "the narrowness of the base of active involvement and . . . the breadth of the more passive mass. . . ."

Other research has turned up variations on Friedlander's theme. The French-Canadian carpet weavers of Woonsocket were led by highly skilled Franco-Belgian anarcho-syndicalists. Among the mostly Irish transit workers of New York City, the key leaders were veterans of the IRA who, as Joshua Freeman remarked, differed from their fellow Irishmen in "matters of personality, politics, and ideology."

To this mix, Ronald Schatz's systematic study of the electrical workers has added an occupational factor. To an unexpected degree, the industrial-union movement seems to have been sparked by craft workers. At General Electric and Westinghouse, the union pioneers were Anglo-Saxon long-service employees activated in many instances by demotions from high-status jobs during the Depression.

We were skilled men on unskilled work! . . . We were just part of the common mass, you might say. And that's what got us really thinking a lot about unionism.

The speaker was vice-president of the UE Erie local, where most of the members were low skilled immigrant workers. The women leaders were more closely representative of female electrical workers in job terms—short-service, young, semiskilled—but they differed crucially in their personal lives: they lived independent lives while their sister workers mostly were dutiful daughters living at home and turning over their pay to their parents. So, consistently, these rank-and-file leaders were unrepresentative workers, and unrepresentative, as Friedlander said, in ways that gave them "more profound ideals of a broadly democratic nature. . . . They shared a 'resentment of injustice.' . . ."

Members of this group made up what there was of a radical American working class. Edmund Kord was a Socialist, and he recruited his entire secondary leadership into the Socialist party. To what purpose? Friedlander stresses the instrumental benefits. The Kord people gained confidence, a sense of direction and purpose, and practical training in the arts of organizing and running a local union.

Did that instrumental logic apply as well to the Communists? Schatz's study of UE pioneers suggests that it did. They did not go from communism to unionism. "Most radical workers traveled in the opposite direction: they were union activists who joined the party for support in organizing." Their indigenous character emerges increasingly in recent scholarship as the key to understanding the CP unionists. It helps, for one thing, to account for the durable support they enjoyed among a non-Communist rank and file. And it throws into a rather different light their relationship to the CP apparatus. They cannot be seen any longer simply as foot soldiers, so to speak, in the march and countermarch from the Third Period to Popular Front to Cold War. The point need not be pushed too far and, in any case, is likely to resist precise resolution. That ways could be found for evading or reconciling conflicting claims can certainly be demonstrated, as has been done, for example, by

Ronald Filippelli's ingenious explanation of the success of the UE's CP leadership: it struck an implicit bargain with the membership, whereby the party line could be followed on the editorial page and in convention, but at the bargaining table primacy went strictly to bread-and-butter issues.

The New Left/social-history orientation thus has had the effect of disengaging CP labor history from the formal party history (just as, on the flip side, it has had the effect of treating the Communist party as an agent of rank-and file containment). The need for relative independence was of a piece with the need for the party connection in the first place. Radical the rank-and-file leadership may have been—but radical in service to the cause of industrial unionism.

What of the shop-floor actions that swept the industrial plants in the first stages of unionization? Here, too, Friedlander's findings have proved prescient. The wildcats and slow-downs in his parts plant sprang not from any class perspective or even from a strongly felt sense of grievance. They were the work of young "new hires" who had little interest in the union and whose activities Friedlander considered "nihilistic." There is a similar, if more variegated, drift to much of the subsequent research into shop-floor militancy.

The sit-downs at Akron's rubber plants, Daniel Nelson found, included after the first wave many that were called for frivolous or nonexistent reasons. "'We didn't care' is a common recollection of the sit-down veterans." Factionalism also contributed. Firestone, lacking the shop-floor turbulence of the Goodyear plant, exhibited a higher degree of solidarity, as measured, for example, by the vote given to labor candidates in the 1937 municipal elections. "Militancy and union power were inversely correlated," Daniel Nelson concluded.

In his study of auto plants during this period, Nelson Lichtenstein found "an inherently parochial and localistic focus" to shop-floor actions. They were mostly limited to strategically placed work groups (not on assembly-line work); they were called over grievances specific to those groups; and they occurred with little regard for the interests of other workers. That shop-floor actions might take a reactionary turn became evident in the wartime wildcats in Detroit auto plants, culminating in the week-long "hate" strike at Packard in 1943, called against the hiring or upgrading of black workers.

As a measure of emergent working-class consciousness, shop-floor militancy becomes increasingly cloudy and problematic. Might it not, however, have signified a more limited kind of struggle—one directed against the collective-bargaining system that was then taking shape under industrial unionism? This notion certainly runs as an undercurrent through the syndicalist visions of New Left scholars. Thus Karl Klare's analysis of the "deradicalization" of the Wagner Act turned on just those cases that gave primacy to the contract and "responsible" collective bargaining, culminating in the *Fansteel* decision (1939), which denied NLRB protection to sit-down strikers:

> *Fansteel* . . . bolstered the forces of union bureaucracy in their efforts to quell the spontaneity of the rank and file. As such, . . . it marked the outer limits of disruption of the established industrial order that the law would tolerate. The utopian aspirations for a radical restructuring of the workplace . . . were symbolically thwarted by *Fansteel*, which erected labor law reform as a roadblock in their path.

How strong a case can be made for the proposition that the shop-floor struggles of the 1930s aimed at "a radical restructuring of the workplace" or, more precisely, at a bargaining system that might result in such a restructuring? There was, first of all, a historical context for such a struggle. Nowhere else, recent scholarship suggests, was the conflict between labor traditions of autonomous work and the Taylorist demand by management for control so sharply joined and so endemic as under American industrialism. The workplace was, in Richard Edwards's nice phrase, "contested terrain."

That mass-production workers seized every chance for shop-floor control seems clear from Nelson Lichtenstein's study of the auto industry during the sit-down era and during World War II and from postwar industrial-relations research into shop-level resistance to the formal contractual system. What has not been demonstrated is the existence of any rank-and file conception of an alternative—say, of the shop-steward system that existed in England, or the even less structured shop-floor relations in Australia.

In their recent *Second Industrial Divide* (1984), Michael Piore and Charles Sabel make a strong case for technologically determined labor relations. The American mass-production system, based on special-purpose machinery and line assembly, called for narrowly defined job structures (in which the job, not the worker, carried the wage rate), orderly job allocation, and hierarchical control. It does not appear that industrial workers challenged these basic, determining elements. One of their earliest demands was for seniority, that is, for a *more* formalized system of job allocation. Grievance procedures were installed in the first GM and U.S. Steel agreements. And narrow job structures very quickly became the framework for wage determination under collective bargaining. The very logic of their work environment would seem (if one follows Piore and Sabel) to have compelled industrial workers to opt for a rule-bound system that militated against shop floor self-activity.

"It could have been otherwise." Staughton Lynd's words are a kind of touchstone to the new scholarship on industrial unionism. From that thought flowed a host of new questions about the known history of the CIO and about the unknown history of America's industrial workers. But that research must in the end be able to show that indeed "it could have been otherwise." Rich though the scholarly findings have been, they have not brought forth the one essential for historical reformulation: they have not revealed the alternative that rivaled the union course that was actually taken. So the field must ultimately be yielded to the liberal conception of industrial-union history.

Liberal historiography, however, is no longer what it was when it came under New Left assault 15 or so years ago. Bernstein's and Fine's central assumption had been the durability of the industrial-union achievement. (This was equally true of the New Left: the dividing line at bottom was whether one valued or deplored the stable collective-bargaining system.) That assumption has fallen increasingly into question in recent years.

Today industrial unionism is in crisis. Its bargaining structure, constructed painstakingly over many years, has begun to unravel. (The latest: May 6, 1985—the major steel firms announce they are ending industry-wide bargaining.) The political strategy pioneered by the industrial unions is also in shambles. (The latest: May 4, 1985—Lane Kirkland denounces the Democratic party for seeking, in the aftermath of the 1984 elections, to distance itself from the labor movement.) Nor have the industrial unions held their own within the labor movement. As a group, they have shrunk by at least a quarter since 1955, and today they constitute scarcely 15 percent of the AFL–CIO. For a labor movement under siege, the industrial unions constitute a weakening battalion in the order of battle.

A perceptible change has overtaken the liberal interpretation of industrial unionism. Early on, in fact, as the AFL showed itself to be the more dynamic unionizing force over the longer term, historians began to downgrade the craft versus the industrial issue over which the CIO had been launched. The heroes of industrial unionism also have lost much of their earlier luster. In Dubofsky and Van Tine's biography, John L. Lewis emerges as a deeply flawed figure, briefly remarkable as the founder of the CIO but incapable of providing it with sustained leadership, and incapable even of keeping political faith with his followers (he plotted for Herbert Hoover's nomination in 1940 before settling for Wendell Willkie). A sad undercurrent runs through the later chapters of John Barnard's fine brief biography of Walter Reuther. For all his social vision and boundless energy, the UAW leader was inexorably defeated by the environment in which he operated.

More telling yet has been the recent treatment of New Deal labor policy. In liberal historiography, the Wagner Act occupied a place of honor: it liberated workers from employer control and paved the way for collective bargaining. Now 50 years of legal evolution have made the National Labor Relations Act seem a straitjacket for the labor movement and increasingly also a tool of modern antiunion employers. One would expect that shadow to be cast back on the formative history of the Wagner Act. So we find James A. Gross's detailed account of the early NLRB devoted to describing the political counterattack that transformed a vigorous, independent NLRB "into a conservative, insecure, politically sensitive agency preoccupied with its own survival and reduced to deciding essentially marginal legal issues using legal tools of analysis exclusively." By 1940, Gross's analysis suggests, we were already on course to the Reagan NLRB.

Christopher Tomlins's new history goes Gross one better. The heart of the matter for Tomlins is not the emasculation of the Wagner Act but the fact that it was in inherent opposition to the voluntaristic basis of the labor movement. Tomlins's hero is not Robert Wagner or John L. Lewis but Samuel Gompers, for Gompers at least understood—in Tomlins's words—that "a counterfeit liberty is the most that American workers and their organizations [could] gain through the state. Its reality they must create for themselves." Perhaps it is time to coin a new historiographical designation, say, along the lines of postliberal revisionism.

And what of the future? Readers will doubtless have been struck by how strongly the unfolding history of industrial unionism has shaped our thinking about the opening struggles for that movement. At some point, past and present begin to disengage. The historian's own world becomes too remote from past events to dictate, in any direct sense, his or her conception of those events. The past can then be understood on its own terms, a lost world to be recaptured in the historian's imagination. That would apply, for example, to the 19th century Knights of Labor, which was the expression of a long-gone small-producer economy. But the manufacturing economy on which industrial unionism was built seems today also on its way to extinction. (The latest: June 8, 1985—the U.S. Commissioner of Labor Statistics reports that 2 million manufacturing jobs have disappeared since 1980.) Are we coming to the time when the CIO—at least in its original incarnation— will become the kind of historical subject that the Knights of Labor is today?

Labor Law Reform and Postindustrial Unionism (1994)

Dorothy Sue Cobble

Sue Cobble (1949–) was born into an Atlanta union family and politicized by the civil rights movement in the 1960s. In high school and college she worked as a waitress, receptionist, file clerk, and union shipscaler. After taking an advanced degree at Stanford, Cobble published numerous books and articles on the history of women's work and trade unionism, both in the United States and abroad. She joined the faculty at Rutgers University in 1986 and soon thereafter founded the Center for Women and Work in the University's School of Management and Labor Relations.

The Clinton administration's 1993 decision to establish a Commission on the Future of Worker-Management Relations has opened a far-ranging debate about the U.S. collective bargaining system. Organized labor generally argues that its priority should be strengthening workers' rights to organize and bargain under the current system. But most academic commentators—and probably a majority of the commissioners—emphasize the need to foster worker-management cooperation and to extend "employee representation" to the 85 percent of workers without unions.

I for one don't see the two streams of reform as necessarily opposed: workers do deserve greater protections in exercising both their collective and their individual rights to representation. At the same time, all of the most prominent labor law reform proposals have a common failing: they do not fully respond to the representational needs of the new service work force, a majority of whom are women and minorities.

In large part, this failure is a result of a policy discourse mired in the present. Ironically enough—given the ever-mounting stacks of labor history monographs and the flurry of scholarship on "postindustrialism"—neither a sufficient sense of the past nor the future informs the debates over worker representation and labor law reform. It is as if labor history began with the organization of mass production workers in the 1930s. The wide range of representational forms devised by workers before the dominance of New Deal industrial unionism has been forgotten. Paralleling this historical amnesia is a blindness to the dramatic ways in which the employment relationships of today (and tomorrow) differ from those of the recent past. The factory floor can no longer be the sole basis upon which generalizations are made. Our current labor relations system must be reconceived in light of the realities of the new service work force.

The labor relations system dominant since the 1930s and 1940s assumed a long-term full-time commitment to a single employer—a fundamentally "worksite" orientation. Union benefits were tied to individual employers and often limited to long-term, full-time employees.

This worksite orientation clearly is inadequate for the new contingent work force, many of whom are highly mobile and only tenuously attached to a single employer. This contingent work force—part-time, temporary, leased, on-call, subcontracted workers—makes up an estimated 25 percent of the work force, and most experts expect the proportion to rise. A disproportionate number of these workers are female. Women account for almost two-thirds of temporary help services employees, and Diana Pearce estimates that 52 percent of women, but only 33 percent of men, work part time or part year.

In addition, firm-based bargaining is not an effective approach for small employers with limited resources. This problem affects women and service workers in particular. In contrast to manufacturing, the service sector (with the exception of governmental services) is often characterized by small firms operating in local competitive markets. And, in the private sector, women are much more likely than men to work for small firms and at worksites with fewer people.

Moreover, many women's jobs in the service sector and throughout the economy are occupationally based, not worksite-based. Women move from employer to employer and from industry to industry more frequently than men do. Women thus rely less on training and promotional opportunities within a firm; they find a better firm or a better employer rather than a better job within the same firm. A collective bargaining system that weds higher wages, benefits, skill upgrading, and employee participation to a specific firm will deny basic employment rights to large numbers of workers, many of whom will be women.

The New Deal labor relations framework is also marred by its adherence to the managerial principles advocated by Frederick Winslow Taylor. Taylorism assumed that production is organized most efficiently through a hierarchically structured, micro-managed workplace with narrow job titles, detailed work rules, and strict separation of managerial and worker functions. In this context, unions were adversaries, not partners with management. In a classic division of labor, management retained authority over the design and organization of work; the union declined (and in some cases was denied) responsibility for supervisory functions, efficiency, and productivity.

As manufacturing shifts toward team work and more flexible computer-based technologies, Taylorist management practices have come under fire. Yet Taylorist notions have always been ill-suited to the realities of the service and white-collar work world, where workers tend to be in situations of close personal contact with their immediate boss. The line between employee and employer is more indistinct than in the traditional blue-collar, mass-production factory; employee-employer relations are largely personal and collaborative rather than adversarial, formalized, and highly bureaucratic.

Management efforts to Taylorize service workers, particularly those involved in direct service encounters, were never as successful or as widespread as in mass production manufacturing. At times, even management realized that friendly service and attentive caring are not best extracted through authoritarian, top-down supervision, and that creativity and problem-solving in white-collar employees cannot be "mandated" from above. Indeed, many non-factory workers, professional and nonprofessional alike, have always engaged in certain "managerial" functions; they work more autonomously or in self-managing teams where the senior member takes responsibility for organizing the flow of work, supervising less skilled co-workers, and maintaining work quality.

Given these realities, a labor relations system that allowed workers to exercise certain managerial prerogatives would be a better match with the practices of service and white-collar workplaces. Organizing and representational processes that emphasized greater participation, less adversarial proceedings, and more consensus-style "win-win" bargaining also would be more appropriate.

Yet efforts to move toward this kind of transformed labor relations system are on a collision course with the Taylorist legacies embedded in our current labor law—a point underscored in the AFL-CIO's recent report, *The New American Workplace: A Labor Perspective* (1994). Under our current legal framework, if unions agree to transform work practices and empower individual workers, they risk bargaining away their members' rights to union representation. The Supreme Court, for example, recently barred a group of licensed practical nurses from organizing because they exercised "independent judgment" in assigning tasks and directing the work of nurses' aides. In the eyes of the court, these "supervisory" functions made them ineligible for coverage under the National Labor Relations Act.

Despite the deep-seated problems with the New Deal framework we have inherited, there are tenets of that same system worth preserving. Let me specify three.

- *First, the old system rightly recognized that collective power for employees was essential for a genuinely collaborative relationship between labor and management. As Adrienne Eaton and Paula Voos argue in* Unions and Economic Competitiveness, the most productive partnerships are between those relatively equal in power. Yet the inequities of power between individual employees and their employers have widened since the 1930s. Employee representational schemes that fail to ensure collective employee participation or that create joint committees in which management retains ultimate decision-making authority are out of touch with the realities of today's workplace. Unionism and collective bargaining, albeit as transformed institutions, should remain at the heart of labor policy.

- *Second, the New Deal framework acknowledged the need for adversarial as well as cooperative encounters between employers and employees.* That need still exists. Arrangements that do not provide a way to express conflict and exert pressure for its resolution would deny the fundamental realities of our economic system.

The issue is not how to do away with "adversarialism" but how to minimize unhealthy and unnecessary adversarialism. Unions must be encouraged to accept more responsibility for the health of the enterprises with which they are linked, whether schools, hospitals, or auto factories. Yet the destructive adversarialism that has thrived in the last twenty years has been fueled not just by a limited unionism but by a management culture deeply skeptical of the benefits of power-sharing and democracy at the workplace. The true American exceptionalism, as Sanford Jacoby noted in *Masters to Managers*, is American management's penchant for unilateral control. Public policy must dampen the current adversarial culture by ensuring the institutional security of unions. Introducing "employee participation committees" or plant-level work councils might help close the "representation gap" for those without union representation. But the widening "union gap" between the United States and other industrialized countries must also be closed if these committees are to function effectively and if a realignment of power and decision-making is to occur.

- *Third, strong, autonomous unions act to overcome gender, class,
  and racial divisions in our society and to further economic justice.*
  Unionization raises wages more for women and minorities
  than for white men; it also helps close the gender and race
  wage gap. Unions with large female constituencies have
  pushed for pay equity, family and medical leave, and other
  advantageous policies for women.

Much of the current critique of the New Deal system equates all
unionism with the form of unionism that became dominant in the
1940s. Thus, the argument goes, if industrial unionism is obsolete,
so is unionism per se. This historical blindness hampers attempts
to create new forms of collective representation. Post-industrial
unionism does not need to be invented out of whole cloth; rather,
we can reshape and extend elements of past and current institutional practice. The practices of what I have termed "occupational
unions" and the nontraditional approaches to representation taken
by female-dominated groups such as teachers, nurses, and clericals
offer the best guide to a post-industrial unionism.

Occupational unionism, the primary model of unionism before
the New Deal, was neither Taylorist nor worksite-based. Although
not every trade adopted occupational unionism in toto, before the
New Deal most organized trades, and virtually every trade that
successfully organized mobile workers, relied upon some of its
elements. Occupational unions recruited and gained recognition
on an occupational/local market basis rather than by industry or
individual job site; they emphasized occupationally based rights,
benefits, and identity rather than worksite-based protections. Longshoremen, janitors, agricultural laborers, food servers, and garment
workers, as well as such classic craft unionists as printers, building
tradesmen, and performing artists strove for control over hiring
through the closed shop and through union-run hiring halls; they
stressed employment security rather than "job rights" at an individual worksite; they offered portable benefits and privileges; and
they took responsibility for monitoring workplace performance.
The line between employee and employer was blurred as well. Not

only did unions take responsibility for personnel decisions, but many organizations (teamsters, musicians, retail workers, for example) included supervisors and small employers.

Occupational unionism flourished because it met the needs of workers and employers outside of mass-production settings. In local labor markets populated with numerous small employers, the unionization of garment workers, restaurant employees, teamsters, and others brought stability and inhibited cutthroat competition. Employers gained a steady supply of skilled, responsible labor and an outside agency (the union) that ensured the competence of its members. Workers did not gain long-term job tenure with a single employer, but they did have the opportunity to develop skills and experience in a variety of worksites. This unionism, then, in contrast to industrial unionism, never developed rigid seniority rules at individual worksites. Occupational unionism was committed to maintaining employee productivity, quality service and production, and to ensuring the viability of unionized firms.

Occupational unionism declined dramatically in the postwar era, in part because of shifts in union institutional practice, as I have detailed for the hotel and restaurant industry in *Dishing It Out: Waitresses and Their Unions in the Twentieth Century*. Legislative and legal decisions also took their toll: the closed shop, picketing to gain employer recognition, secondary boycotts, the removal of members from the job for noncompliance with union bylaws and work rules, and union membership for supervisors all became illegal. Unions lost their ability to organize new shops, to maintain multi-employer bargaining structures, to set entrance requirements for the trade, to oversee job performance, and to punish recalcitrant members.

Of course, the industrial model should not be abandoned wholesale, but it is essential that we begin to think once more in terms of multiple and competing forms of unionism. A single model of labor relations cannot meet the needs of all workers. What transformations in public policy would help make possible new unionisms for the postindustrial future?

Expanding the definition of "employee" under the Wagner Act is of primary importance. By my estimates, a third of the private sector work force (some thirty-two million workers) is now explicitly exempted from exercising collective bargaining rights. Domestic and agricultural workers, the self-employed, and others were originally excluded under the Wagner Act in 1935. Later legislation and legal rulings have rescinded the bargaining rights of supervisors, managers, professional employees deemed "managerial," and "confidential" employees (those with access to information considered confidential by the employer). The law must not discriminate against those such as domestic and agricultural workers whose worksites are still linked to the household economy. Nor should categories of workers be excluded simply because they exercise certain "managerial" or "supervisory" responsibilities. In a post-Taylorist workplace, virtually every employee will participate in decisions once thought to be managerial prerogatives.

In addition, many workers are "effectively barred" from collective representation because they have nonstandard employment relations. Many part-timers, temporaries, and other casuals are exempted from participating in National Labor Relations Board (NLRB) elections because they lack a sufficient "community of interest" with "regular" employees. The problem is not just one of eligibility and expanded coverage but of making it easier for employees to secure contracts with their employers. The most frequently mentioned recommendations include increased penalties for employers who fire union activists, expedited election procedures, enhanced worksite access for union organizers, card-check recognition (which requires employers to bargain once a majority of workers have signed cards favoring unionization), and requiring arbitration when negotiations over a first contract break down—all of which would do much to "level the playing field." Yet more fundamental reforms are required.

If a mobile, decentralized service work force is to gain union representation, unions must once again have the ability to organize "top-down" and to exert many of the economic pressures on employers that were once legal. The millions of nonfactory workers—teamsters, longshoremen, waitresses, cooks, musicians, and others—who successfully organized between the 1930s and the

1950s relied on mass picketing, recognitional picketing (prolonged picketing with the explicit goal of gaining union recognition), secondary boycotts (putting pressure on one employer to cease doing business with another), "hot cargo" agreements (assurances from one employer that "he" will not handle or use the products of another nonunion or substandard employer), and pre-hire agreements (contracts covering *future* as well as current employees)—all tactics now illegal under current labor law. Making them legal again would facilitate the organizing of workers from domestic cleaners to the millions of fast food workers toiling for minimum wages. McDonald's, for example, is unionized in Denmark, Finland, Mexico, Australia, and other countries in large part because of the legality of secondary boycotts and other kinds of economic pressure. Unionized employees at milkshake supply centers, and those working as truckers and printers all helped bring McDonald's to the bargaining table by refusing to produce and deliver goods to the chain.

Yet even when employer recognition is achieved, the small bargaining units typically decreed by the NLRB make meaningful bargaining difficult. Decentralized, firm-based bargaining fuels employer resistance by heightening the economic burdens on the few unionized employers. It divides employees, and it demands an inordinate degree of union staff and resources. The Hotel Employees and Restaurant Employees, for example, cannot negotiate individual contracts with the thousands of independent and family-owned eating establishments that exist in even one major metropolitan area.

Changes in the law would help remedy this situation. Marketwide, multi-employer bargaining could be encouraged by certifying multi-employer bargaining units, by penalizing employers who withdraw from voluntarily constituted multi-employer agreements, and by implementing "sectoral bargaining" legislation. Sectoral bargaining mandates that the minimum standards of an agreement be extended to other employers on an industry, occupational, or geographical basis. Broader-based bargaining would also be facilitated by removing the restrictions on the economic weapons allowed to labor. Increasing the power of unions has often meant that employers—especially small employers in highly competitive markets—voluntarily sought multi-employer bargaining.

Lastly, other deeply rooted industrial union traditions must be reconsidered if a postindustrial unionism is to be born. Survey data show that although the majority of workers want collective representation, they are not satisfied with the way most unions respond to their need for promotional opportunities and their desire for recognition of individual achievement. In the past occupational unions rewarded individual initiative through pay schedules that combined seniority-based scales with wages pegged to skill. The performing arts unions still negotiate a collective contract that sets minimum standards while allowing individuals to bargain supplemental enhancements. Likewise at Harvard, the new Union of Technical and Clerical Workers there negotiated a collective bargaining agreement in which rigid, detailed work rules became less important in an environment in which decision-making had been shifted downward and in which trust and good relationships were deemed of value. Harvard employees relied on large bargaining teams during contract negotiations and set up a system of joint problem-solving councils that have involved hundreds of workers. These new mechanisms for bargaining were effective in large part because the local union vigorously maintained ties with its own members and relied on well-organized and traditional economic pressures when necessary.

Work-force diversity is not new. Over its century and a half of existence, the American labor movement has accommodated that diversity, as the variable practices of organizing and representation among teachers, nurses, construction workers, waitresses, janitors, truck drivers, and others attest. The test of the labor movement in the twenty-first century service society will be whether it can recover and extend that tradition of multiple unionisms.

Frontline Caregivers: Still Struggling (2012)

Eileen Boris and Jennifer Klein

*Eileen Boris (1948–) was born to a lower-middle-class fam-
ily in Boston and politicized by the civil rights movement and
its feminist offspring. A Brown PhD in American Studies, she
is the author of numerous books and articles on the relationship between home, work, and social reproduction. Most of her
teaching career was spent at Howard University and the University of California, Santa Barbara. Jennifer Klein (1967–) was
born in Miami and educated at Barnard and the University of
Virginia. Her books and writings have explored the character of
America's public-private welfare state. She teaches at Yale and
has been active in the New Haven labor movement. Boris and
Klein are the authors of* Caring for America: Home Health
Care Workers in the Shadow of the Welfare State *(2012).*

Flora Johnson takes care of her adult son Kenneth, who suffers from
cerebral palsy. She used to work as a cashier at a unionized grocery
store and made enough to buy a home in the Washington Square
neighborhood on the South Side of Chicago. After she retired, her
home became her workplace; she was paid by the State of Illinois
to be the primary caretaker for her son. The state also helped her
afford a lift to enable Kenneth to enter and leave their house in his
wheelchair as well as to install safety bars in the bathroom.

But home care is low-wage work, and Johnson found she lacked
funds to make additional home improvements to keep her son
healthy. She obtained a second mortgage to pay for such upgrades

as replacing a leaky roof and removing the carpet, a constant impediment for Kenneth. Trapped in the predatory loan market that fed on black neighborhoods, she took on a second mortgage with a balloon trigger that soon escalated her payments from around $900 to over $1,400 a month. Eventually, she faced foreclosure on her home. "It would have been devastating if I had lost it," she explains. "I just couldn't see myself being in an apartment with him. They won't let you add a lift and things like that." As the former president of her union local, the seventy-eight-year-old Johnson knew how to fight back.

When Johnson became a full-time care provider, she joined a Service Employees International Union local, now known as SEIU Healthcare Illinois, which had its roots among community organizers who had long fought predatory lending. Together with allies in a neighborhood group called Action Now, she confronted the bank that would strip her and others like her of their homes.

In the late spring of 2010, a dozen community activists accompanied Johnson to a local branch of Countrywide, the giant mortgage firm that held her note. When the bank representative claimed there was nothing to be done, a leader from Action Now emphasized the importance of Johnson's home as a necessary locus of caring, insisting, "Oh yes, you can do it. She has a son with cerebral palsy. She needs to stay in her own home." Turning that into a particular moral and political claim, backed by collective action, they succeeded in forcing Countrywide to eliminate the higher interest rate, bring the mortgage more in line with actual home value, and reduce monthly payments to what she could afford. Over the past two years, Johnson and her fellow and sister activists have repeated this tactic at dozens of banks that threaten the homes of other poor and working-class Chicagoans.

The Great Recession has hit home-based workers like Johnson with a triple whammy. The housing and mortgage crisis threatened their very workplace—their homes or the homes of those they cared for; the fiscal crisis of the state led to cuts in funds that paid their wages through long-term care programs; and the conservative political backlash and Republican ascent of 2010 opened an assault on their hard-won collective bargaining rights, wage increases, and recognition as "workers."

Poor black women like Johnson have long cared for the elderly, ill, and disabled—whether in their own homes or in the residences of others. Sometimes, they do it out of love; many have referred to care work as "a calling." Often, it is the best job they can find. Elsewhere in the United States, Latinas and other recent immigrants make up a third of those who perform daily tasks—bathing bodies, brushing teeth, putting on clothes, cooking meals—that enable people to live decently in their own homes. But in Chicago, African Americans still dominate this workforce. They mostly care for elderly and disabled people who qualify for Medicaid and SSI (Supplemental Security Income).

These workers are America's frontline caregivers. They number over 1.7 million nationwide. Home care workers earn just a bit more than the minimum wage and historically have had little or no job security, health benefits, or even workers' compensation. Government programs began subsidizing home care in the 1930s. Yet in every decade since then, policymakers and welfare administrators have acted on the presumption that the intimate labor of caregiving should be the loving and unpaid duty of wives, mothers, and daughters. So home care aides, defined as elder companions rather than workers, are still excluded from the nation's primary wage-and-hour law, the Fair Labor Standards Act, more than seven decades after it was enacted in 1938. Moreover, because they are often poor women taking care of people receiving public assistance, the suspicion and taint of "welfare fraud" has been used to cut their hours of service or pay in times of fiscal anxiety.

Since the late 1970s, however, hundreds of thousands of caregivers have demanded recognition of their worth as well as more funding for their clients—and achieved some notable successes. In Illinois and California, the SEIU took the lead in organizing this workforce. In New York, first Hospital Workers Local 1199 and then the SEIU obtained better reimbursement rates from state legislatures for vendor agencies, which in turn led to improved worker pay through more robust collective bargaining contracts. Elsewhere,

the American Federation of State, County, and Municipal Employees (AFSCME) and the Communications Workers helped home care
workers achieve similar gains. About 500,000 home health workers are unionized. At least 275,000 home child care providers also
have moved into unions. Where they are state-recognized, home
care unions have achieved density, that is, they represent nearly all
workers in the sector.

Their most critical demand is for an adequate income. In the late
1950s and 1960s, home care workers became public employees, with
standard hours and benefits. Yet once they joined with the rising
militancy of other public sector workers, local and state govern-
ments in the 1970s increasingly turned to contracting out the service to private agencies or classifying the workers themselves as
independent contractors, leading to greater casualization of the
job. A worker employed by a nonprofit (or, after 1981, a for-profit)
firm could never count on a fair wage for hours worked; indeed,
it was difficult to even get enough hours to add up. She might be
assigned to help an elderly person to get out of bed in the morning,
get dressed, and eat breakfast, and then travel, at her own expense,
to tend to another client for a few hours. And if it took her longer to
finish her tasks, she wouldn't receive overtime.

Unions developed a strategy that gradually changed the way
state authorities treated home care workers. To overcome the lack
of a common workplace and exclusion from national labor laws,
organizers marched on state capitols and lobbied their representatives. They sought to elect legislators and governors who would
improve working conditions that also enhanced the quality of care.
They formed coalitions with relatives of their clients, with disability rights activists, and with advocates for senior citizens. The
outcome of this long struggle was the recognition in many states
of home-based care workers as quasi-public employees, paid from
public revenues. In some states, unionization efforts preceded a
change in policy, whether executive order or legislation. In others,
governors signed executive orders allowing for (and thus sparking)
union elections.

Where the union developed a grassroots culture, it transformed working for these state programs into a collective experience that turned caregivers into workers and workers into trade unionists. Amanda Carles, a California woman who cared for an adult daughter with Down Syndrome, explained that she had "become much more aware of all the things you do [for the person you're taking care of]. Once you actually have to document your hours to get paid . . . you see how much work you do." The union became the place where, one Russian-speaking immigrant told us, "you can step forward, have a voice, you can have free speech." Bay Area home attendant Rosie Byers became a shop steward and eventually a union vice-president in the 1980s. The union trained Byers and her co-workers to organize others and read contracts. "We started telling people . . . you'll be able to speak up and speak out about the contract. You can even have a say on the contract," Byers said. "That really had a big impact." They were able, in the words of many union members, to "come out of the shadows" and be "invisible no more."

All these efforts depended on the ability, as well as the desire, of politicians to devote public resources to workers' welfare. But the Great Recession has jeopardized these advances. Even as home care has become one of fastest growing sectors of the economy, the major achievements of union members—greater employment security and benefits for clients—are threatened by reductions in hours and funding.

Barack Obama's economic stimulus helped stabilize programs and wages through 2010, but major reductions in hours (and thus income) began in 2011. Agency employees in Illinois, for example, average only twenty hours of paid work a week, but workers have clients who require more assistance. Those taking care of family members can't extend their hours because they can't leave a homebound relative to go to another person's residence. State agencies are recalculating what family members would supposedly provide anyway, thus recalibrating the allotment of support based on expanding the range of unpaid labor. They are also reducing the hours a worker is allowed to spend with each client.

These cutbacks can take subtle but insidious forms, such as

undercounting the time it takes to give a bath or do laundry. Workers can't leave their charge in the middle of a bath because the allotted minutes are up, but they don't get paid for the "extra" time. Some workers use their own money to buy food for clients or take them to the doctor. States exploit the fact that it's an intimate, relational job.

Some states are also narrowing what kinds of labor they will compensate. In particular, they have targeted housekeeping. There's always been an ambiguity about which aspects of home care should be paid: bodily services and personal care; housekeeping; the emotional labor of chatting, sharing stories, spending time, and being a friend. When judges, agency administrators, and politicians previously sought to deny state responsibility for the conditions of employment, they renamed the job—as visiting housekeeper, homemaker, home attendant, or home aide—in order to get another federal program or level of government to pay for the service. Workers saw through that ruse and testified before courts, Congress, and public agencies that no matter what they were called, the work was the same, part manual and part emotional, personal tending and housekeeping. Over time, they won payment for cleaning houses as well as people.

The current economic crisis has given state officials an opportunity to constrict this broader recognition and thereby reduce hard-won gains. In early 2011, Governor Scott Walker and the Republican majority in the Wisconsin legislature stripped all bargaining rights for home-based care workers as part of their larger rollback of rights for public employees. Rick Snyder, Michigan's Republican governor, sided with home child care contractors who didn't want to withhold union dues from employee paychecks after the anti-union National Right to Work Legal Defense Fund took up their cause. The Governor ruled that state-subsidized home health care workers, twenty thousand in number, were not public employees. In Ohio and Indiana, Republican governors rescinded state executive orders that had fostered unionization of these home care workers. Even Governor Jerry Brown of California, a Democrat who relied on union support for his victory in 2010, got the legislature to cut funds for home care and vetoed a bill giving bargaining rights to home-based child care providers.

As Flora Johnson can testify, care workers and recipients are equally threatened by the collapse of the housing bubble. Since 2008, Cook County has experienced over 40,000 home foreclosures every year. In Roseland, Englewood, and South Shore, neighborhoods near Johnson's home in Washington Square, "you drive down a block and you might see only two houses occupied and all the others boarded up. People just can't afford it," one union official explains.

Care workers are struggling to hold on to their homes amid increasingly dangerous conditions; yet they must stay in them. For years, the independent-living movement has emphasized the right to live at home and in the community—winning these rights through political action and court cases. For child care providers, state licensing guidelines often require that they make modifications to the house in which they live, so these workers often have a significant investment in the home. It is their workplace and essential to carry out their work. This merger of home and work thus turns the foreclosure threat faced by other poor people into a particularly acute crisis for home care workers.

As a nation, we seem to believe that only through cheap labor can we "afford" to provide long-term care. We think about the needs of recipients but not about those who do the work. The Great Recession and Republican ascendancy are shaking the very programs that made home-based services possible. Can we let these forces make life more precarious for all of us? A majority of Americans will at some point depend on a care worker, often one who has long labored in poverty and struggled to balance her own and others' social needs. The absence of public support and labor standards may hasten the day when no one will be available to care.

"It's Business, Man!" Unions and "Socially Responsible" Corporations (1999)

Liza Featherstone

Liza Featherstone (1969–) was born in Washington, DC, and grew up near Boston. Educated at the University of Michigan, she has been a labor journalist and teacher at New York–area universities. She has published books on the antisweatshop movement, working conditions at Walmart, Hillary Clinton, and the history and culture of focus groups. She is a member of the Democratic Socialists of America.

"How do you feel?" roared Jerry Greenfield, CEO and co-founder of Ben & Jerry's, the ice cream company that has (in the public imagination, at least) long epitomized corporate social responsibility. He posed this question a few years ago to the audience at the company's folk music festival, held annually in mansion-packed Newport, Rhode Island. "I feel good!" roared back the Teva- and tie-dye-clad crowd. (Greenfield opens the company's staff meetings with the same ritualized call and response.) The folk festival—featuring countercultural icons like Joan Baez and accessorized by petitions supporting legislation to "Save the Family Farm"—was vintage Ben & Jerry's. Greenfield's performance was designed to assure the festival's upper-middle-class audience that Ben & Jerry's, maker of flavors with trippy names like Cherry Garcia, is not a bunch of grim stuffed shirts in a boardroom, but a downright groovy (and ethical) little company. The skeptical observer, however, couldn't help wondering: what happens if you don't feel so good?

Last year, a group of maintenance employees at the Ben & Jerry's plant in St. Albans, Vermont, found out. These workers wanted time and a half for work on weekends and for any work that exceeded the standard eight-hour day. Company policy was to pay the federal minimum: time and a half only after forty hours have been worked in a week. (This means, for example, that maintenance workers might be scheduled for ten-hour shifts on the four days following Labor Day or Memorial Day, but collect no overtime.) In early November, after months of frustrating discussions with management, some of the maintenance workers, who earn, on average, about $17 an hour, approached the International Brotherhood of Electrical Workers' Local 300, and launched a campaign for representation.

Ben & Jerry's fought back. Asked how the company's anti-union campaign compared to those he's encountered from other, less "socially responsible" firms, Local 300's Tim Watkins, who coordinated the drive, called it "very aggressive." Some of the campaign followed a textbook union-busting formula: management held closed-door meetings with employees who had signed union cards, and told them that if they joined the union, they'd be spending all their time on picket lines, and would be "expected to go on strike at the drop of a hat," says Watkins. The union filed no unfair labor practices charge with the National Labor Relations Board (NLRB), because, as Watkins explains, "they always stopped just short enough of illegality."

None of this is unusual; employers fight unions every day, and they fight them unscrupulously. According to analyses of NLRB data by Cornell labor researcher Kate Bronfenbrenner, about a third of companies have illegally fired union supporters during elections. In this context, the behavior of Ben & Jerry's certainly wasn't as bad as a company's can get.

But Ben & Jerry's had a formidable and complicated weapon at its disposal: a "socially responsible" image. Started in 1978 by Ben

Cohen and Jerry Greenfield, two longhairs who have been friends since junior high gym class, Ben & Jerry's is now a multinational corporation with more than 170 stores in the United States, and has been famously socially conscious for over a decade. The company's mission statement, written in 1988, advertises its dedication to the "new corporate concept of linked prosperity" and declares a "deep respect for individuals inside and outside the company and for the communities of which they are a part." Through the Ben & Jerry's Foundation, the company redirects 7.5 percent of all pretax profits to nonprofit organizations. The company's best-known campaign has been "1% For Peace," a crusade to redirect 1 percent of the U.S. defense budget to "peace-promoting projects." Ben Cohen brought an eleven-foot ice cream pie to Capitol Hill to protest inadequate social spending and appeared on ABC's *The View* calling for cuts in the defense budget.

Ben & Jerry's argued that its employees didn't need a union because they had better-than-average benefits (including paid family leave and health club memberships, as well as three pints of ice cream daily). Central to the company's campaign, too, was the argument that the maintenance employees shouldn't be trying to organize a bargaining unit that included only themselves; all 150 workers in the plant, Ben & Jerry's lawyers argued, should be given the chance to vote on union representation. With this objection—the basis of Ben & Jerry's challenge to the union before the NLRB—Ben & Jerry's appeared to be promoting democracy in its workplace. But that rhetoric was disingenuous, because the union's support wasn't as strong among the production employees in the plant. Furthermore, the electrical workers' union was a logical choice for the maintenance employees because they are electrical workers. Had the production workers wanted to unionize, another union, one that had some experience in their field, would have been more suitable. In December, the NLRB rejected Ben & Jerry's challenge and ordered an election at the company.

In January, the maintenance workers voted for the union, eleven to eight, becoming the first unionized Ben & Jerry's employees in the company's twenty-year history. But Watkins says that the Ben &

Jerry's campaign was so relentless that if the pro-union employees "hadn't been so solid, we would have lost them." Bargaining hasn't been easy, either; by early July, seven months after the election, there had been more than a dozen frustrating negotiation sessions, none lasting longer than three hours, and a satisfactory contract was nowhere on the horizon.

Given that Ben & Jerry's professes concern for—and even puts some serious money toward helping—the poor and marginal, the company's anti-unionism seems curious. But in balking at unions in its own workplace, Ben & Jerry's is far from unique among progressive employers. Businesses with an explicit mission of "social responsibility" (SR)— of which Ben & Jerry's is probably the most famously liberal—have been proliferating since the late seventies. In addition to Ben & Jerry's, such companies as Borders Books and Music, Starbucks, Noah's Bagels, Whole Foods, Newman's Own, Working Assets, and the Portland, Oregon–based Powell's Books have recently been mired in acrimonious labor disputes. "It's business, man!" says Marty Kruse, a used-book buyer and one of the initial Powell's organizers, who thinks it's foolish even to make an issue of SR union-busting. "We don't live in some anarcho-syndicalist utopia. If you're disappointed that they're resisting, you're being naïve."

"It's very frustrating," says Paul Couey, another Powell's Books employee and leader of its union drive, of the myriad paradoxes involved in organizing workers in an SR context. Employees and union representatives agree that when workers are trying to organize, a company's PC image is at best a mixed blessing—and sometimes a flat-out curse. The rhetoric of "social responsibility" can be a company's Achilles' heel—laying it wide open to charges of hypocrisy—but it's also an insidious union-busting tool.

Like Ben & Jerry's, many progressive employers use their SR image against the union. This was certainly the case in the campaigns by booksellers and other employees of Borders Books and Music—efforts that started in 1996 and petered out last year. Founded by two Ann Arbor hippies in the 1970s, Borders is now the second-largest book retailer in the world. But when employees in Philadelphia, Chicago, Bryn Mawr, Ann Arbor, Harrisburg, Evanston, Des Moines, Seattle, New York City, and Stamford, Connecticut, sought union representation, the company skillfully evoked the long-running perception that it was a progressive company. Borders corporate flacks loudly touted the domestic-partner benefits the company offered to gay and lesbian couples (never mind that those benefits included a health plan most employees couldn't afford).

In numerous public statements, Borders officials praised the noble history of the labor movement but insisted either that unions were irrelevant to the contemporary workplace, or simply "inappropriate for Borders." In Philadelphia, where employees had petitioned to join the Wobblies (yes, a tiny remnant of the IWW still exists), one manager (a self-identified socialist) posted a flyer on the employee bulletin board headlined: "The Days of Joe Hill Are Over!" Of course, such posturing wasn't the only reason Borders ultimately wore down its agitators; the company also deployed the decidedly uncrunchy tactic of hiring Jackson, Lewis, one of the leading union-busting law firms in the nation, to stop the organizing. But employees agree that Borders' phantasmic liberalism helped management immeasurably.

More recently, employees at Powell's Books, a six-store chain in Portland, Oregon—who, at $7 an hour, were making no more than Portland's average fast-food worker, and had just been denied an expected wage increase—faced a similar, though more restrained, counterattack when they wanted to join the International Longshore and Warehouse Union's Local 5 (ILWU). Owner Michael Powell is a prominent progressive in Portland who is active in the local Democratic Party and an outspoken free-speech advocate. His bookstore is a favorite meeting-place for the Portland left, and at least appears to celebrate diversity of all sorts. This summer's in-store readings included lesbian poet Minnie Bruce Pratt and ecofeminist Charlene Spretnak, and the store's Web site is run in close partnership with the *Utne Reader*. So last fall, employees and customers alike were surprised that Powell fought the union. He sent out a letter to all his employees' homes accusing the union of corruption (actually confusing it with a different union); later, he campaigned against the ILWU's long record as a defendant in discrimination suits. "You say the word 'union,' and everyone's supposed to feel all squishy. I don't get it," Powell insists. "I understand if you're organizing farm workers, or people in Bangladesh. But this is not that kind of situation."

The union won in April 1999, 161 to 155—a very close margin. Paul Couey, who works in the store's corporate accounts department, says Michael Powell's bluster hurt the union. "He [Powell] framed it as a human rights issue," says Couey. "He said the union would quell free speech. He used all this jargon that sounded progressive—saying that we were a small, organic institution, and could respond more flexibly [without a union]." Says Couey, "Most of the flexibility to which he was referring was managerial. We wanted some flexibility in our own finances!" Because Powell was known to be progressive, employees were at first confused when he talked about unions in what Couey calls "such stereotypical" terms. "In early meetings, some of us felt that if we could explain it better maybe he would understand. But as it continued it became clear that he wasn't misinformed; it was a tactic."

So what's going on here? Like New Age religion, that other cultural pathology of the 1980s, the SR business movement reflects that period's lack of left political vision and analysis. In its implicit notion that consumerism could substitute for politics—aptly reflected in the title of that Bible of corporate social responsibility, *Shopping for a Better World*—it was, at best, a lazy and naïve idealism. At worst, it cynically played on the reality that, in the 1980s, as now, many people were unhappy with a world centered around corporate profits, yet could imagine no alternative. It played on most Americans' desire to believe that capitalism, without any major, messy overhaul, could be a force for good, if only the people in charge meant well. The movement has spawned many of what futurist and SR guru Hazel Henderson calls "cleaner and greener" small firms, and increasingly, large corporations are jumping on the marketing bandwagon; even Wal-Mart is now a member of Business for Social Responsibility. The buzzword itself is revealing. "Responsibility" suggests that, like parents or benign dictators, people running businesses should make compassionate and sensible use of power—while the *fact* of that power should go unchallenged.

As prescriptions for social change go, then, SR is uninspiring, inadequate, and unambitious. But it's also a ready-made rationalization for union-busting; after all, if the people running the show are the ones who bear all the responsibility, and are cool progressive folks, why would workers need a voice of their own? Local 5's Michael Cannarella, who coordinated the Powell's drive, has organized many nonprofits "run by fairly liberal people." "The reaction is universally the same," he says. " 'Hey, we're taking care of these people, how dare they?' It's like, 'I'm the dad, you're the kids.' Sometimes the more liberal they are, the worse their reaction to the union because they're the ones who take it the most personally."

Michael Powell, for one, has taken the union victory very personally indeed. "I thought I was a compassionate employer," he says. "I thought I tried to reward my employees as best I could. That point of view was rejected. It shakes your confidence in who you are and what your values are."

"Even employers who want to do good end up acting like employers," observes Paul Mishler, a New York–based labor educator. "That's why you need unions." As for employers who claim that they already treat their employees so well that a union isn't necessary, Mishler says, "That's like asking, would you need democracy if you always had a nice president? It's a silly question. The fact is that dictators always end up doing bad things, and employers are the same. Without a union [an SR workplace] is a benevolent dictatorship."

Listening to Michael Powell, it's clear that either he's genuinely anxious that a pack of sweaty longshoremen are going to invade his genteel bookstore or, just as likely, he's playing on his workers' status anxieties. "We're not on the docks," he says. "I don't want an assembly-line work environment. I want to be able to talk collegially to my employees." Says Mishler, "A lot of people who emerged from that period of the sixties have this idea that middle-class niceness is better than working-class roughness. You know, 'they're not

our type of person, they listen to the wrong music, they eat meat.' "
Not only do such attitudes preclude these employers' empathy with
workers, they inform a cornerstone of SR anti-unionism: the assumption that conflict itself is destructive. Borders' management, in
trying to discourage employees from unionizing, continually dis-
paraged unions as "divisive," and disruptive to company "culture."
Such narratives exploit employees' utopianism; most people would
like to believe in the possibility of a non-exploitative workplace
in which workers' and companies' interests are the same. This is
probably a pipe dream in firms without full worker ownership. But
rather than inspiring employers at least to try to approximate such
a vision, the rhetoric and practice of corporate socially responsibility actively undermines it.

Still, the outlook for SR employees who wish to unionize is certainly no bleaker than that for any other workers—and they do
have some points in their favor. One advantage to organizing SR
workplaces, for the union movement and for employees, is that it
provides a political impetus to create better unions—these are employers that will call a union on a lack of democracy or other, often
very real, political flaws. Michael Powell wasn't wrong to point out
unions' history of racism, sexism, homophobia, xenophobia—nearly
every imaginable form of exclusion; such a history exists, and it's
shameful. Having opponents with the vocabulary to recognize
such problems is probably constructive for the labor movement. SR
businesses, however vague their own politics, also tend to attract
politically conscious employees, the kind of people who could turn
out to be lifelong labor activists, and at the very least, could help
unions to work in left coalitions and rebound as a political force.

As the first group of employees in the ILWU's new local, Powell's
employees have the opportunity to create a democratic structure;
it's a responsibility they're taking seriously as they draft their new
local's constitution. The pro-union employees knew that choosing
a decent union was crucial, not only because they knew that Michael Powell would play the "unions are corrupt" card, but also because progressive workers, far from being knee-jerk pro-unionists,
tend to be skeptical about institutions. "When you're organizing a

progressive business, it's especially important to have a [union] record you can defend—many unions really don't have a democratic structure," says Couey. "We would not have won if we had gone with a less democratic union."

[Editor's note: Workers at Powell's bookstore won their collective bargaining contract, likewise the maintenance employees at Ben & Jerry's. Borders went bankrupt in 2011.]

Janus *v.* Democracy (2018)

Joseph McCartin

Joe McCartin (1959–) grew up in Troy, New York, and took degrees from the College of the Holy Cross and the State University of New York at Binghamton. Since 1999 he has taught history at Georgetown where he directs the Kalmanovitz Initiative for Labor and the Working Poor. Among his many books, articles, and journalistic interventions, he is the author of Collision Course: Ronald Reagan, the Air Traffic Controllers, and the Strike That Changed America *(2011).*

Draining union finances will not be the most significant outcome of the Supreme Court's decision in *Janus v. AFSCME*. It poses a serious threat to our democracy, which President Trump and his right-wing enablers have already put in peril.

To be sure, *Janus* will hurt unions, as the anti-union Liberty Justice Center and the others who funded the plaintiff's case intended. Today, nearly half of all union members work for a government, and the vast majority live in states where, prior to the court's decision, unions were able to collect representation fees from all those for whom they bargained. Anti-unionists are already *encouraging* those workers to opt out of paying fees. Worried unions with large public-sector memberships began cutting staff and budgets months ago, putting efforts like the fast food workers' Fight for $15 on life support. As these cutbacks suggest, public-sector unions are not the only victims of *Janus*. It will further erode worker bargaining power in an economy where more than half the national income already goes to the top 10 percent of earners.

Yet *Janus* constitutes an even more significant setback—for democracy.

For most of the twentieth century, the advance of political democracy went hand in hand with efforts to make the workplace more democratic. Progressive Era reformers predicted that democracy would die in a world dominated by corporate behemoths unless workers secured *industrial democracy* in the workplace. In 1915, the chairman of the U.S. Commission on Industrial Relations warned that "Political freedom can exist only where there is industrial freedom; political democracy only where there is industrial democracy."

New Dealers embraced that logic. When Senator Robert Wagner drafted the National Labor Relations Act in 1935, he believed collective bargaining was "at the heart of the struggle for the preservation of political as well as economic democracy in America." That wisdom also guided those who extended union rights to government workers in the 1960s. Denying civil servants the right to bargain collectively was "more fitting to a benevolent despot than to the world's greatest democracy," as one reformer, Wilson R. Hart, put it.

The reasoning of these reformers was sound. As workplace democracy expanded, so did political democracy. Racial, age, gender, and income restrictions on the electorate all fell as collective bargaining spread.

Yet in the middle of the last century, the tide began turning against the mutually reinforcing expansion of the two forms of democracy. In 1947, the Taft-Hartley Act empowered states to forbid union contracts whose beneficiaries bore the costs of representation equally. Today twenty-eight states have these misnamed "right-to-work" laws.

With *Janus*, the 5–4 right-wing majority on the court has sought to turn that long war into a rout. As Justice Elena Kagan put it in her dissent, with *Janus* "that healthy—that democratic—debate" over the wisdom and justice of "right-to-work" laws "ends." The court has ended it not by making all government workplaces "right-to-work"—even before *Janus*, no government workers were required to join a union or pay dues. What it did was to turn the interdependent relationship between workplace and political democracy on its head. According to Justice Samuel Alito's majority opinion, "public-sector agency-shop arrangements violate the First Amendment" because bargaining by government unions addresses "matters of public concern," and is therefore political. He argues that majorities of government employees, no matter how lopsided, may not secure contracts whose beneficiaries share their costs, lest some workers' free speech rights be infringed. It matters not to Alito and his colleagues that the "First Amendment was meant . . . not to undermine but to protect democratic governance," as Kagan eloquently put it, and it matters even less that healthy democratic governance—in work relations no less than government—depends on systems of fair taxation.

Not coincidentally, the same one-vote majority on the court that just stripped workplace majorities of their rights recently approved assaults on democracy in the polling place. Earlier this month, in *Husted v. A. Philip Randolph Institute*, the right-wing justices greenlighted the tactics of Republican secretaries of state who have been purging registration rolls of qualified voters. Fittingly, the deciding vote in both of these anti-democratic decisions was cast by Justice Neil Gorsuch. He took a seat kept open by the Senate's refusal to vote on an Obama nominee, and was appointed by a president who lost the popular vote in an election which he won with the help of a foreign power and a wayward FBI.

By squelching democracy both at the polls and in the workplace, the court has sown a bitter wind. Recent uprisings by teachers in states like Oklahoma and West Virginia, which already banned union fees, suggest that it might one day reap a whirlwind.

As those inspiring walkouts showed, rampant injustice can rouse even formerly quiescent people to action—whether their unions are well-funded or not. If public-sector bargaining is simply a form of politics, as this court holds, teachers and other government workers should use *their* free speech rights to challenge any legal restrictions on what demands are legally permissible to make at the bargaining table. They should join with community allies and begin to use collective bargaining wherever it still exists to confront government policies that are privatizing and beggaring public services and further concentrating wealth at the top. Some unions have already begun doing this in an effort they call "Bargaining for the Common Good." The *Janus* decision should give their initiative an urgent new impetus.

Their fight is the same one waged by our forebears who believed democracy in the workplace and in politics must either stand or fall together. As we come to grips with *Janus*, it is clear that the fight for democracy in the twenty-first century has suddenly become both more perilous and more necessary than ever.

PART IV

New Frontiers

When the socialist founders of *Dissent* looked to the labor movement, they carried with them certain assumptions about the type of worker they were likely to find. That was the archetypal industrial proletarian of the mid-twentieth century, one who made or moved goods that had likely been manufactured or mined, and whose struggles centered on earning a wage sufficient to support *his* nuclear family. In this they strayed not very far from the dominant intellectual currents of their time, those which ensured, as the historian and *Dissent* contributor Alice Kessler-Harris once put it, that "the culture we associate with class is sharply gender-defined"— and defined along the lines of other ascriptive identities as well, like race, national origin, and sexuality. Nothing threw into sharper relief the limitations of the original *Dissent* style of radicalism than this presumption of what the working-class looked like.

In part, the problem stemmed from the composition of the *Dissent* crowd itself. Through the 1960s, men authored no fewer than 95 percent of the pieces published, and as often as not entire issues went to print without a single woman's name appearing in the table of contents. It took eighteen years before the editorial masthead included any women, with Patricia Cayo Sexton and Edith Tarcov—the latter of whom, despite a heavy workload, had been listed as "editorial assistant"—joining in 1972. Even in 1985, Joanne Barkan could describe the magazine's board as "pretty old, very male, professionally homogenous (many academics)," and, in the sole indicator of diversity, "politically heterogenous (socialists, social-democrats, liberals, and a few heading farther to the right)." It was also almost entirely white.

Gradually, broad-based social struggle opened the pages of *Dissent* to heretofore overlooked segments of the working class—as it did with other publications of the left. The civil rights and women's movements forced a reckoning with the relationship between class exploitation and other forms of oppression, while the campaign against the Vietnam War drew attention to the political economy of imperialist adventurism. At the same time, union drives and strikes by public sector and service employees changed the complexion of the labor movement, and encouraged an overdue reconsideration of what exactly constituted the world of work. By the century's end, immigrant workers' organizing efforts stood as one of the few sources of hope in an otherwise bleak landscape of defeat, a trend that continued into the new millennium. With these developments came a widening range of labor coverage in the magazine, as the selections included in this section attest.

In our first selection, we reprint an essay originally published in the 1959 labor issue, in which Dan Wakefield offers a moving account of the citywide hospital strike that placed Local 1199 of the Retail Drug Employees Union a on firm footing. Later celebrated by Dr. Martin Luther King Jr. as his favorite union, 1199 represented, in the words of historians Leon Fink and Brian Greenberg, a post–McCarthy era "reassertion of a labor-based vision of social reform." The successful struggle waged by these workers—who were, until 1974, unprotected by federal labor law and widely considered to be impossible to organize—would inspire unionists for years to come.

The greeting these new voices received from the institutional labor movement was mixed, and sometimes tragic—perhaps never more so than during the 1968 New York City teachers' strike, the subject of the Thomas R. Brooks article reprinted next. Fought over the implementation of "community control" in the NYC Board of Education–established Ocean Hill–Brownsville experimental district, the conflict pitted the United Federation of Teachers (UFT), with its heavily Jewish membership, against civil rights groups and black parents frustrated by the glacial pace at which school integration efforts had progressed. What exactly democratic educational governance was, or how it ought to look, meant very different things to these social forces. And reconciling the competing viewpoints, it turns out, may have been easier said than done. "No event in recent history has so embittered and divided the people of New York," wrote the *Dissent* board in a preface to Brooks's piece, "and this division has also shown itself among the intellectuals, within the union movement, and on the Left." Given the controversial nature of the subject, the editors used that preface to invite submissions offering alternative perspectives on the strike. None that they deemed worthy of publication appear to have been received.

Not long after health care and public employees arrived on the scene, however, the labor movement in general entered a period of steep de-cline. But throughout those dark days, one group of workers did sustain the tradition of civil rights unionism that had been practiced by 1199: immigrant workers in the burgeoning service sector. From the 1990s on-ward, some of the most dynamic organizing has been led by foreign-born workers in building services, industrial laundries, hotels, and other low-wage industries. Their workplace struggles, though powerful in their own right, were from the outset intertwined with an equally impor-tant movement that has challenged the nation's draconian immigration policies. In a selection reprinted here, the sociologist Ruth Milkman evaluates the legacy of these efforts and takes to task the reactionary position—adopted even by some who purport to side with the left—that immigrants bear responsibility for the poor condition of the U.S. labor market and union movement.

While unions like SEIU and UNITE HERE have been the organizations most visibly aligned with this immigrant worker movement, E. Tammy Kim draws attention to the inability or unwillingness of organized labor as a whole to commit to recruiting the most marginalized members of the working class into its ranks. Their absence has called forth a number of worker centers and alt-labor organizations that operate outside the bounds of national labor law and on shoestring budgets. These disadvan-tages, Kim notes, may well offer opportunities of their own, enabling a range of strategies and tactics that all-too-cautious established unions have thus far eschewed. Indeed, groups like the New York Taxi Workers Alliance and the Los Angeles–based Koreatown Immigrant Workers Al-liance have used just this kind of scrappiness to develop into durable and formidable organizations.

Among the most well-known models for this type of labor organiza-tion is the National Domestic Workers Alliance. Women who performed waged services in the homes of others were one of the two groups of workers to be explicitly written out of New Deal labor and employment law; the second was those who worked in agriculture. While the NDWA has mounted impressive campaigns in this area, including successful legis-lative battles to win a Domestic Worker's Bill of Rights in four states, care work—inside and outside of private residences—remains as poorly paid and challenging a job as one can find. In her contribution to this section,

Michelle Chen explores the appalling conditions that prevail in child care workplaces and asks what sort of strategy, aside from day care–by–day care union drives, stands the best chance at improving things.

In the popular imagination, graduate student workers may not stand as comparably disadvantaged as some of the other groups mentioned, but in terms of pay and precarity, their situation is not altogether different. They too, moreover, have had to struggle to be seen as employees of universities and thus as entitled to protection under labor law. To conclude this section, we reprint an essay by Gordon Lafer on the protracted battle waged by these academic workers through the 1990s to win union recognition. Three years after Lafer's article appeared, a George W. Bush–appointed majority on the NLRB declared this group to be "students," not "employees," thus allowing the private institutions described to ignore the democratic will of these graduate workers. More than a decade after that, a Barack Obama–appointed NLRB reversed that decision and restored graduate workers' rights—opening the door to the monumental wave of successful university organizing drives in the years following the pandemic.

Hospital Workers Knock at the Door (1959)

Dan Wakefield

Dan Wakefield (1932–2024) was born and raised in Indianapolis, where he got his journalistic start as a sportswriter for the Indianapolis Star *while still in high school. Soon after graduating from Columbia University, Wakefield was dispatched by* The Nation *to Mississippi to cover the Emmitt Till murder trial. He went on to publish a number of books, novels, and screenplays, including* Island in the City: The World of Spanish Harlem *(1959) and* Going All the Way *(1970).*

Pinned on the basement walls of a temporary union headquarters during New York's hospital strike last spring was a two-page, full color advertisement torn from *Life* magazine. It showed a gentleman of the New Leisure stretched in a hammock, drinking a pink frothy mixture that appeared to be an ice cream soda. His face reflected such ecstatic contentment that a casual observer might wonder if there weren't perhaps a couple of jiggers of gin in the mixture. Below the ad, printed in ink on a piece of scrap paper were the words, "We want this life too!"

Around the room on folding chairs sat a sprinkling of the aspirants to membership in the advertised affluent society; the most underpaid and poorly benefitted workers in the richest city of the richest nation of the world. They were mostly Negroes and Puerto Ricans, their ages ranging from the teens to a time at which the counting of years is superfluous, the faces beaten and drawn beyond any other category but Old. They gathered for six weeks in basement rooms and rented halls near the hospitals that employed them, fanning themselves against the heat and the boredom, rising up to shuffle into place on the picket lines, coming periodically back to strike headquarters to claim the bread and canned food that union sympathizers contributed during the seige.

The plight of these several thousand striking workers, from the ranks of the 30,000 employees who do the laundry, kitchen, maintenance, service, and laboratory work in New York's 81 "voluntary" hospitals (supported mainly by charity) drew both sympathy and shock from most of the city's citizens, especially union members, and the local union leaders who like to refer to New York as a "labor city." These striking workers, organized by Local 1199 of the Retail Drug Employees Union (an affiliate of the RWDSU), commonly averaged $34 a week without unemployment and disability benefits, without seniority, without union representation, and in some cases, with a six-day week. In an era when labor demands are centered more and more on the shorter week and special benefits, and blue collar workers increasingly are faced with the split-level problems of their white collar brothers, the sudden "discovery" of the forgotten hospital workers provided a shot in the arm and a common, uncontroversial cause to the recently merged New York labor council, which got behind the strikers with unanimous aid and enthusiasm. As one observer of the labor scene described the strike, "This is the most clearcut social issue since the revolt of the gladiators."

Few people disagreed with that sentiment, and a no less sober voice than that of a Justice of the New York State Supreme Court told the hospital management on June 12 that their refusal to recognize the union was "an echo of the nineteenth century." And yet, despite what seemed a majority of support from public opinion, as represented by leading citizens who urged that the union be recognized, and despite the combined efforts of the merged union strength of this "labor city," the settlement that ended the strike after six weeks was anything but clear-cut. To the end, the hospital management refused to grant outright recognition to the union, and the settlement provided principally for the less than revolutionary concessions of raising wages to at least a minimum of $1 an hour, providing for impartial grievance machinery and arbitration through outside representatives of the workers' choosing, and a review board of hospital and court-appointed members which will take up requests for improved standards in the future. After a summer of working under these conditions, the union is far from satisfied.

Throughout the strike the workers' meetings were alive with the kind of militant spirit that has rarely been seen in labor since the thirties—and indeed, the issues involved in a strike have rarely been so basic since then. Typically revealing of the spirit of the striking workers was the meeting they held after roughly three weeks on strike, to vote on the first proposals of settlement offered by the Hospital Association.

The meeting was held on the stifling May night in the ballroom of the Hotel Diplomat, a high-ceilinged cavern done in nickelodeon baroque, with gilded cherubs and scarlet draperies. Into it were packed nearly 2,000 strikers (double the number alleged by the hospitals to be on strike at the time) and they sat in silence that was broken increasingly by jeers and catcalls as Harry Van Arsdale, president of the New York merged labor council, read the "Hospital Benefit Plan" which had been submitted by management as a substitute for unionization. It is hard to think that the men who wrote it would have had the guts to read it before the audience of striking workers. It provided for "improvement in literary and cultural pursuits," instructions for the workers in "the rules and obligations of citizenship in a free democracy," a contribution of $100,000 from the United Hospital Fund for scholarship assistance to workers and their children, and other amenities which were as far removed from the needs and desires of a man who makes $32 a week as the promise of membership in the Racquet Club. The plan offered a wage increase of $2 a week. There was general laughter, and it was not pleasant laughter.

When the votes on the proposal were cast and being counted (it was voted down overwhelmingly), the floor was opened to strikers who wanted to say a word or so to their fellow workers. Within a few moments, the line to the microphone was jammed. A worker from Brooklyn Jewish Hospital pointed out that if the hospitals meant what they said, they wouldn't be afraid of having a union. He had already had experience with hospital promises: "I was on a grievance committee the hospital set up once and when we went in to tell them our grievances, they showed us a movie."

A Puerto Rican worker from Beth David came to the mike to say, simply: "Estados Todos Unidos."

A worker from Brooklyn Jewish said, "We'll walk till our shoes wear out."

A social worker arose to say, "Don't let them tell you it's only non-professional workers on strike. Many professional people are out, and we're proud to be with you."

A Negro lady who barely reached the mike stood on her toes and said in a high, joyous voice: "Brothers and Sisters—Hallelujah!"

They roared back, "Hallelujah."

They were brothers and sisters of poverty, and for the most part of color—as well as of a union—and the special shame of the strike was that their battle had to be waged against the wealthy who claim to be their benefactors as well as their bosses. The difference between the hospital bosses and the bosses of the past lay not in their proclamations of anti-union sentiment (the hospital bosses were as adamant against a union as were the bosses in the days of the Knights of Labor) but in their personal backgrounds and records. Rather than the profiteering bosses of old who were fighting the union in order to grind more pennies from the sweat of their workers, these were volunteer citizens helping to operate non-profit medical institutions for the welfare of the community. Many of them are philanthropists, humanitarians, and, in many cases, "Liberals." They are men who build gymnasiums for under-privileged kids and then pay their parents $32 a week and scream bloody murder when they try to join a union. Evidently they saw no discrepancy between their past actions of philanthropy and humanitarianism and their battle to keep the hospital workers—many of whom earn so little that they hold down full-time jobs and still have to have supplementary relief from the city—from choosing a bona fide union to represent them.

The pious proclamation on the part of management that hospitals were "different" and unions would be detrimental to their proper functioning—perhaps even create danger to the lives of the patients—was ridiculous from the start. The city-supported hospitals have been organized for a number of years, and the voluntary Maimonides Hospital, organized for several years under Local 1199, as well as Montefiore, which was organized by that union the first of this year, have gone on about their business without any lack of efficiency or danger to patients since recognizing the union. In fact, Dr. J.A. Katzive, executive director of Maimonides Hospital, stated in an interview in the *Wall Street Journal* that in his experience with the union "things have been entirely satisfactory." In the same article, Ray Emberg, president of the American Hospital Association and director of the University of Minnesota Hospital, was quoted as saying, "The calibre of the workers has improved since the union came in. The union gave security and we got more stable people."

Yet the representatives of the hospital boards never ceased to act as if the coming of the unions was comparable to the coming of the Black Plague. Their rage and fervor in fighting the union was a strange thing to behold from men who are philanthropists. When underpaid workers at several of the hospitals were kicked out of hospital-owned rooming houses because they had gone on strike, Mr. Benjamin Buttenweiser (Lenox Hill Hospital), of the National Urban League, the Federation of Jewish Philanthropies and the American Jewish Committee, was asked by the press to comment on the evictions. He said it was a "practical step."

Roughly 80 percent of the 30,000 workers of New York's voluntary hospitals are Negroes and Puerto Ricans, and in the first week of the strike, Harry Van Arsdale said that the withholding of union recognition to these workers was a "slap at an abused minority." Mr. Buttenweiser's answer was: "How ridiculous can you get?"

It is hard to imagine that anyone who followed the strike very closely or attended any of the workers' meetings could have found the charge ridiculous. At the last meeting of the strike, when the workers accepted the hospital settlement, one of the New York union leaders got up to say that one result of the strike was the unity that the workers had gained—not only with each other but with officials and members of other unions. He said he imagined that this was the first time many of the people in the audience who were Negroes or Puerto Ricans had ever really met and worked in a common cause side by side with white people. The audience clapped and cheered in affirmation, and there were shouts of "Yes, yes."

Another factor that increased the bitterness of the strike was that it pitted the poorest people of the city against the richest people. The hospital directors have pointed out the complex financial burdens of the institutions, and said that the whole thing had to do with the economics of modern medicine, rather than the issues of rich people and poor people, colored people and white people. The economics are of course at the heart of what set things off, but once set off, the issues were far more deep and personal than questions of Blue Cross rates and patient payment. The several bitter scuffles that broke out among strikers and policemen sprang from deeper passions. One of the biggest of the outbreaks occurred when a class of medical students marched in a parade up Fifth Avenue past the Mt. Sinai Hospital and workers, with their picket signs proclaiming the desire of a decent life, joined in the lines of march and had to be torn away by policemen.

How messy and disturbing it is when the poor people spoil our parades and demand their own place in the affluent society the magazines tell them they live in. Perhaps one of the many things the strike of the hospital workers proved is that the clean, conscience-easing rites of professional Charity are no substitutes for the more difficult and awkward procedures of allowing the poor to join together and speak and act for what they need. The term used to describe the settlement that the hospital directors finally agreed to was "backdoor recognition" of the union. Well, they are back there, and they aren't going away. Soon they will be at the front door, asking to be let in, and not even Charity will be able to shut them out.

Tragedy at Ocean Hill (1969)

Thomas R. Brooks

Thomas R. Brooks (1925-2016) worked as a farmhand and factory worker and served as a rifleman in the Tenth Mountain Division in 1943–46, before using the GI Bill to go on to Harvard, where he served as campus president of the Society for Industrial Democracy. Later a union organizer, labor editor, and president of the League for Industrial Democracy, Brooks published scores of articles and several books on labor and politics, including Toil and Trouble: A History of American Labor *(1964) and* Communication Workers of America: The Story of a Union *(1977).*

One wishes that the 1968 New York teachers' strike had not happened. The social fabric of the city was severely tried and suffered grievous wounds. Reconciliation is to be hoped for, but I fear it is unlikely, pretty much for the same reasons that made the strike all but inevitable. Still, there is no need to repeat history in quite the same dismal fashion, here or elsewhere. So, one attempts analysis. Perhaps the tragic conflict will yield some measure of understanding.

It was the United Federation of Teachers that brought decentralization to Ocean Hill–Brownsville, a grim, run-down corner of Brooklyn. With roughly 8,000 pupils—75–80 percent Puerto Rican with a sprinkling of "others"—in five elementary schools (kindergarten through fourth grade) and two intermediate schools (fifth through eighth grade), Ocean Hill–Brownsville is one of three experimental districts set up with an assist from the Ford Foundation.

Decentralization and community control by now are loaded

political catchwords, lacking precise definition. How they came to be that way is a story of frustration and anger, a consequence of fruitless attempts to get action from the circumlocution office that passes for a Board of Education in New York City. As a result of the Board's betrayal of promises to move forward on integration, parents at an intermediate school in one of the experimental districts voiced demands for "quality segregated education" and for a black principal. The Board, however, opened the school with a white principal, then transferred him out, precipitating a walk-out of black and white teachers in protest. Meanwhile, agitation for a larger parental voice in the affairs of the school mounted. The Board cautiously announced its desire "to experiment with varying forms of decentralization and community involvement in several experimental districts of varying sizes." At this point, The UFT became involved, and the first of the decentralization plans evolved.

The plan called for a two-year program. It provided for a governing board composed of ten parents and five teachers (one from each school in that particular district) to be elected by parents and teachers respectively; five community representatives were to be selected by the parent members; and a representative by the supervisors. After training, the board would select a full-time administrator to hire and fire teachers and to set educational goals. The elementary schools were to become a part of the More Effective Schools (MES) program, which was sponsored by the UFT and in effect in 21 other schools throughout the city.

Since the Board would have had to underwrite the expansion of the MES program into experimental districts, it balked. The reason was economic: *per-pupil cost in the UFT-sponsored MES schools is roughly $915 as against the estimated city-wide average of $485.* The Board dangled the prospects of "community involvement" before the parents and community activists, saying in effect, "If you don't play our way, no game." The UFT fought for the educational advantages and lost. Community activists, however, were eager for control almost on any terms.

The role of the Ford Foundation, at this point, is unclear. But it apparently put up little or no fight for MES, although it came up with roughly $173,000 for "planning" in each of the three districts.

Within all three districts parents and teachers fought, often bitterly, over the "how" of the experiment. Teachers were divided. The UFT leadership tended to view the boards as potential employers and therefore held that teachers ought not to sit on boards as members. However, some UFT chapters in the experimental districts did elect representatives to sit on the new boards, while other chapters refused all along to do so. Some teachers cooperated with the parents until they could no longer take the verbal abuse, and then quit. Others still cooperate, despite conflict. A sizable minority of the union continues to disagree with the course taken by the majority on this matter.

The teachers' disenchantment with the "experiments" was reinforced by their experience with the governing boards during the 1967 two-week contract strike. Some of the teachers active in the planning for the experiments hoped that the parents would back the UFT in its negotiations with the Board of Education since several key demands were aimed at improving education—expansion of the MES program, smaller classes, and the like. Ironically, one of the demands turned down by the Board was a UFT proposal for a public review board to hear parental complaints against the teachers. The UFT believed—and still believes—that such a review board would provide due process for teachers, enable parents to air their grievances, and enable the system to rid itself of incompetents. The parents, however, refused to give their backing. Like most parents, they did not like school strikes, which are especially hard on working parents who need the schools not only to educate their children but to watch over them while they are at work. Parents also tended to blame the UFT for going on strike rather than blame Mayor John Lindsay for his ineptness. (The Mayor, after all, could have forced talks to proceed at a more intense pace much earlier in the summer. But he apparently thought the teachers would follow his advice to remain in school rather than pursue their own self-interest as teachers and trade unionists. Neither the parents nor the Mayor is very strong on labor relations.)

Behind the natural inclination of the parents toward disapproval, however, there is some evidence of social-worker manipulation pushing experimental district boards into a hard line against the strike. In one case, for example, staff members of the Parent Development Program, an antipoverty agency training parents for paraprofessional tasks in the schools, issued a leaflet in the name of community parents that viciously attacked the teachers for striking. The leaflet was later withdrawn since its social-worker authors had not bothered to consult with the parents.

The three experimental districts were the locus of the only serious attempts at union-busting during the contract walkout. They were not successful, despite the urgings of the antipoverty warriors. For example, only a minority of the three districts' black teachers crossed picket lines, and attempts at running classes with parents failed, as they did elsewhere in the city. A certain lasting bitterness, however, was engendered. The UFT, for its part, made a major blunder when it demanded that the teachers be given the right to oust "disruptive children" from their classes. Black militants immediately charged that the demand was aimed at black children. The UFT subsequently proposed an eminently sensible and fair solution to an admittedly difficult problem. Unfortunately, the so-called disruptive child issue did poison the atmosphere. Within the decentralized districts, governing board members vowed vengeance. Teachers in one of the districts (I.S. 201) who participated in the walkout were told that they would face an "in-depth screening" on their return to work. An appeal by UFT president Albert Shanker averted a mass walkout of 490 teachers in Ocean Hill–Brownsville at the end of the contract strike.

Ironically, as it turned out, Rhody McCoy, the black administrator heading Ocean Hill–Brownsville, told me, "We have no intention of screening teachers. We will exercise the same prerogatives that superintendents and principals have at any other school in the city of New York [in appraising teacher performance]. We'll see to it that they are transferred out [if warranted] *only after due process*" (my italics). The teachers, in turn, were pleasantly surprised by McCoy's appointment of one Puerto Rican, one white, and three blacks

as principals of the Ocean Hill–Brownsville schools. Two were selected for praise in an article on decentralization by Eugenia Kemble in the *United Teacher*. When David Lee, principal of P.S. 178 in
Ocean Hill–Brownsville, could not get the Board of Education to
remedy physical defects in his school, UFT president Albert Shanker wrote a letter to the Board and made it public as a means of
exerting pressure for the needed repairs.

McCoy is a warm, likable man. Evidently anxious to do a good
job, he was at the time I interviewed him an exceedingly frustrated
man. He needed, I suspect, a substantial gain, a major educational
accomplishment, to demonstrate that the project was working—and
to head off the extremists on his flanks. But he was frustrated, in
part, by the hostilities between his staff and the Governing Board
following the September 1967 strike (hostilities that he had, with
UFT support, succeeded in cooling somewhat) and by lack of support from the Board of Education, from which all things still flowed.

Here's how McCoy described the situation to me last winter (December 1967):

> For three months, we've been in a state of persistent anxiety.
> We've got all the ingredients for a meaningful change right
> here in this District. But the question is, how much longer
> do you expect these people to string along? The faculty asks,
> where are the innovations, the new curriculum? But I'm not
> the local government. Every dime was spent before we came
> into existence. I'm not saying that decentralization means more
> money, but it does mean control over money. If the money is
> controlled already, we're not decentralized.

By spring, the situation worsened. In *The Burden of Blame*, a report
on the Ocean Hill–Brownsville controversy put out by the New
York Civil Liberties Union (NYCLU) on October 9, 1968, the UFT
was charged with

> escalation of rhetoric, [which] exposed the deep fears and hos-
> tility that existed between the white middle-class educational

establishment and the black community. The community began to accuse the teachers of scuttling the experiment, and the teachers, having resigned from the Local Governing Board, began to talk about black extremists and black racism.

That is the accepted view among liberals. However, the truth is something else again and a good deal more complicated. As Maurice Goldbloom points out in a critique of the NYCLU report distributed by the Ad Hoc Committee to Defend the Right to Teach, the activities of the "extremists" and "militants" "had become a serious problem well before the establishment of the Ocean Hill–Brownsville district."

In May 1967, the preceding year, Robert "Sonny" Carson of Brooklyn CORE had announced that he considered the five principals in the area "fired" and demanded that at least half of the teachers in the area be black. Demonstrations were held to enforce this demand. At that time, threatening and racist literature began to crop up in teachers' letter boxes and has reappeared off and on since.

The tenor of this scurrilous stuff may be gleaned from the following quote from several handbills:

Get off our backs, or your relatives in the Middle East will find themselves giving benefits to raise money to help you out from under the terrible weight of an enraged black community. . . .

[This, from another handbill:] It is impossible for the Middle East murderers of colored people to possibly bring to this important task the insight, the concern, the exposing of the truth that is a must if the years of brain-washing and self-hatred that has been taught to our black children by those blood-sucking exploiters and murderers is to be overcome.

The handbills cropped up again last spring. Significantly, in the spring of 1968, Leslie Campbell, vice-president of the Afro-American Teachers' Association, was transferred to I.S. 271, the center of much of the controversy this year. He helped to polarize the situation in Ocean Hill–Brownsville. As the final speaker at a school assembly following the murder of Martin Luther King, Campbell whipped up the already aroused, deeply disturbed students with cries, "Don't steal toothpaste and combs, steal things we can use. You know what I mean, brothers. . . . When the enemy taps you on the shoulder, send him to the cemetery. You know who your enemy is." (This for twelve- to fifteen-year-olds!)

Can we describe this as the UFT, to quote the New York Civil Liberties Union's statement, fanning "the flames of social fears" as it increasingly harped on "extremism," the "militants," and "black power"? After Campbell's speech, bands of youths roamed the school's corridors. Three teachers were attacked; one was taken to the hospital with a concussion.

The district was shut down for several days. Understandably disturbed, the UFT leaders in the district met with McCoy to explain the problem and seek ways of preventing repetition of such provocative acts. McCoy said that any action would have to be taken by the Governing Board and that he would arrange a meeting. Later, he said such a meeting was not possible.

Then, on May 9, midmorning, registered letters were delivered to 19 teachers and administrators on their jobs, stating: "The Governing Board of Ocean Hill–Brownsville Demonstration School district has voted to *end your employment* in the schools of this District. . . . This *termination of employment* is to take effect immediately" (italics added). No reasons were given for the firings in the letters. Subsequently, McCoy said, "They were suspected of trying to sabotage the demonstration project." Other reasons were advanced at various times to different reporters—discriminating between Puerto Rican and Negro children, endangering the safety of the children, inability to maintain order, etc. Not one of the charges was ever supported by evidence. As a New York Urban League advertisement put it, "What the governing board found wanting in these teachers was a genuine desire to teach the children in their charge. . . . *And it is a very difficult charge to prove in a court of law. How do you document a sneer? How do you prove a tone of voice? How many witnesses are needed to convict teachers of the failure to love their children?*"

How indeed! Professionals may well ask themselves how you *disprove* such charges. The UFT properly insisted that the 19 (10 teachers, 9 administrators) be reinstated, or that charges be filed. It is important to note that there was a minority on the Governing Board who thought the teachers should have a hearing.

Over the summer, Judge Francis Rivers, himself a black, heard the cases against seven teachers. Three other cases were dismissed because lawyers for the Governing Board were unable to produce witnesses or evidence supporting the allegations. Judge Rivers ruled that the cases against the other seven teachers were "unproved," and he ordered their return to continue teaching at their schools. Meanwhile, the Ocean Hill–Brownsville Governing Board recruited new teachers, 75 percent white and mostly Jewish, to take the place of the 350 on strike. It refused to take back the ousted teachers, as well as all those who walked out. In September, the UFT struck the system to enforce Judge Rivers' arbitration award and the Superintendent's orders that all the teachers return to their posts.

That strike supposedly ensured that due process would be built into any decentralization plan. The settlement provided for the return of the ousted teachers, full salary payments for the teachers who engaged in the spring stoppage, and a guarantee that any teacher dismissed or disciplined by a local governing board could appeal to a three-man arbitration panel. But when the teachers returned to work, the Board of Education could not—or would not—enforce its part of the agreement. Teachers seeking to return to I.S. 271 were blocked by "the community," a euphemism for "Sonny" Carson of Brooklyn CORE and his young men, assorted antipoverty staff, and others from outside the district, a scattering of residents, and a handful of parents. The union charged the Governing Board with sabotaging the agreement and struck once more. Again, a settlement was reached: this time, it entailed the suspension of the Governing Board until the ousted teachers were reinstated. Violence broke out at I.S. 271; nine people were arrested (most of whom did not even live in the district) and ten policemen suffered minor injuries in a clash between Ocean Hill–Brownsville supporters and the police, seeking to open the schools to students and teachers.

The Board of Education again suspended the local Board and sub-sequently suspended McCoy and seven of the district's eight principals for failing to comply with an order to reassign the returning teachers to their classrooms. Observers were assigned to the disputed schools, too. On October 11, for no good reason, the Board of Education, in its composition now a Lindsay Board, reinstated McCoy and the seven principals and ordered I.S. 271 reopened. The union charged the Board with breaking its agreement and encouraging vigilantism. The third strike followed.

This time the strike stretched out until it looked as though the whole mess would land in the lap of the state legislature, and the atmosphere in New York City became appallingly tense. The position of the UFT hardened; it now insisted on the removal of McCoy, the Governing Board, and those "scab" teachers who had threatened UFT teachers with what Mayor Lindsay termed "verbal abuse." But, in reality, no one really wanted the dispute to go to the legislature. Ocean Hill–Brownsville feared that such a step might well mean the death of decentralization and the UFT that it could also mean a stiffening of the state's Taylor Law, which bans strikes among public employees but as of now provides comparatively light penalties for violations.

The way to a settlement was cleared when Superintendent Donovan took action against four teachers accused of harassing union members when they last returned to their posts. Then, the Appellate Division of the State Supreme Court upheld three to two a lower-court ruling that the Ocean Hill–Brownsville principals had been illegally appointed. This cleared the decks for the basic settlement—which called for the appointment by the State Board of Education of Associate State Commissioner of Education, Herbert F. Johnson, as trustee of Ocean Hill–Brownsville; the establishment of a three-man committee with the responsibility of ensuring teacher rights and the power to act where violations occurred; and the addition of 10 days to the school year, and 45 minutes to the school day to make up lost time. In all, the three strikes had kept 50,000 teachers and 1 million pupils out of school for 36 of the first 48 days of the fall school term.

Conventional liberalism sometimes preening itself as "radical," advances two reasons for the strike—one is the teachers' white racism; the second is the UFT's alleged opposition to decentralization. The evidence for the latter rests solely on the UFT's public fight against the so-called (McGeorge) Bundy plan. At present, the city has 30 districts (plus the three experimental districts), each averaging roughly 30 schools with 36,000 pupils (roughly the size of the Evansville, Indiana, school system). An analysis of the racial composition of grades one through eight prepared by the Bundy panel's staff shows 13 predominantly (50 percent or more) white, 6 black, 4 Puerto Rican, and 7 Negro-Puerto Rican. Minority-group children make up just over 50 percent of the total school population. The percentage of black or Puerto Rican administrators, however, is virtually nil and for teachers only slightly better, roughly 12 percent.

The Bundy panel recommended up to 60 autonomous districts, which might mean districts on the order of the Norwalk, Connecticut, school system—say, 16,000 pupils each. The Bundy recommendations, however, were not as radical as many seem to think. The aim was to decentralize the system but not necessarily make way for community control.

Indeed, Bundy's proposal for the formulation of district boards is quite conservative. Financially, the district boards would be empowered "to determine needs, develop programs, and apportion available funds among the programs." But funds are to be distributed "under a city-wide objective formula," not on the basis of any given community's need. Finances are so structured that it would be difficult for the community boards to pressure the city, or the state, for additional funds.

This was the decentralization plan fought by the UFT. The union wanted—still wants —*elected* school boards. It favors 15 districts on the grounds that this is economically more feasible and would prevent administrative costs—district superintendents, for example, get $30,000 a year—from eating up additional money that will become available when decentralization takes place. In addition, although this is provided for in the Bundy plan, the union wanted strong guarantees that it would not have to go back to the year Alpha in collective bargaining. Indeed, I believe it would be a serious error for the city to allow bargaining to take place on money, benefit, and basic working conditions on a local board-by-board basis.

All of the several possible consequences of such a labor policy in a decentralized school system, I believe, would work to the disadvantage of the politically weak districts—and there are bound to be several of these.

All of the above is subject to honest differences of opinion and the city needs more, not less, debate over decentralization. Unhappily, the UFT not only lobbied, which was its right, against the Bundy-Lindsay plan, but it also sought to punish its "enemies" in the legislature politically in last spring's primaries, which was unwise. It sought the defeat of some perfectly good legislators. Luckily, it lost.

Before the March on Washington in 1963, Michael Harrington and Bayard Rustin argued, convincingly I believe, that the movement of black people in America could serve as a catalyst for a new era of progress. The idea was to build a coalition that might do something about jobs, education, housing, health problems, even possibly affect the inequitable distribution of wealth. As we all know, the coalition has fallen apart; what's more, the two key wings of the coalition—the labor movement and the civil rights movement—are being egged on to fight each other.

As radicals, we have always recognized the existence of racism among white workers, condemned it and at the same time tried to point out how it worked against the best interests of working people. Clearly, racism has been used by employers, demagogues, and the less fussy elements of the establishment to prevent black and white workers from working together for common goals. All this is rather elementary but I raise it because we are now being told that white working men—and especially their unions—are the *cause* for black people being locked into black ghettos.

If slums are caused by racism, then we need to look no further than at the teachers, plumbers, or steel workers. There is no need to concern ourselves with such esoteric matters as the oil depletion allowances, or tax loop holes allowing millionaires to escape scot-free from income tax payments, or even to consider that David Rocke-feller of Chase Manhattan is in fact a much more powerful man than the mayor of our city. So what if taxes are inequitable, incomes maldistributed, and housing conditions determined by banks, in-surance companies, and real estate magnates? All we need to do is bust a union!

If you think this oversimplifies what is going on, listen to John Doar, Lindsay's appointee to the Board of Education and its pres-ident, as quoted in *Fortune*, January 1968. One can imagine how pleased *Fortune* readers must feel as they read, "Union concepts of security and seniority were formulated in the period of strug-gle between company and union. Now the struggle is between the Negroes and unions." A few paragraphs later, Doar adds, "It is our position that a basic conflict exists between labor union concepts and civil rights concepts. Something has to give."

Lindsay and Doar, the Ford Foundation and the establishment have been trying to make something give these last few months in New York. And it is not racism—black or white. They escalated a localized—admittedly complicated—conflict into a city-wide near disaster. Instead of mediating, for example, Mayor Lindsay fostered the spread of conflict. His Board of Education, instead of working in the interests of all the parents of the city, has actively sided with a minority faction within a minority community in a struggle for control over that community.

When the UFT shut down the schools, the Mayor and the Board might have taken a leaf from sophisticated management-labor rela-tions, recognized the reality, and sat down to negotiate. The closing of schools would have generated broad pressure from parents and the public for settlement—and conceivably one more to the liking of the Board than the union. What in fact did the Board do? It de-clared the schools open, named the first teacher in as principal, and invited angry parents to slug it out with their teachers who were forced, as the Board must have known they would be, to mount mass picket lines. If the devil himself had desired it, no other pol-icy would have succeeded so well in spreading racial antagonism throughout the city.

We are, I believe, in for more of this sort of action. The new man in the White House has already talked favorably about "black capitalism." There has been a sudden flow of foundation and corporate money into "black capitalist" ventures. Separatist tendencies within the black community are being encouraged. After all, if the overwhelming majority of blacks voted for Hubert Humphrey and by extension for inclusion in our society, where else are Republicans to go? "Community control" is big this year with the foundations. Hopefully, blacks will soon realize that "community control" is another bag woven by Whitey, that the only way to escape manipulation by the white upper-class establishment is to make common cause in fruitful political action with one's natural allies, those "others" who also suffer the consequences of an inequitous economic and social system, as well as with organized labor, urban and urbane liberals, other minorities, youth, and the "new South."

Reconciliation in New York City may indeed be the first step in rebuilding on a stronger foundation the coalition of conscience that has been the source of all our progress in recent decades.

Immigrant Workers Didn't Kill Your Union (2019)

Ruth Milkman

Ruth Milkman (1954–) grew up in Annapolis, Maryland, where her politics were shaped by her mother, the daughter of Jewish immigrants from Eastern Europe whose worldview reflected the left-wing milieu of 1930s Brooklyn. Milkman was part of the socialist-feminist movement at both Brown and UC Berkeley, where she took her PhD in sociology. She has taught at Queens College, City University of New York; at UCLA, where she directed the Institute for Research on Labor and Employment; and then again at CUNY where she teaches sociology and labor studies. Her books include Gender at Work, Farewell to the Factory, L.A. Story, *and* Immigrant Labor and the New Precariat.

Immigrant organizing stood out as a rare bright spot on the otherwise dismal U.S. labor scene in the late twentieth and early twenty-first centuries. To the surprise of many observers, starting in the late 1980s low-wage foreign-born workers, including the undocumented, eagerly welcomed opportunities to unionize and infused the labor movement with new energy. Immigrants also helped to galvanize the "alt-labor" movement, flocking to worker centers across the nation that deployed new strategies to challenge wage theft and other employer abuses in sectors where obstacles to traditional unionism were especially formidable. Largely in response to these developments, union leaders abandoned their longstanding support for restrictive immigration policies; by the turn of the century organized labor instead had become a vociferous champion of immigrant rights.

Yet some unionists dissented from this stance, especially in the relatively conservative building trades, many of which are still overwhelmingly made up of U.S.-born white males. The Pennsylvania building trades have lobbied for legislation to penalize construction firms that hired undocumented workers, while an upstate New York carpenters' union representative admitted that his union routinely reported the undocumented on construction sites to immigration authorities. These unionists, like many ordinary Americans, were convinced that immigrants, and especially the undocumented, lowered wages and took jobs away from U.S. citizens.

On the surface, their view may seem plausible. Construction has suffered severe deunionization over recent decades, leading to lower pay and degraded working conditions, especially in the residential sector of the industry. Employers launched a vigorous anti-union assault as the residential industry recovered from the recession of the early 1980s, using a variety of tactics to expand the non-union segment of the industry. When that happened, U.S.-born building-trades union members abandoned the jobs affected, typically moving from the residential to the commercial sector of the building industry—the latter was booming in the 1980s and remained heavily unionized. Meanwhile, employers recruited immigrant workers, both authorized and unauthorized, to fill the newly degraded jobs in residential construction. Thus the employment of immigrants did not *cause* the labor degradation in the industry; on the contrary, it was the *result* of the employers' anti-union campaigns. Similar processes unfolded in many other industries as well. But rank-and-file workers, as well as some unionists, unaware of this dynamic, often blamed immigrants instead for the degradation of jobs.

Such scapegoating has become even more widespread since the rise of Donald Trump and the aggressive attacks on immigrants that propelled him into the presidency. His gratuitous attacks on birthright citizenship and "chain migration," as well as his unfounded claims that "illegals" raised crime rates and committed voter fraud, famously arouse the latent xenophobia and racism of many white workers. In addition, after taking office, the Trump administration systematically promulgated an array of draconian anti-immigrant initiatives: the Muslim travel ban, new limitations on refugees and asylum-seeker admissions, family separations at the border, large-scale ICE sweeps, and increased arrests and deportations.

Some on the left point to continuity in regard to the last of these: not for nothing had Obama earned the moniker "deporter-in-chief." Immigration and Customs Enforcement (ICE) arrests were up 42 percent in the first eight months of the Trump administration, compared to the same period in 2016, but the numbers were even higher in 2010 and 2011, under Obama. Yet most deportations in the Obama era involved new arrivals apprehended at the border, or immigrants with serious criminal records. By contrast, under Trump ICE prioritized "internal removals" of the undocumented, often sweeping up those with no criminal records and others who had resided in the United States for many years. ICE agents became increasingly aggressive, apprehending undocumented immigrants in courthouses and outside schools, locations it had avoided under earlier administrations. Workplace raids, rare in the Obama years, were revived. Trump has also taken steps to curb *legal* immigration, for example, seeking to end "temporary protected status" for Haitians, Central Americans, and others. All these policies are relentlessly trumpeted in the president's speeches and tweets, along with his beloved border wall proposal.

As detentions and deportations became increasingly arbitrary and unpredictable, fear and anxiety in immigrant communities spiked to levels not seen for half a century. In California, the state with the largest undocumented population as well as a much-vaunted sanctuary law (introduced immediately after Trump's election and signed into law in 2017), "thousands exist in a cordon of terror," as Michael Greenberg reported in the *New York Review of Books*. "Paranoia has infiltrated every aspect of life. Civic activity [among the undocumented], such as attending town meetings and other public events, has ground to a virtual halt."

Not surprisingly, despite his populist rhetoric, Trump is no friend to organized labor. Still, many unionists welcomed (albeit warily) his posture on trade, resonating to the critique of NAFTA and the "tough" approach to trade with China. Labor leaders also harbored hopes that Trump's stated commitment to rebuilding the nation's infrastructure (which soon proved to be "fake news") would generate a raft of new union jobs. Yet there was no retreat from the AFL-CIO's or the Change to Win (CTW) federation's support of immigrant rights, with the notable exception of the unions representing ICE agents and border control officers, both of which endorsed Trump in 2016 and ever since have been cheerleaders for "zero-tolerance" immigration policies. Indeed, organized labor mobilized in support of immigrants threatened with deportation, for example in the Working Families United coalition, formed in 2017 by the Painters union, the hotel workers' union UNITE HERE, the United Food and Commercial Workers, the Teamsters, LIUNA, as well as the Bricklayers and Ironworkers. That same year the AFL-CIO developed a toolkit to assist unionists threatened with workplace immigration raids. Several individual unions launched their own training efforts to educate members about how best to respond to raids or the threat of deportation.

While most segments of the labor movement have continued to support immigrant rights, if less vocally than in earlier years, the liberal consensus on immigration policy has begun to weaken in the wake of Trump's success (and that of right-wing populists in Europe) in winning working-class support by demonizing immigrants. For example, Hillary Clinton warned in an interview shortly after the 2018 midterm elections that "if we don't deal with the migration issue it will continue to roil the body politic." And in his 2018 book, *The Nationalist Revival*, John Judis confessed his sympathy for Trump's nationalist agenda, arguing that low-wage immigration inevitably reduces the leverage of the U.S.-born working class. "Enormous numbers of unskilled immigrants have competed for jobs with Americans who also lack higher education and have led to the downgrading of occupations that were once middle class," he declared. This type of left-wing nationalism is even more widespread in Europe.

Similarly, Angela Nagle's provocative essay, "The Left Case against Open Borders," published in the pro-Trump journal *American Affairs*, harkened back fondly to the days when organized labor embraced restrictive immigration policies, pointing out that the main supporters of open borders have been free-market ideologues like the Koch brothers, along with employers reliant on cheap labor. Historically, she added approvingly, trade unions took the opposite view:

> They [unions] saw the deliberate importation of illegal, low-wage workers as weakening labor's bargaining power and as a form of exploitation. There is no getting around the fact that the power of unions relies by definition on their ability to restrict and withdraw the supply of labor, which becomes impossible if an entire workforce can be easily and cheaply replaced. Open borders and mass immigration are a victory for the bosses.

The attack on the left for supporting "open borders" is a red herring; this stance remains on the margins of the progressive mainstream—but most progressives *do* oppose the restrictive policies favored by Trump and his acolytes. Moreover, the labor movement abandoned the perspective Nagle articulates two decades ago. Despite their painful awareness that many rank-and-file union members voted for Trump in 2016, the AFL-CIO leadership and that of the CTW federation, as well as the vast majority of their affiliates, have not wavered from the pro–immigrant rights stance they adopted at the end of the twentieth century.

There are compelling economic reasons for progressives to align with labor in this regard. As the journalist Eric Levitz has noted, immigration obviously does expand the labor supply, but it also creates additional economic demand; and in the context of an aging population, the immigrant influx, disproportionately comprised of prime-age workers, contributes to the fiscal sustainability of programs like Social Security and Medicare. This is the consensus among most experts, but as Levitz observes, the case for restrictionism put forward by commentators like Judis and Nagle is "primarily an argument about politics, not economics," pivoting on the susceptibility of U.S.-born workers to right-wing populist appeals.

To meet that challenge, the most urgent task for progressives and the labor movement alike is to push back against the right-wing narrative that blames immigrants for the reversal of fortune suffered by white U.S.-born workers over the past four decades. Progressives need to promote instead a counternarrative that highlights the ways in which business strategies from the 1970s onward have reduced wages and undermined the labor movement—strategies that have been rendered invisible or irrelevant for the many U.S.-born workers who have been persuaded by Trump and his supporters to scapegoat immigrants. In a nutshell, the task is to redirect the entirely justifiable anger of those workers toward employers instead of the foreign-born.

The case that immigration was a key driver of working-class distress does seem plausible at first glance, especially in regard to timing. Not long after the passage of the 1965 Hart-Celler Act ended four decades of highly restricted immigration, the economic status of white male non-college-educated workers, most of whom had prospered in the postwar years, began to spiral downward. In the same period, inequality surged as well.

These trends are indeed interconnected, but the line of causality runs in exactly the opposite direction from what Trump's and Judis's anti-immigrant narratives imply. Immigration was not the cause of the neoliberal economic restructuring that began in the 1970s or of the accompanying explosion of inequality and labor degradation. On the contrary, the influx of low-wage immigrants was a consequence of these developments. U.S. employers' efforts to externalize market risk through various forms of subcontracting, and at the same time to actively undermine labor unions, generated a surge in demand for low-wage labor. That, in turn, led millions of immigrants, both authorized and unauthorized, to enter the bottom tier of the nation's labor market to fill "jobs Americans won't do."

The primary driver of labor migration, past and present, is

economic demand. While "push" factors in sending countries do spur emigration, it materializes on a significant scale only in response to employers' search for new sources of labor. The 2008 financial crisis is revealing in this regard: as the U.S. economy imploded, and jobs in sectors like construction and manufacturing evaporated, the number of unauthorized migrants crossing the border decreased dramatically. Prior to the Great Recession, immigration grew in direct response to rising employer demand for cheap and pliable labor. Starting in the late 1970s, new business strategies drove down labor costs through expanded subcontracting, deregulation, and efforts to weaken or eliminate labor unions.

In industries like taxi driving and trucking, where deregulation led to union decline and wage cuts, as well as in deunionized construction, manufacturing, and service industries, many U.S.-born workers voted with their feet to reject the newly degraded jobs, and then immigrants were hired to fill the vacancies. If migrants did not arrive on their own in adequate numbers to fill the demand, employers routinely sent recruiters to Mexico and other parts of the Global South to find them, often in blatant violation of immigration laws and regulations. In short, immigration was the consequence, not the cause, of declining labor standards.

Demand for immigrant labor also expanded in the domestic and personal services sector in this period. Here the key driver was not employment restructuring and job degradation but instead a combination of demographic changes and rising income inequality. As maternal labor force participation grew, the nation's increasingly prosperous professional and managerial classes devoted a growing part of their disposable income to purchasing services from housecleaners, nannies, and eldercare providers, as well as manicurists and other "personal appearance workers." Many affluent households now included two adults with long working hours, thanks to the feminist movement's success in opening the professions and the corporate suite to upper-middle-class women in the 1970s, even as changing expectations of parenting and the aging of the population stimulated growing demand for care work inside the home. Yet in the same period, the traditional labor supply in domestic labor occupations was evaporating, as the civil rights movement opened up lower-level clerical and service jobs and other options to African-American women. Black women thus began to shun domestic work just as demand for it began to rise, leading many households to replace them with immigrant women, who were increasingly available in this period as permanent family settlement came to dominate over the earlier pattern of male-dominated circular migration.

Some of the biggest concentrations of Trump's U.S.-born white working-class supporters in 2016 were in the Rust Belt. No one can seriously suggest that immigrants should be blamed for the massive wave of plant closings that swept across the Midwest starting in the 1970s. In this context jobs were not degraded, they simply disappeared. Yet immigrant scapegoating does not necessarily have to be rooted in reality. Native-born "anger at displacement, blamed on 'aliens,' sometimes rested on actual experience but more often on imagination and fear stoked by demagoguery," Gordon points out. "We know this because the Klan flourished in areas with few 'aliens.' "

The right-wing anti-immigrant narrative has in effect distracted attention from the actual causes of declining working-class living standards. The white working class has every reason to be alienated and enraged by rising inequality and the disappearance of good jobs, but their anger has been profoundly misdirected. It should focus not on immigrants but on the deliberate actions of business interests to degrade formerly well-paid blue-collar jobs and to promote public policies that widen inequality. Rather than opportunistically jumping on the anti-immigrant bandwagon, labor and progressives hoping to regain support from the white U.S.-born workers who supported Trump in 2016 should devote their energies to shifting the public conversation in this direction.

Organizing the Unorganizable (2015)

E. Tammy Kim

E. Tammy Kim was born on a U.S. military base in Korea, the birthplace of her immigrant parents, and grew up in Tacoma, Washington. Educated at Yale and the NYU School of Law, Kim worked as an attorney for low-wage New York City workers before pursuing a career in journalism. Now a contributing writer at the New Yorker, *she also serves as contributing editor at* Lux *magazine and previously co-hosted the weekly podcast* Time to Say Goodbye. *Long active in the labor movement, Kim is a member of the Freelance Solidarity Project of the National Writers Union.*

In September 2013, the AFL-CIO, a giant labor federation comprising fifty-six unions and 12.5 million U.S. workers, held its quadrennial convention in Los Angeles. There was plenty of what one might expect from such a gathering: lapel pins and hats with jaunty slogans, rousing speeches, and middle-aged toughs talking working-class politics. There was also a parade of low-wage workers, none of them formally members of the AFL-CIO. Immigrant nannies, Walmart clerks, day laborers, and taxi drivers appeared on stage, cheered by a sincere, if slightly flummoxed, union crowd. The intended message was clear: this is the future of the labor movement. Welcome them and pay attention.

To understand how a once marginal coterie of low-wage immigrant workers came to be courted by mainstream unions, one must go back to the adolescence of our globalized, outsourced, service economy. In the 1990s, a wave of small nonprofits opened, first in New York then across the country. They were called worker centers—community groups that organized underclass laborers, often of the same ethnic background, and with a focus on particular industries or neighborhoods. These groups tended to be far left and non-hierarchical, turned off by the bureaucratic bloat and corruption of large unions.

Worker centers provide clues to the future of organized labor, particularly in this moment of capitalist crisis. They now number in the hundreds, representing Chinese prep cooks and West Indian cleaners as well as African Americans doing drywall. Compared to major unions, worker centers have few members and even smaller budgets, but they are determined. Long before the 2007–09 recession and Occupy Wall Street, they forced inequality into public discourse and told personal stories of migration and hardship. The Chinese Staff and Workers' Association (the first worker center, founded in 1979) led aggressive pickets against restaurants and garment factories in New York's Chinatown. Community Voices Heard organized unpaid municipal employees exploited by the 1996 welfare reforms. Damayan, a Filipina worker center, exposed the indentured servitude among live-in nannies. And the Restaurant Opportunities Center and the National Mobilization Against Sweatshops fought for their members—kitchen staff and cleanup workers, respectively—to receive just compensation for the health and economic impacts of 9/11.

These grassroots and immigrant-led campaigns had a visceral appeal. The general public, for whom unions were mostly anathema, could relate to the reasonable, basic demands of low-wage laborers. City-dwellers were stunned to learn that their deliverymen and nail-salon workers were paid less than minimum wage, and surprised to see them wield handmade signs, day after day, yelling in front of their bosses' homes.

I've followed what might now be described as the "worker-center movement" for the past decade of their thirty-year trajectory. As a law student, then lawyer, I worked closely with the groups in New York City, several of which have grown and "gone national." More recently, as a journalist, I've covered their campaigns and traced their relationship to traditional unions. It is impossible not to be impressed by worker centers—or to worry about the trade-offs they currently face.

As many labor watchers have pointed out, worker centers, in concept, are nothing new. Vulnerable workers—immigrants, women, and racial minorities—have always formed their own movements. At the turn of the last century, before laws governing unions were put in place, low-wage workers assembled in alleyways, settlement houses, churches, and synagogues. The earliest unions recognized that every job had the potential to be decent and dignified: a garment worker could sew ninety hours a week for poverty wages, or forty hours and earn an adequate living; a welder could risk losing his arm and his livelihood, or labor under safe conditions with health insurance and a pension.

But there was a long period in which this foundational idea— organize to improve—was abandoned by "big labor." Complacency set in during the postwar manufacturing boom, when nearly one-third of employees worked under a collective bargaining agreement, and in the subsequent decades of bust, globalization, and deregulation, industrial unions focused on protecting what they'd already achieved. The 1965 immigration reform drew unprecedented numbers of foreigners to fill low-wage jobs; yet, in 1986, the labor movement supported a provision that ultimately criminalized these workers. The "employer sanctions" law, embedded in that Reagan-era immigration reform, aimed to penalize the act of hiring unauthorized labor. In practice, however, it gave bosses carte blanche to threaten employees with deportation, giving rise to countless workplace raids.

Worker centers organized this migrant underclass. Like their late-nineteenth-century counterparts, they began as tiny non-profits: understaffed, poorly funded (by foundations instead of member dues), and in some cases, limited by their members' exclusion from the labor laws. Taxi drivers are considered independent contractors, for instance, and nannies and farmworkers have no right to collectively bargain. Nevertheless, worker centers—led by charismatic immigrant women and people of color such as Linda Oalican of Damayan, Bhairavi Desai of the New York Taxi Workers Alliance, and Lola Smallwood Cuevas, whose Black Worker Center focuses on the construction trade—have organized individuals and small groups of employees, protested loudly, and used wage-and-hour lawsuits and media strategies to get their message across. In contrast to unions, worker-center leaders are not of the rank-and-file. They are predominantly middle-class, highly educated, professional organizers—a consequence, perhaps, of the groups' dependence on foundation and government grants.

Perils of fundraising aside, the legal structure of worker centers has given them certain advantages over traditional labor: no bureaucratic layers or restrictions on protest; no need to rely on an increasingly feeble National Labor Relations Act. Under current law and practice, unions are extremely hierarchical and depend on a slow, inefficient election process to organize new workplaces. Caselaw prohibits them from conducting "secondary boycotts" (any protest against entities that do business with the employer in question) and, in most contracts, they give up their most valuable weapon: the right to strike. Still, the labor movement claims millions of members, and the collective bargaining agreement remains the most powerful tool for raising industry standards.

What, then, have worker centers accomplished? For thousands of low-wage immigrants, a great deal. At Adhikaar in Queens, New York, Nepali domestic workers gather for lunch, meetings, know-your-rights presentations, and English classes. In Los Angeles, members of the Koreatown Immigrant Workers Alliance discuss labor concerns as well as affordable housing and gentrification. And near Baltimore, CASA de Maryland, an immigrant rights organization, protests violations of employee rights and lobbies for Dreamers.

It is harder to gauge the wider societal impact of worker centers. Because they generally operate as independent non-profits, they have not yet organized enough members or workplaces to transform industry conditions. (A significant exception is the New York Taxi Workers Alliance, now the de facto bargaining representative of the city's yellow cabs.) Worker centers have, however, mastered public relations, built relationships with unions and government agencies, won precedent-setting lawsuits, pushed through major pieces of legislation, and trained some very impressive member-leaders. In New York, we can thank the Chinese Staff and Workers' Association for honing picket-line techniques and successfully litigating subcontractor liability. Domestic worker groups in several states have secured industry-specific bills of rights. And the New Orleans Workers' Center for Racial Justice routinely advises government agencies on migrant labor issues.

One East Coast union leader I interviewed called these media-heavy tactics spectacle, not movement. "How many dues-paying members do they actually have?" she asked, criticizing the non-profits' limited reach and reliance on foundations. But even critics cannot deny the groups' influential style and gravitational pull. Worker centers have posed an implicit challenge to unions: to organize the "unorganizable," to embrace immigrant workers, and to think beyond the contract.

Some in the traditional labor movement were already doing this. In the late 1980s, the Service Employees International Union (SEIU) began organizing low-wage home health aides and, most famously, custodians in corporate towers. The Justice for Janitors campaign led marches and sit-ins that froze major intersections; there were police beatings and arrests. And in contrast to the Old Left industrial unions, the SEIU saw the immigrant identity of the majority Latino/a janitors as a rallying point, not a divisive liability.

It is no coincidence that this same SEIU, which split from the AFL-CIO in 2005, is the primary backer of the fast food protests launched after Occupy Wall Street. Despite the far-off goal of a McDonald's contract, the union has spent untold millions on a worker center–style campaign: grassroots organizing, yes, but also litigation to fight retaliation and establish joint-employer status, bills to raise local and state minimum wages, and the public-relations magic of Berlin Rosen. At the same time, SEIU has stayed largely behind the curtain, deferring to worker centers and reconstituted ACORN (Association of Community Organizations for Reform Now) chapters in every participating city. It's a logical move for the union. Community-based groups enjoy "street cred" that big labor doesn't, and they cost much less to operate (they pay their staff organizers very little and need not budget for lobbying or member benefits). The SEIU relies on these non-profits to canvass workplaces, host meetings, and plan one-day strikes tailored to local conditions. At protests in Charlotte, for example, the North Carolina NAACP has championed African American fast-food employees, calling Fight for 15 "the new civil rights movement."

Meanwhile, the AFL-CIO has had its own courtship with worker centers. In 2000, the confederation renounced its support of the "employer sanctions" law and, under the leadership of Richard Trumka, has advocated for immigration reform, a higher minimum wage, and other priorities for low-wage laborers. The OUR Walmart campaign, run by the United Food and Commercial Workers, operates under a non-union structure very similar to that of the fast-food movement, and other AFL-CIO entities have donated generously to worker centers, breeding some resentment among dues-paying members. Trumka has proclaimed domestic workers and freelancers an integral part of the labor movement. In 2011 he even granted a charter to the non-union National Taxi Workers Alliance, an outgrowth of the New York worker center.

The AFL-CIO and SEIU are employing the tactics used by immigrant worker centers to organize Burger King fry cooks, Walmart "associates," and warehouse laborers outside the union framework. It's at once strategic borrowing and an adaptation to a bleak landscape. Today, every job seems temporary and precarious, half the states are "right to work," and only 6.7 percent of the private sector is protected by a collective bargaining agreement. Unions want and need new members.

The fast food campaign is in many ways a test case for the future of labor. Since the financial crisis and ensuing Great Recession, we have seen middle-aged parents resorting to jobs behind the counter; we have seen mass unemployment and the death of "good" jobs. Whereas the first immigrant worker centers made us think, "How, in America, could this be?" the fast food movement highlights what we already know, and what no longer shocks us, about the economy.

It remains to be seen if mass organizing is possible in a dispersed, private industry like fast food. Is a national union feasible? Or will the current structure—a labor-community hybrid; a centralized web of non-profit worker centers—prove sustainable in the long-term?

Just as traditional labor has returned to pre–New Deal methods, worker centers have inched toward the union form. In the last ten or fifteen years, quite a few have formed large coalitions: the National Taxi Workers Alliance, Restaurant Opportunities Center United, National Domestic Workers Alliance, and the National Day Laborer Organizing Network, to name a few. As these nationals mature, they will have to sort out their purpose and relationship to member groups, especially in terms of funding and movement goals. I've heard the same frustrations, off the record, from multiple locals: why, they ask, do the nationals get all the funding and acclaim? What about the members and organizers on the ground? Whose campaign should have priority?

In the union context, locals collect dues and send money upstream. But the same types of conflict—political and strategic—frequently arise. A national coalition might agree to an immigration reform package its more radical member groups cannot abide. A local worker center might target a neighborhood cafe with very few employees, to the chagrin of an umbrella organization eyeing a national restaurant chain.

As one union member told me, it was only a matter of time before worker centers started dealing with the same problems as traditional labor. There are risks inherent to going national: corporatization, hierarchy, warring egos, and a lost connection to the rank and file. Worker centers have made it big. What we don't yet know is if they'll maintain the spirit of being small.

The Care Gap (2016)

Michelle Chen

Michelle Chen (1981–) was born in New York City to Chinese immigrant parents and grew up hanging out in their shop in Manhattan's Chinatown. Holding a PhD in history from the CUNY Graduate Center, Chen is the author of a number of scholarly publications in addition to her work as a journalist on labor and immigration issues. She has been a contributing writer for The Nation *and* In These Times *and a contributing editor at* Dissent. *A longtime co-host of the* Belabored *podcast (with Sarah Jaffe) released by* Dissent, *Chen is also the co-producer of the Asia Pacific Forum podcast. Previously, she served as literary editor of* CultureStrike, *a media and arts project focused on the culture and politics of immigration. Chen has been a postdoctoral fellow in history at the Cornell University School of Industrial and Labor Relations.*

For all her working life, educating young children has been LiAnne Flakes's calling. When she started working in the 1990s, practically anyone could get a job teaching preschool. "Now," the Florida-based early childhood teacher said in a recent interview for the *Nation,* "you're being required to go to school." Flakes earned additional educational credentials accordingly, developing expertise on the developmental pathways of the children she teaches—their first letter and number recognition, how they learn to socialize, and how each day's lessons at her publicly subsidized daycare center shape their minds for the rest of their lives. "They're developing personality, they're developing temperament, they're developing all of that at this age. So as preschool [teachers] we are the ones that help to shape them for the future," she says.

But while she's proud of how her field has matured, she's disappointed that her wages have lagged. "I think we're just as important as an elementary school teacher," she says, "we're just as important as a high school [teacher] or college professor." There's a bitter subtext: she currently earns $12.50 an hour, or less than two-thirds the pay rate of a typical public high-school teacher.

For most of Flakes's career, the wages for workers in her field, which includes childcare workers as well as certified preschool teachers, have stagnated. As far as teachers and educators are concerned, says Flakes, "We are the most underpaid workers in America."

Preschool teacher paychecks look even thinner when compared to the swelling cost of raising a child. But while childcare costs have soared—spending in the sector has doubled, with about $2.4 billion a year spent on early childhood care and services—wages in the industry have stayed flat, and nearly half of childcare workers rely on public benefits to survive. Why is the labor of educating children worth so little?

Overall spending for early childhood services is driven by a variety of factors, including the rising cost of elite private programs, the growing demand for childcare among working parents, and higher standards for early childhood programs, which make regulatory compliance costlier. But whatever fuels the "market" for care, the money isn't trickling down to workers like Flakes, who foster this increasingly precious phase of child development. Ironically, many poorer children are underserved by the childcare and preschool systems. Investments in early childhood are stratified by class, as is public funding for daycare and pre-K programming. Overachieving parents purchase state-of-the-art private childcare and "enrichment" activities for their kids, designed to prepare them for a lifetime of success. Meanwhile, middle-class and poor families struggle to pay for the basic daycare and preschool services they need in order to work. Poor families spend close to a third of their incomes on childcare.

Though federal and state subsidies under the Child Care and Development Block Grant—distributed through states in the form of vouchers—help some poorer households cover childcare costs for working parents, this generally excludes parents who are not in the workforce. Childcare burdens can keep a parent from going out to search for a job. Limited childcare subsidy vouchers exclude families earning above a modest eligibility threshold (well short of a family living wage in many American cities). And since a growing share of all workers have irregular or part-time schedules that may vary week to week, childcare may be unavailable regardless of price, since there's no daycare that fits a night-shift schedule.

Faced with such barriers, many parents rely on grandparents or other relatives or friends to babysit for free, as people always have. But increasingly, both government policy and families themselves prefer institutional childcare. Yet even in its professionalized form, childhood services are outsourced to low-wage female workers. About 95 percent of childcare workers and 97 percent of preschool teachers are women. Both the demand for services and the supply of caregiving labor are driven by women at both ends of the economic hierarchy—and the dichotomy between those receiving care and those giving it gets obscured in public discourse about work-life balance, a concept often associated with "career women" and not everyday workers. Women's achievements in the white-collar workplace have often depended on the undercompensated labor of poorer peers.

The low wage floor in the field of early childhood care acts as a subsidy for wealthier parents purchasing top-quality childcare. And here's where class divides intertwine with care gaps: poorer teachers and caregivers who are raising children of their own can't afford the high quality of education they're trained to provide for other people's kids. And so, like many other working-class parents, teachers' children too fall into the yawning developmental gap between rich and poor kids, a gap that is created before they even learn how to count. As childcare becomes more professionalized but wages stay low, the gulf expands between well-off families, who offload care work onto daytime surrogates, and the service workers who absorb the burden, often for poverty wages and at the expense of their own kids.

Achieving real equity means state support for working conditions that allow for healthy parenting and a decent livelihood. Investing in early education benefits everyone involved, whether they are paying, earning, or learning.

Whatever form childcare takes, economic insecurity is toxic to the developing mind. Children who grow up in an impoverished environment without intellectual stimulation tend to enter school already disadvantaged, and they may never catch up. According to the Center for American Progress, "Much of the achievement gap that we see in later grades has its origins in the gap that exists at age 5."

As early childhood development becomes more important and established, the economic and social stakes of not receiving it are getting higher. Researchers have reevaluated how "early" one should intervene, and public education authorities have sought to further formalize preschool—districts are beginning to introduce curriculum models to track kids toward the standard K–12 system—as a pathway to elementary education.

But it's an uneven path. Unstable state and federal funding streams are spread thinly across both private and public providers. As a result, according to W. Steven Barnett, director of the National Institute for Early Education Research, "you end up with situations where some children get higher quality [care and education] because they get there first." In other words, only the children of parents who sign up for limited slots on a first-come, first-served basis benefit; the rest scramble for slots in free programs. During a hot enrollment period, "you find parents in Georgia camping out overnight to get a place for their child in a public school pre-K."

Meanwhile, workers tasked with providing a nurturing and stable environment for other people's children face constant economic anxiety. Surveys by Berkeley researchers found that over a period of more than two decades of flatlining wages, a childcare labor force that earns "barely more than fast food cooks" often struggles with stress over income instability and "not having enough food for their families."

Venetta Strickland of North Carolina started working in child-care about thirteen years ago, while looking after her young son with cerebral palsy. He's now nearing high school graduation, with three siblings coming up behind him. She's still scraping by on $12.45 an hour from a small daycare center that she says has been tight-fisted about giving raises.

"Just working with kids as a whole is very rewarding," she says. "But at the end of the day . . . when it's time to clock out, the real life hits back, and hey . . . how am I going to feed my kids?" She's managed to move out of her mother's home, but struggles to keep up with rent for her two-bedroom apartment, and still sometimes leans on her mother to provide her own family's informal daycare. Meanwhile, she says, student debt looms ahead as she studies for an online education degree. "There's been many times that I don't even make it to the next pay day."

Between her days guiding preschoolers' first forays into count-ing and reading, Strickland knows what her daughter does with-out: the field trips, the carefree playtime, the kind of enrichment the family has briefly glimpsed on the days Strickland's employer has allowed her to bring her daughter to work. As the educator who takes care of other people's children for eight or nine hours a day, she worries that her own kids are missing out.

For another preschool teacher, Desiree Gonzales in Albuquer-que, her school schedule clashes with her working-mom schedule. The mother of three says she gets by with a state childcare subsidy and the roundabout convenience of enrolling one of her children at the school where she works, so the subsidy essentially goes toward teaching her own toddler (like many working-class single parents, she can only work with the subsidy, otherwise, the teacher would stay home, priced out of daycare herself). But she recently had to give up a new, higher-paying teaching job when she realized that it would not allow her to take a break to fetch her older son from school in the afternoons, like her previous employer had.

The catch-22 of struggling to teach others' children in order to raise her own eventually led her back to her old job. "I feel like I'm at work too much, and not home enough," she says, but at the same time, "if you're not working as much . . . you're not getting paid as much."

The financial stress takes a physical toll: as childcare provider Carolyn Carpenter recalled in an essay published by the advocacy coalition Raising California Together, parents sometimes had to drop off sick kids at her daycare, since they couldn't take time off from work to stay home with them. Carpenter was in the same position: "I also lack paid leave and sick days, and am left to struggle whenever I or my child gets sick . . . we working moms find ourselves on the verge of losing it all."

Labor activists are becoming more vocal in their demand for fair pay in the childcare sector. The Fight for $15 campaign, a broad community-labor coalition supported by the Service Employees International Union, has branched into organizing childcare workers, including Flakes, to press for $15 an hour as a starting wage, in tandem with similar calls for higher wages for fast-food workers, homecare workers, and others in historically non-unionized, low-wage jobs.

Testifying at a public hearing on the Fight for $15 campaign in Raleigh, North Carolina, Tolanda Barnette talked about being a childcare worker who never made more than $10 an hour over her twelve-year career. While her classroom was a sanctuary, she slept in a shelter because she couldn't afford a home for her family:

> There is something really ugly about being someone who is passionate about caring for children, goes above and beyond to care for children, but not being paid enough, to be able to have enough, to care for my own. . . . I want to give them the world; $15 an hour won't make us rich, but I could finally feel like my family and I are going to be alright.

While it's unlikely Congress would agree to dramatically subsidize childcare in the current hostile climate on the Hill, preschool remains one area that draws rare bipartisan interest: many states have established universal pre-K programs, including Republican strongholds like Florida, Georgia, and Oklahoma. Building fair wages into childcare reform may symbolically start braiding together labor and family interests in the policy discussion over the future of care.

Equalizing the working conditions for childcare providers requires a more holistic conception of education. As the field of early childhood development shifts toward higher, more sophisticated standards, workers need tailored professional education programs to lift them into higher-paying positions. But financial hardship and a dearth of specialized training programs leave many early-childhood workers in a career rut.

Another way to advance the workforce is for educators to organize, but collective action is hard to cultivate in a climate of chronic instability. Marcy Whitebook, a childcare policy researcher, says unionization remains hampered by the early learning sector's precarious working conditions and by such variation in program sizes and structures. With early childhood services scattered across small community centers, churches, and schools, she says, "The main challenge is the size of the organizations and the turnover—in addition to the overall negative climate for unions."

Gonzales has campaigned with PEOPLE for the Kids, a community-labor coalition that has sought to link the three pillars of New Mexico's childcare infrastructure: providers, which are often small, privately run organizations; union and non-union educators and staff; and families. Together, they've petitioned state lawmakers to fund childcare comprehensively, so workers can earn a decent wage while parents receive subsidies that cover the cost of quality care—that way, childcare centers won't have to squeeze wages or cut hours to keep the lights on. Bridging parents and educators, the campaign has sought to keep legislators from triangulating on childcare funding—resisting the state's tendency to expand classroom slots but scrimp on teacher wages. Campaigners want it all for their kids—and for those who care for them.

Matthew Aber-Towns, an organizer with the American Federation of Teachers, which has supported the campaign, says the overarching goal is to ensure "all the stakeholders in the industry are organized and united." Currently, while childcare center operators struggle to sustain themselves on inadequate funding, he explains, among the staff, "you have the worker voice that's saying, 'look, you need quality, and you can see these need to be good jobs.' . . . [And parents are] saying, 'We need access and flexible options for early learning.' "

Bringing up a child has evolved from a domestic duty to one of the fastest growing sectors in the education system. Between wanting the best for our kids and demanding fairness for all caregivers, preschool teaches the hard lessons of inequality that politics easily forgets.

Graduate Student Unions Fight the Corporate University (2001)

Gordon Lafer

Gordon Lafer (1960–) grew up in New Jersey and earned a PhD in political science at Yale University. There he helped organize the union for Yale grad students and then spent two years as research and communications director for the coalition of unions representing Yale employees during a long contract fight and strike. Lafer then worked for the Building Trades Organizing Project in Las Vegas before joining the faculty of the University of Oregon's Labor Education and Research Center. He is the author of The Job Training Charade and The One Percent Solution: How Corporations Are Remaking America, One State at a Time.

In the spring of 2001, graduate students at New York University made history when they won recognition for the first graduate student union at a private university. To accomplish this feat, students had to overcome the political and legal opposition of virtually every elite school in the country. In a series of hearings before the National Labor Relations Board, arguments opposing the union were voiced not only by NYU's own administration but by those of Yale, Princeton, Columbia University, the Massachusetts Institute of Technology, Stanford, Johns Hopkins, Boston University, the American Association of Universities, the American Council on Education, and the Council on Graduate Schools. In a series of landmark rulings, the NLRB rejected the arguments of these scions of higher education and opened the door to a new wave of organizing on the nation's campuses.

The fact that the entire organizational leadership of elite higher education mobilized against the NYU union indicates what was at stake in this fight. In fact, though, the NYU decision was only one of several late-1990s decisions marking a sea change in academic labor relations. These rulings have helped to spur an unprecedented boom in graduate student organizing, activities that come on the heels of what is already a fast-growing movement. Between 1995 and 2001, the number of graduate student unions in the country grew from ten to twenty-seven, leading some 20 percent of all graduate employees to be covered by union contracts.

Although the legal decisions have been important, the recent boom in organizing activity is primarily a reaction to dynamics within the university itself. The traditional ideal of college education pictures a setting that is specifically outside the rat race—an opportunity to explore ideas, make friendships, and develop a sense of one's self in ways that are not possible amid the dog-eat-dog pressures of commercial life. However, universities have moved progressively away from this community-of-scholars model, fashioning themselves instead in the image of private corporations. Rather than pursuing the romantic vision of the classroom as an encounter between seasoned scholars and eager young minds, administrators across the country have radically shifted teaching duties away from regular faculty and onto the shoulders of graduate students and adjunct instructors. The economic logic of this strategy is simple to grasp: graduate student teachers earn considerably less than full-time faculty members. Not surprisingly, the number of tenure-track faculty was cut by 10 percent between 1975 and 1995—a period during which overall enrollment was expanding significantly—while the number of graduate teaching assistants increased by nearly 40 percent. Nationally, it is estimated that a majority of all teaching hours are now performed by graduate students and other contingent teachers; an undergraduate signing up for an introductory English class has less than a one-in-four chance of being taught by a tenure-track professor. And in both natural science and humanities departments, graduate students are responsible for 90 percent of the grading. As administrators have been increasingly driven by bottom-line considerations, graduate students have become an indispensable ingredient in the financial calculations of every major university.

These same dynamics that make graduate students such a good buy while they are in school make them increasingly unemployable after they complete their degrees, leading a coalition of national faculty associations to bemoan "the vanishing traditional faculty member." The wholesale substitution of casual teachers for tenure-track positions has marked the decimation of the academic job market. In the natural sciences, the turn to commercially sponsored research has likewise encouraged a more corporate structure in which a limited number of principal investigators oversee a large staff of graduate students and postdoctoral fellows. As a result, the number of faculty positions has decreased while the time one is expected to apprentice in the purgatory between graduate school and a junior faculty slot has lengthened, with Ph.D.s in the biological sciences now spending an average of four years in low-wage postdoctoral "fellowships." The Commission on Life Sciences warns that "many graduate students entered life science training with the expectation that they would become like their mentors: they would be able to establish laboratories in which they would pursue research based on their own scientific ideas. The reality that now faces many of them seems very different."

Finally, even those ultimately lucky enough to land tenure-track positions find that they are still not inhabiting the lives of their mentors. While other professional salaries have soared over the past three decades, downsizing has enabled university administrators to cut faculty pay, despite significant growth in the higher education market. This, then, is the contradiction that lies at the heart of the corporatization process: the very dynamics that make graduate students so useful to the business mission of the university are also destroying the academic careers that are supposed to justify the long haul of earning a Ph.D.

In the 1980 *National Labor Relations Board v. Yeshiva University* case that largely banned faculty unions at private universities, Justice William Brennan's dissent warned of the dangers of leaving academia a union-free environment. Removing the possibility of faculty organizing, he predicted, "threatens to eliminate much of the administration's incentive to resolve its disputes . . . through open discussion and mutual agreement . . . [and] removes whatever deterrent value [labor law] may offer against unreasonable administrative conduct." Decades later, it appears that graduate education has fallen victim, in part, to just this unchecked administrative power feared by Brennan. Given a free hand to unilaterally mold the university to their own liking, administrators have produced a system that—while financially successful—has undercut much of what used to stand at the heart of academic life.

Administrators across the country have relied on a common set of arguments to oppose granting their graduate students the same rights afforded secretaries and librarians: that graduate teachers and researchers are "students, not employees," that the tasks they carry out are "training, not work," and that unionization would destroy the collegiality of campus relations. The single most counter-intuitive argument launched against unionization is the proposition that unions threaten academic freedom. NYU asserted that all the working conditions of teachers—including salary and workload—were "educational policy" issues that could not be subject to collective bargaining without undermining fundamental freedoms. Yet the university already negotiates over terms of employment with individual graduate students, as individuals are free to reject teaching positions if they deem the salary inadequate. Thus, NYU's real concern was to avoid negotiating terms of employment *collectively* rather than individually, presumably based on the fear that collective bargaining would prove more expensive. But this has nothing to do with academic freedom and, on the contrary, amounts to a direct refutation of the very purpose of federal labor law—to provide workers the ability to negotiate on a more even footing with their employers. The administration's argument, the Clinton NLRB concluded, "runs directly contrary to the express purposes of the [National Labor Relations] Act."

The argument that most strains credulity may be that of Yale Law School dean Anthony Kronman (1994–2004), who suggested in the pages of the *New York Times* that a union might stunt the intellectual development of its members. Graduate students "are working to become individuals with distinctive views and voices," Kronman explains. "Collective bargaining, with its demand that one voice speak for all, is [not] compatible with the individualism of university life—the life the students have chosen precisely because it leaves them free to follow their own path and to speak for themselves." The notion that unionization might prevent individuals from finding their own intellectual voice requires such a dramatic suspension of belief that one almost feels insulted by the demand to treat this as a serious proposition. Perhaps Kronman has never heard of Albert Einstein—a member of Princeton's American Federation of Teachers faculty union; or never been impressed by the work of any graduates of the University of Michigan, University of Wisconsin, or other unionized schools; or never known anyone who teaches at Rutgers, the University of Massachusetts, or other campuses where faculty are organized.

Indeed, all the arguments about academic freedom ring hollow for a simple reason: this problem has already been solved. Administrators often talk as if the prospect of academic bargaining is a new problem, fraught with unknown procedures and unpredictable pitfalls. In fact, the correct response to this worry is: been there, done that. Both graduate student unions and faculty unions have been conducting negotiations for decades; in all this time, there has never been a suggestion that academic freedom was compromised. "After nearly 30 years of experience with bargaining units of faculty members," the NLRB concluded in 2001, "we are confident" that issues of academic versus employment considerations can be easily resolved.

Nevertheless, there is a meaningful—and disturbing—conception of "academic freedom" that animates administrators' opposition to unionization. Take for instance the case of Yale, where faculty and administrators threatened striking graduate student workers in 1996 with bans from future teaching assignments; suggested that participants could be kicked out of graduate school; and adopted a policy allowing faculty advisers to write negative letters of recommendation on the basis of strike participation. These reprisals led the federal government to file charges against Yale administrators and faculty and to resolutions of censure against the school from the Modern Language Association, the American History Association, and the American Association of University Professors (AAUP). Ultimately, the government dropped most of its charges based on a technicality regarding the particular form of this strike—withholding undergraduate grades at the conclusion of the fall semester—even though such threats would clearly be illegal in the context of a normal teaching strike. For most of the academic community, academic freedom consists precisely in the protection against such threats. Yale provost Alison Richard, on the other hand, saw it this way: "These restrictions on what could be legally discussed with an employee," Richard insists, "would strike at the freedom of expression central to the whole conception of the university as an intellectual community."

In the minds of campus administrators, then, the principle of "academic freedom" has been reformulated along frighteningly Orwellian lines. The revised principle seems to boil down to the right of administrators to threaten those lower down the academic food chain. This debate over contrasting visions of academic freedom points, at the deepest levels, to what is at stake in campus organizing campaigns. Beyond the immediate economic issues of wages and benefits, this is a fight over the extent to which universities will be democratized. The romantic vision of the medieval university run by its scholars is long gone. But the difference between a democratized and corporatized university remains more critical than ever as universities face the future.

The second front of the graduate unionization struggle is the administrators' war for the hearts and minds of campus faculty. Graduate student unions have repeatedly insisted that their conflict is solely with the central administration. Faculty have, in fact, found unions easy to work with. In a comprehensive survey of faculty at universities with established graduate student unions, 95 percent of faculty stated that graduate student collective bargaining did not inhibit the free exchange of ideas between faculty and graduate students; an overwhelming majority reported similarly that graduate student unions had not created an adversarial relationship, and that the union had not inhibited their ability to advise or mentor their own students. Administrators, though, have adopted a conscious strategy of placing faculty at the fulcrum of union conflicts. Thus, one school's recommendation to fellow administrators was to stock the university's negotiating committee with a majority of *faculty members*—even though they would have no final say over university positions. By forcing graduate students to negotiate with those who hold the most immediate power over their coursework, grades, and ultimate career prospects, administrators seek to gain an edge in intimidating graduate employees into substandard settlements. Faculty are encouraged to play this role, in part, by administration suggestions that unions threaten the freedoms of faculty themselves.

In fact, faculty may find that the biggest threat to academic freedom comes from above. Administrators' anti-unionism has too often led them to impose the equivalent of an academic state of emergency, in which the normal protections of faculty and graduate students are suspended, with everything subject to the single goal of beating back organizing efforts. Increasingly, these anti-union campaigns have threatened the liberties of faculty as well as graduate students. For instance, the dean at the State University of New York at Buffalo removed Professor Barbara Bono from her position as chair of the English department after she refused to sign a letter threatening striking graduate student teachers with being banned from future employment. Professor Bono explained, "I was not going to turn to threatening my students." One might view this as a noble defense of the mentoring relationship. In the eyes of the administration, however, department chairs are delinquent in their duties if they refuse to be part of the anti-union machinery. Thus, Dean Charles Stiger explained that he removed Professor Bono because "she expressed considerable sympathy for the students' situation and didn't see that forceful action was required."

Just as administrators may have feared, the success of graduate student unions has spurred increased organizing among other academic employees, including both adjunct and tenure-track faculty. The *Yeshiva* decision drastically restricted faculty organizing on the basis that, in the model of medieval scholarly communities, faculty hold primary decision-making authority and therefore are themselves managerial employees with no right to organize. "If there were a single group comprising the essential heart of management," Yeshiva's lawyers insisted, "it would be the faculty." If this description of faculty-run universities was dated in 1980, it has by now become utterly untenable. As the president of NYU's AAUP chapter noted, "Today it's undeniable that universities . . . are modeled not on medieval guilds, governed by their members, but on modern corporations." At some point, a new faculty union will force this principle to be considered once more; and when this happens, the administrators who have remade the university in the decades since faculty were cut out of collective bargaining will be hard-pressed to keep a straight face while suggesting that faculty still run the place.

PART V

What Is to Be Done?

How to renew and reanimate the labor movement has been a perennial question for decades. Indeed, for the better part of *Dissent*'s existence, its contributors have been grappling not with the issues posed by the magazine's socialist founders but rather with the more fundamental challenge of how to revitalize the union movement—or simply how to defend it from annihilation. Always closely connected to questions of union democracy, the content and tone of *Dissent*'s labor coverage has in this regard converged over time with that appearing in other publications close to the labor-left—like *In These Times*, *Jacobin*, and even *Labor Notes*.

Events in the years since the global financial crisis have lent these long-standing debates around union renewal a new sense of urgency and dynamism. The valiant 2011 campaign waged by Wisconsin workers against then governor Scott Walker's revanchist assault on public sector unionism—the prelude to the *Janus* decision—may have been unsuccessful, but it did serve as an inspiration to unionists far beyond that state. From there, the 2012 Chicago teachers' strike, Occupy Wall Street, and eventually the Bernie Sanders presidential campaigns, along with a number of less well-publicized struggles, helped working people around the country—and especially those in the generational cohorts entering a dismal post-2008 workforce—think more clearly about power, and about how to build it. Tens of thousands responded by flocking into the Democratic Socialists of America (DSA), the political organization most closely aligned with the *Dissent* intellectual project. Suddenly, this dusty old style of democratic socialism was hip.

Yet on the strategic question of how, exactly, to translate these scattered successes and raw energy into lasting power, there is no shortage of perspectives. Since the New Voice leadership assumed the reins at the AFL-CIO in 1996, many organizers have insisted that resource-rich organizing campaigns, often recruiting young people, would yield increasing union density. Intransigent employer resistance and endless legal obstacles, however, have remained the central challenges in the way of this approach. Others have emphasized the importance of linking unions to other social movements—struggles for workers of color, immigrants,

women, as well as those in pursuit of a green transition and against imperialist war. If the organizational payoff of these efforts has been small,
the political significance of organized labor's move to the left has been
notable indeed. So too with campaigns like the Fight for 15, and related
living-wage fights around the country, which have meaningfully improved
the conditions of low-wage work even if they have done little to add to
labor's membership rolls. Finally, in the years since the Bernie Sanders campaign and especially in the aftermath of the pandemic, organizers have increasingly returned to the enunciation of an aggressive set
of wage and working condition demands, often backed by union strike
power. If the level of working-class militancy pales in comparison to that
which prevailed in the 1970s, it has at least, for a few years, headed in
the right direction.

In the first selection reprinted here, Nelson Lichtenstein draws attention to the notable ways in which organized labor has moved to the
left in recent decades. Whereas the AFL-CIO, when at the height of its
power during *Dissent*'s early years, hesitated to embrace causes championed by the social movements of 1960s and early 1970s (and often
enough viewed them antagonistically), the federation now proved a reli-
able participant in progressive coalitions. Lichtenstein situates this political evolution within the context of the rightward political shift that has
taken place over the past generation or more. Faced with enemies hell-
bent not just on containing labor's power but on destroying every shred
of social protection that working people have won over the past century,
unions have become, as Lichtenstein puts it, "reluctant radicals."

The climate crisis has done as much as any other issue to force a reckoning with the character of capitalism both inside and outside of the
labor movement. Yet the challenges associated with achieving a truly just
transition remain as serious as ever. In the next essay, Trish Kahle con-
fronts these contradictions head-on through an exploration of the past
and present of "labor environmentalism." Ecological degradation, Kahle
argues, must be understood as part of the broader neoliberal onslaught
on working people and the public sector, for "austerity and sustainability
are antithetical concepts."

Some of the most celebrated recent battles against austerity have
been led by public education workers, as Eleni Schirmer and Sarah Jaffe

remind us. Schirmer's article documents the efforts by the Milwaukee Teachers' Education Association to develop what would be understood as a common-good organizing and bargaining strategy in the wake of passage of the antiunion Act 10 measure in Wisconsin. Jaffe, a veteran labor reporter and co-host of the *Dissent* podcast *Belabored*, provides a detailed and in-real-time account of the historic West Virginia teacher strike that kicked off the Red for Ed movement that spread from places like Oklahoma and Arizona to Chicago and Los Angeles.

Finally, no discussion of union renewal would be complete without consideration of the bankrupt nature of the existing labor law regime. As meaningful reform of the National Labor Relations Act, for instance, has been and will likely for some time remain stymied by the U.S. Senate, organizers and scholars have undertaken a productive debate about alternative legal strategies.

In a thought-provoking essay on sectoral bargaining, Kate Andrias looks to the New Deal origins of the Fair Labor Standards Act and identifies an attractive precedent for the development of tripartite boards that could be authorized to set standards across entire industries. Instead of committing resources to the arduous task of organizing worksite-by-worksite as mandated by the firm-centered NLRA, the approach proposed by Andrias holds the promise of enabling a more genuinely class-wide style of unionism that seeks to reshape the political economy itself.

In contrast, Veena Dubal contends that the concept of sectoral bargaining and related labor law reforms put the cart before the proverbial horse. The profound disempowerment of working people from the 1970s onward, she insists, cannot be understood apart from the structural, macroeconomic policy regime that tolerates—even pursues—persistent employment insecurity. A more comprehensive political economic vision, anchored by the demand for the right to a job, ought to lie at the center of the labor movement's strategy in the years to come.

Why Labor Moved Left (2015)

Nelson Lichtenstein

Nelson Lichtenstein (1944–) was born in Frederick, Maryland, to parents who were both refugees: one fleeing Nazi Germany, the other Mississippi's gothic culture. He took a PhD in history at the University of California, Berkeley, where his politics were shaped by a brief but intense engagement with the International Socialists, later Solidarity, many members of which "industrialized" in the 1970s. Lichtenstein remained an academic, writing books and articles on the mid-twentieth-century industrial labor movement, including a biography of the UAW's Walter Reuther. In the 1990s he was a principal organizer of the "teach-ins with the labor movement" that helped reconcile academic leftists with a new generation of union leaders. In the twenty-first century he taught at the University of California, Santa Barbara, where he directed its Center for the Study of Work, Labor, and Democracy.

Hard times sometimes have a silver lining. As American unions have come under unrelenting assault, the left is "enjoying" a historic victory, but one most labor partisans would rather do without. If one considers the political landscape in the United States over the last half century, then American unions have moved—or been moved—to the left margin of mainstream thinking and action. They have gotten there primarily because of the shifting political and economic landscape on which they stand; for the most part, their leftism represents no conscious insurgency. Organized labor has become, instead, the domain of reluctant radicals.

The decimation, over the past few decades, of the industrial relations system that was a bulwark of Cold War liberalism has forced even some traditionally conservative unions—such as the Teamsters, the United Brotherhood of Carpenters, and the old Retail Clerks (now the UFCW)—to take stances once adopted by left-wing unions in the 1940s: participating in liberal-led coalitions, advertising their multiracial character, and "blaming and shaming" corporate adversaries. Labor's capacity to play the role of an insular, conservative interest group stands in inverse proportion to its organizational strength. Meanwhile, and ironically, a few of the "new social movements" spawned by the New Left—environmentalists, "lean-in" feminists, and some elements of the now triumphant gay rights movement—have shifted to the center. Corporations and even some elements of the GOP court them, even as those same companies and politicians remain steadfastly hostile to trade unionism.

Left and right are malleable, historically specific concepts. In some eras, they refer to economic positions, in others, to those of culture or foreign policy. But by almost any criteria, a snapshot of trade unions in 1965 would locate them firmly in the center of American politics. Unions did back the civil rights laws of 1964 and 1965, but the AFL-CIO itself failed to endorse the 1963 March on Washington (which the United Auto Workers, under Walter Reuther, helped finance). AFL-CIO President George Meany had a visceral hostility to anything resembling a mass mobilization of the rank and file, where the left, old or new, might make its presence felt. He and other top labor officials were staunch Keynesians, but they did little to challenge corporate power except in the routinized world of collective bargaining. The corporations were nearly always the aggressors—as in the 1959 steel strike, the longest and largest in American history, which began when all the big steel companies made a determined effort to "speed up" the work and recapture some of the job control they had lost to the unions in the 1930s and 1940s. In this case, the corporations lost.

That the unions stood for the industrial relations status quo also became apparent in their response to the challenge they faced from the civil rights movement. This was not just because of white working-class racism, although there was certainly plenty of that. As the legal historian Reuel Schiller has demonstrated, the dual systems of workplace justice that arose from the mid-1960s onward were destined to clash. Labor's was based on the industrial pluralism and representational democracy at the heart of the Wagner Act; the other was based on the rights-conscious regime established by Title VII of the Civil Rights Act. In this conflict, most unions became de facto opponents of a deeper level of racial justice on the job—not just affirmative action, but the whole idea that industrial justice was predicated upon a set of individual rights, and not collective, majoritarian power and decision making. Their opposition was reinforced by the cultural and social proclivities of the white, male, blue-collar workers who still composed a plurality of the rank and file and a large majority of officials. Nor were the academic spear carriers for the labor movement critics of the status quo. The then Industrial Relations Research Association (now, the Labor and Employment Relations Association), a potent scholarly group out of whose ranks came university presidents such as Clark Kerr and cabinet members such as George Shultz was just about the only academic organization in the early 1970s with no radical caucus.

In the 1960s, New Leftists were first prodding and then hostile critics of the house of labor. SDS's Port Huron Statement sadly chided unions for a failure to fulfill their liberatory promise: "Today labor remains the most liberal 'mainstream' institution—but often its liberalism represents vestigial commitments, self-interestedness, unradicalism. In some measure labor has succumbed to institutionalization, its social idealism waning under the tendencies of bureaucracy, materialism, business ethics." The very concept of "participatory democracy," for which the Port Huron Statement became well known, rhetorically countered the "industrial democracy" which had seemed a radical vision from the First World War through the Great Depression. But its radicalism quickly drained away in the postwar decades to devolve into the system of collective bargaining facilitated by the Wagner Act and practiced by big unions and giant corporations. SDS therefore endorsed Daniel Bell's classic essay, "The Subversion of Collective Bargaining," first published in *Commentary* in early 1960. Bell saw the great steel strike of 1959 as a sham, largely useful to corporations, which responded to the long shutdown by instituting higher prices.

Radicals of the 1960s rebelled against the entire system of collective bargaining. They viewed grievance procedures as legalistic displacements of the raw shop-floor conflict they hoped to mobilize. Collective bargaining ratified the power of unresponsive elites, both corporate and unionist. Industry-wide bargaining, a *bête noire* for corporate conservatives, was also seen by the left as an iron cage that limited local autonomy and insurgent activism.

Then, in the early 1970s, some New Leftists made a "turn toward the working class." Intellectuals like André Gorz and Staughton Lynd linked a systemic critique of capitalism and mass society with a quest for workers' power and the abolition of alienation at the "point of production." At the same time, a younger generation of New Leftists added a critique of corporate power, routinized work, union bureaucracy, and the racism and sexism endemic to working-class culture, with a sense of the agency and insurgency they had earlier glimpsed in the civil rights and antiwar movements. There was some cooperation between the New Left and liberal or radical unions like the Hospital Workers Local 1199 (now United Healthcare Workers East), AFSCME, the United Electrical, Radio, and Machine Workers, and, above all, the United Farm Workers. Many veterans of the student movement became activists within these organizations. However, to be among the relatively few leftists who even thought about trade unionism was to seek its transformation. Unions did not recruit students to be organizers in those days, and the students who "industrialized" did so to overturn not just the union leadership but the entire structure of collective bargaining.

Of course, these grand ambitions became a good deal less plausible in the 1970s as the unions encountered a new set of headwinds, which have never abated. As a result, most unions retreated to the left for one or more of three reasons—structural, political, and ideological.

Structurally, many of the institutions that had undergirded

centrist pluralism were virtually destroyed. A combination of capital mobility, management hostility, and political reaction ravaged private sector unionism. The smaller the trade-union movement became, the more corporations viewed it as intolerable. If you are managing a firm with a union contract in a sea of non-union competitors, then your desire to get rid of the union has an overwhelming urgency. Industry-wide collective bargaining has vanished in auto, steel, meatpacking, and other formerly well-organized industries. Today, it exists only in major league sports, among some Hollywood professions, and on the West Coast waterfront.

Organizing in the traditional sense has become nearly impossible. For more than a generation now, the courts have legitimized virtually every anti-union ploy and tactic that corporate managers and a cohort of anti-union law firms and think tanks could dream up. Even with a liberal majority now at the National Labor Relations Board, a paltry 30,000 workers win union recognition each year through use of its procedures. As a result, union leaders have lost the legitimacy that once backed up their power in the pluralist liberal order. In the 1950s Reuther often asserted, "First we must organize them, that's the easy part, then we must unionize them, that's the hard part." By "unionize" Reuther meant what we would call "consciousness-raising." Today, the tasks are reversed, which means that the persuasive talents of smart leftists are more desperately needed than ever before; union organizing now requires, above all else, an ideological mobilization both of workers and of the communities in which they live.

The evisceration of collective bargaining, in both the private as well as the public sector, shifts labor to adopt a strategy of popular mobilization. Under the Wagner Act, bargaining was designed to depoliticize the relations between labor and capital, insulating them from both the judiciary and from partisan rivalry. In practice, that was never the case, and unions have always been active in elections and in lobbying for policy changes. But as long as a semblance of the yearly bargaining system still functioned, they did not have to stake quite so much money, time, and prestige on the ebb and flow of election results.

Today, collective bargaining has, at best, a minimal payoff. It has no capacity to set standards for other workers in the same industry, as it once did in the early postwar era. Nor can it generate substantial dividends for even the most self-interested or conservative groups of workers. Public-sector austerity and the deunionization of the private sector mean that unions are almost always on the defensive when it comes to bargaining with city officials or individual corporations.

Thus unions have to be political, not just in terms of electing one "friend of labor" over another politician, but in a fundamental strategic sense, in which contests over state policy become the central arena of economic and social combat. Victory in the Fight for $15 campaign, for example, will not be measured in new union members or new contracts, but in new laws raising the minimum wage, preventing wage theft, establishing a livable set of working hours, and reforming overtime-pay rules. This dynamic moves labor onto a battlefield long occupied by civil rights and gay rights advocates as well as feminists and environmentalists. It means a "Europeanization" of American labor relations, in which the state, albeit on a local level, has come to play a much more prominent role in structuring the world of work.

Conservatives understand this dynamic well, which is why their assault on unionism has been so unremitting. Moreover, conservatives are now attacking all the surviving institutions of industrial pluralism, which the labor left once considered the essence of accommodation and ensnarement. These include grievance procedures, the dues check-off, the union or agency shop, exclusive jurisdiction, industry-wide bargaining, and the National Labor Relations Board itself. In the imagination of the right, the very concept of collective action is a coercive "racket" that subverts both the market and the will or faith of individual workers.

For American conservatives, there is also a larger principle at stake. They disdain organized labor because the union movement stands explicitly for a set of ideas and social impulses they find abhorrent: social solidarity, employment stability, and limits on the workplace power of corporate ownership, plus a defense of the welfare state, progressive taxation, financial regulation, and a government apparatus energetic enough to supervise the health and safety of American workers and consumers. Even when it comes to issues of immigration, race, and gender, American unions, despite a highly checkered history, today stand on the left side of the political divide.

Even if official labor has shifted to the left, it is nevertheless a shadow of its former self. The steady decline in union density and social power, from about one-third of the non-farm workforce in the early 1950s to a little more than 10 percent today, is a trend of great significance. Private-sector union density is now below 7 percent, a figure not seen since the late nineteenth century when unionism had only a semi-legal status, police and courts routinely broke strikes, and politicians and the daily press demonized labor leaders.

Such changes have left radicals inside the unions with little room for critical distance between themselves and union leaders who are struggling for survival. With strikes practically nonexistent and the GOP eager to make labor as impotent as possible, it is hard to generate an oppositional movement within any individual union—something that was commonplace between the late 1960s and the 1980s. What's more, as leading unions adopt the program of the left—immigration reform, defense of gay rights, a critique of a militarized foreign policy, and a rejection of the racism still inherent in many police departments—the space for the kind of criticism once put forward by the drafters of the Port Huron Statement has shrunk. Indeed, the most sophisticated defense of collective bargaining and industrial militancy is now found in *Labor Notes*, the periodical that has been an influential voice of the left within many unions for thirty-five years.

So is radicalism still possible within the unions? Of course. But now, as in Gilded-Age America, the union cause itself is increasingly that of a radical democracy struggling to be born. American trade unionists may have become reluctant radicals, but they are radicals nonetheless.

Austerity vs. the Planet: The Future of Labor Environmentalism (2016)

Trish Kahle

Trish Kahle arrived at radical politics through the antiwar movement in the early 2000s. A rank-and-file leader in the Fight for $15 movement while working at a Whole Foods Market in Chicago, Kahle went on to help organize the graduate workers union at the University of Chicago, the institution from which she took a PhD. She has written for and edited a number of left publications and is the author of Energy Citizenship: Coal and Democracy in the American Century *(2024). Kahle is now assistant professor of history at Georgetown University–Qatar.*

In December 2015, members of the International Trade Union Confederation joined other civil society activists in a mass sit-in at the COP21 talks in Paris. Unionists and their allies, some 400 strong, filled the social space adjacent to the negotiating rooms for several hours, in defiance of a French ban on protests that remained in effect in the wake of the November 13, 2015, terrorist attacks. The ITUC delegation demanded the negotiators go back to the table and make a serious effort to incorporate labor's demands for a just transition—which, at its heart, is concerned with making sure workers in environmentally unsustainable industries are retrained and put to work building a new, sustainable economy.

The action, even as it generated energy and media buzz, failed to convince the negotiators. The "just transition" clause of the Paris agreement remained stuck in the preamble (not in the body of the agreement itself, as the ITUC members had demanded), more of a hat tip than grounds for international action. But at least it got a mention—unlike the fossil fuels largely responsible for the climate crisis in the first place. Nowhere in the Paris agreement or its preamble do the words fossil fuel, coal, oil, gas, or pollution appear.

As the talks wrapped up and global leaders hailed a "historic turning point" in the world's relationship to ongoing climate disruption, environmental activist Chris Williams pointed out that "twenty-one years of treaties and negotiations have all been stepping around the main problem, which is the production of fossil fuels." For all the pomp and circumstance, this agreement was no different. Meanwhile, the consequences of two decades of inaction become clearer each day. A few weeks after the Paris agreement was signed, scientists confirmed that 2015 was the warmest year on record, with global temperatures approaching 1°C above the twentieth-century average. And those already feeling the worst effects of this climate disruption, predominantly poor people of color, continued to have the least say in how to combat it.

All this takes place in the context of a weakened labor movement that has failed to maintain workers' expected standard of living in the face of ongoing restructuring in the world economy and, particularly in the United States, political backsliding. The degradation of work and the destruction of the environment have proceeded hand in hand. Good jobs keep going away, but fossil fuels haven't gone anywhere. And yet the industry-propagated myth of "jobs versus the environment" persists. From the moment Congress debated anti-pollution legislation in the early 1970s, fossil fuel industry leaders promised such regulation would destroy the heavily unionized employment in the industry. In 1971 the Chamber of Commerce warned that the passage of the Clean Air Act could lead to the collapse of "entire industries," while auto industry lobbyists prophesied "business catastrophe." Four decades later, the talking points remain the same.

The problem with this story is that environmental regulation never got the chance to destroy whole sectors of "good jobs," as opponents of pollution regulation promised it would; the fossil fuel

companies themselves, with the winds of free-market fundamen-
talism at their backs, destroyed them instead. A decade after the
passage of the Clean Air Act, the United States was producing more
cars and fossil fuels than ever, and employing a record number of
workers to do so. Another decade later, as the Cold War was ending, U.S. fossil fuel production was still going strong, but the jobs
were evaporating.

It wasn't just fossil fuels, of course. The decline in manufacturing
jobs, union density, and real wages wrought by neoliberal restructuring hollowed out the prospects of the entire American working
class. In the wake of the 2008 financial crisis, the resulting misery
has only been exacerbated by government austerity and anti-union
measures, as manufactured scarcity is marshaled to frighten workers into concessions.

In cities like Flint, Michigan, built around the auto industry, the
consequences of this restructuring are all too vivid. Globalization
and the rise of "lean production" have turned the city, once an industrial powerhouse, into a waking nightmare for the people who
remain: forty years of stagnant wages, reduction in public welfare
and services, and then a recession that gutted the few middle-wage
jobs left. In today's Flint, the generalized decline of American
working-class living standards has turned into a life-or-death crisis. In 2014, emergency city manager Darnell Earley, appointed by
Governor Rick Snyder with no democratic accountability to the
residents of Flint, funneled untreated corrosive water into residents' homes in order to cut the city budget. The result? The corrosive water leached lead and other contaminants from pipes. The
amount of lead in the blood of Flint's children doubled in the space
of a year. At least eighty-seven people contracted Legionnaires'
disease—nine of whom died—and the residents of Flint, who are
overwhelmingly black and low-income, will now face the consequences of irreversible lead poisoning. The situation was so dire
that the *Daily Show*'s Trevor Noah appealed to African nations to
"save an American village." In effect, the governor's emergency
management team poisoned a black working-class city to save a
mere $100 a day. Earley could have paid the difference out of his

own salary and still taken home $143,500 a year—$102,000 more than Flint's median income. And yet Flint residents still somehow pay among the highest prices for tap water in the nation.

About seventy miles southeast of Flint, a story different only in the particulars is unfolding in Detroit, where teachers led a fight against toxic and dangerous school buildings. It's another story where industrial disinvestment has played out as sheer environmental racism. In photographs posted on social media, teachers showed schools where mushrooms grew from the walls and rats roamed the hallways. The showdown over school safety and budget cuts has also become a labor dispute: teachers have organized at least four sick-outs in the first half of the school year alone. On January 20, 2016, the largest sick-out to date shut down almost the entire Detroit public school system. By withdrawing their labor to demand safe working conditions (and healthier learning conditions for their students), the teachers of Detroit stand in a long tradition of union activists organizing outside of their contracts and developing a broader vision for society. The sick-outs built unity among educators and students, between workers and communities, but the state still showed no sign of relenting, instead moving to punish the teachers involved and rule the sick-outs an illegal work action. For Republican governor Rick Snyder and his administration, poisoned water and moldy schools were apparently acceptable side effects of realigning the state budget in the service of private-sector growth.

What the struggles in Detroit and Flint made clear is that neither neoliberalism nor austerity is only a social or political project—they are ecological projects, remaking our relationships with our (built) environments. Whether through contaminated water or infested schools, ecological degradation goes hand in hand with economic and labor restructuring. Moreover, the state leadership and investment, not to mention global cooperation, that would be required to wean the world energy system off fossil fuels cannot emerge as long as social and fiscal austerity remains the order of the day. Austerity and sustainability are antithetical concepts.

The cases of Flint and Detroit point to a deeper link between neoliberalism and the climate crisis. The same forces that devastated both cities, gutting U.S. manufacturing alongside organized labor and the welfare state, have left workers nationwide desperate for even the dirtiest jobs. In this way, they have heightened longer-standing contradictions in the working-class relationship with fossil fuels.

From the mid-eighteenth century on, the industrial-scale use of fossil fuels that accompanied the growth of capitalism increased the standard of living and life expectancy for a vast swath of people around the world. These gains and improvements were far from evenly distributed, and came with their share of previously unknown ills. Nevertheless, they helped the burgeoning working class secure real social power, and the consolidation of the fossil fuel economy fostered cornucopian visions. Demands for a decent standard of living, rooted in much higher energy consumption than had ever before been possible, translated into working-class mobility and leisure time. In a world where energy was already cheap—and where atomic scientists promised it could be cheaper still, even free—workers' visions for themselves included not only a greater share of the fruits of their labor in terms of wages, but in terms of the social distribution of energy.

In the 1960s things began to change, as rapidly growing energy use forced a reorganization of production. With energy consumption doubling in the span of two decades, the industry struggled to keep up with demand. Scheduled nuclear plants were slow to come into public use and hadn't lived up to their initial promise, and anyway, the public remained skeptical of the atom, which, especially during the Cold War, raised the specter of mutual annihilation and nuclear meltdown. The future of energy looked incredibly frightening and uncertain, and the companies took action to protect the energy regime that had made them so fabulously wealthy. Although they would continue to be identified primarily with that sticky black substance, the oil companies bought up coal and gas at a rapid rate, skewing the balance of power between the companies and workers, who remained in unions organized along increasingly blurred industrial lines. Coal miners and oil-rig workers both extracted energy for the same companies but remained organized in different unions without a shared strategy for labor action across the industry.

The destruction of workers' power went hand in hand with energy-industry efforts to protect profits from other potential threats, including regulation of pollution and greenhouse gases. By 1979, nearly every major American oil company had joined in an American Petroleum Institute initiative to share research about the potential impact of climate change. Realizing the gravity of the problem, they buried their data and turned to extensive propaganda campaigns to shape public opinion about emerging climate science. If the planet had to burn to protect the bottom line, so be it.

With energy companies steeling themselves for an uncertain future, the outlook for their workers was decidedly grim. Companies often cited new pollution regulations as the cause of layoffs, and leveraged fears about the future to extract concessions from workers. But the real forces driving down employment were mechanization and strip mining. Over the course of the 1950s, mine mechanization had put nearly two-thirds of the nation's miners out of work. Employment continued to sink in the 1960s, even as production climbed and profits soared. Since the 1970s another two-thirds of the remaining mining workforce have lost their jobs. As Paul Krugman has noted, the "real war on coal, or at least on coal workers, took place a generation ago, waged not by liberal environmentalists but by the coal industry itself. And coal workers lost."

Caught in a period of transition, and rightly convinced the energy companies had neither workers' nor the environment's interests in mind, some miners took it upon themselves to formulate their own solution to the energy crisis. Known as Miners for Democracy, they were a rank-and-file-caucus of the United Mine Workers of America (UMWA), and their vision (true to their name) tied labor, environmental, and social demands to the need to democratize their union.

The Miners for Democracy emerged from a crucible of tragedy. In 1968, seventy-eight miners were killed by an explosion at the Consol No. 9 Mine in Farmington, West Virginia. The disaster brought long-running grievances over workplace safety to a head, leading one UMWA activist, Jock Yablonski, to mount the first opposition campaign against the union's autocratic president, Tony Boyle. As deaths racked up from mine explosions and black lung disease, Yablonski charged Boyle with failing to secure a safe workplace for the nation's miners. But he signaled a problem that extended far beyond the mines. Announcing his campaign platform to "end environmental mayhem," he argued:

> Every union should have a vision of the future. . . . Unions represent men and women who are part of communities, are citizens of states and a nation. The public environment affects the well-being of miners and their families. What good is a union that reduces coal dust in the mines only to have miners and their families breathe pollutants in the air, drink pollutants in the water, and eat contaminated commodities?

Yablonski did not have long to put his vision of labor environmentalism into practice. On December 31, 1969, three weeks after losing to Boyle in an election that was widely seen as rigged, he was murdered in his sleep, along with his wife and daughter, by three hitmen. Boyle struggled to maintain control of the union as its members revolted against the sacrifice of their lives, land, and labor to an economy that did little for them in return, and five years later, he was convicted of the Yablonski murders.

In the meantime, the Miners for Democracy built on Yablonski's legacy to challenge Boyle once again in 1972. "Lives, land, and labor" remained at the heart of their vision. They also embraced Yablonski's broader goal of environmental protection, particularly in relation to two increasingly prevalent practices: strip mining, which had ravaged the Appalachian hillsides, and coal gasification, a major focus of energy industry research and development. Energy companies presented gasification projects as a way to wean the American economy off of imported fossil fuels. The MFD opposed them—even though they would have created jobs for miners put out of work by mechanization and the rise of strip mining—because the process was environmentally destructive and threatened to contaminate soil and water supplies. Most gasification plants were proposed for the American West, where they would have over-whelmingly impacted poor people and Native Americans who faced massive political barriers to fighting the plants on their own.

In addition, some miners went as far as to call for a national ban on strip mining. In place of expanding their dirty industry, MFD proposed adding jobs to the economy by *enforcing* anti-pollution laws: reclaiming land that had been destroyed by coal companies and repairing the damage done by strip mining, they argued, could create thousands of new union jobs. "Tough reclamation laws are essential, and we must insist that they are enforced," Arnold Miller proclaimed as he campaigned for union president on the MFD ticket, "If the state won't do it, the union will."

The MFD's platform carried them to victory in the 1972 election. Their environmentalism, however, faded quickly, as did that espoused by other industrial unions in the 1970s, notably the Oil, Chemical and Atomic Workers Union (OCAW) and the United Auto Workers (UAW). Today, the UMWA leads the charge on pro-coal politics, and parrots the industry line that EPA rules necessarily lead to job loss and impoverishment. It's hard to blame the workers who have accepted this narrative, and continue to stand with employers and politicians against environmental regulation—especially since, at the moment, there are no large-scale jobs programs on the table to replace their current dirty jobs. But history shows that the Faustian bargain offered by their employers is a false one.

The situation in Appalachia today is desperate. As of 2016, median household income in Harlan County, Kentucky, is $18,665, while unemployment stands at almost 12 percent (twice the national average), and a third of the population lives below the poverty line. Residents need jobs, and the energy companies (along with affiliated machinery and chemical industries), the largest economic forces in the area, shape the public narrative of how to bring jobs back. Workers must sacrifice to keep the industry profitable, the story goes, or the jobs will go away for good. Private-sector unions, desperate for a boost in membership after a fifty-year decline, do whatever it takes to defend the few jobs that remain. And not just in coal: whether it's the AFL-CIO announcing its support for the Keystone XL pipeline or unions standing with the American Petroleum Institute to support fracking development, unimaginative union leaders in a hostile environment have chosen to tie the fortunes of workers to those of the energy companies.

This strategy hasn't exactly paid off for organized labor. Thanks largely to the fracking boom, U.S. fossil fuel production and employment grew steadily over the last decade, and weathered the recession well; altogether, from 2004 to 2014, oil, gas, and mining jobs grew by 60 percent. Over that same period, union membership rates in the industry fell by almost the same proportion, dropping from 11.4 to 4.8 percent. (In 2015 jobs took a dive again along with oil prices, while union density got a slight bump.) This puts union density in the fossil fuel industry even lower than in the private sector overall.

Clinging to the fossil fuel industry can only lead to a dead end for workers. It is time for a different approach. Already in recent years, several unions have hinted at such a method, echoing the all too short-lived efforts of Miners for Democracy. In February 2015 more than 6,500 oil workers joined in a strike at fourteen refineries and a chemical plant spanning from Ohio to California. The strike, led by the United Steelworkers, was primarily a conflict over workplace safety: USW Vice President Gary Beevers pointed out that workers were being put at risk by "onerous overtime; unsafe staffing levels; dangerous conditions the industry continues to ignore; the daily occurrence of fires, emissions, leaks and explosions." But it went far beyond that, with the workers positioning themselves as the first line of defense against spills and pollution in surrounding communities. Steve Garey, president of a USW local in Washington, explained that by outsourcing maintenance work to less experienced, non-union contractors who lacked the training and work protections provided by the USW, the industry was also putting communities and the environment at risk.

The workers who took part in the strike would know. Some of them had witnessed a 2005 explosion at BP's Texas City refinery, which killed fifteen workers and injured 180 others after management bypassed safety procedures during hasty repairs. Others had witnessed the 2014 oil spill at BP's Whiting refinery, which dumped as much as 1,600 gallons of oil into Lake Michigan, Chicago residents' source of drinking water.

In a critical step forward for U.S. environmentalism, several key green groups expressed support for the strike, including the Sierra Club, 350.org, and Oil Change International, as well as smaller grassroots organizations like Rising Tide. In Martinez, California, members of Communities for a Better Environment as well as of the local nurses' union joined refinery workers on the picket line. At the end of the six-week strike, the USW claimed victory, citing "vast improvements in safety and staffing." There were signs that the strike could also lead to a more enduring militancy within the union. The USW's threat of a nationwide strike, if unrealized, was itself notable at a time when this tactic has all but disappeared from unions' arsenal. During the strike, Beevers said, "Our members are speaking loud and clear. . . . If it takes a global fight to win safe workplaces, so be it."

In the wake of the strike's success, the USW called for unions to help steer the economy away from profits and toward a system "based not on selfishness, greed, and contempt, but on ethics, on giving people the justice they deserve." This, at its core, is what a just transition is all about: reframing the economy entirely, placing workers at the center instead of profits. "The successful strike by the oil refinery workers," the article continued, "is on behalf of that justice and shows that unions still have power."

Indeed, behind workers' apparent vulnerability lurks enormous potential. As they extract fossil fuels, load them onto railway cars and into tankers, transport them thousands of miles, refine and process them, package and sell them, workers have a unique ability to bring the industry to a halt. And, thanks to the deep integration of fossil fuel products into the modern economy, if the fossil fuels stop moving, so does the rest of the world.

From teachers to nurses to rig operators, the array of workers confronting the nexus of social and ecological destruction is rapidly growing. But much remains to be done. Environmental politics must become generalized in the labor movement, and vice versa. The language of climate justice has already begun to infuse a sense of class politics into environmentalism, and green groups' support for recent labor struggles is a promising step forward. Initiatives like the Labor Network for Sustainability, Trade Unions for Energy Democracy, and the BlueGreen Alliance are helping to connect the dots. But environmentalists must go further, acknowledging that there can be no real solution to the energy crisis without the input and leadership of the people who already do the work. Understanding the climate crisis as part of neoliberalism's larger attack on public welfare and democracy (with the impacts, like all social failings in the United States, experienced more acutely by people of color and particularly by African Americans) can help expand the terrain on which both unions and climate activists struggle.

Ultimately, we live in the world we build. That world is both social and ecological, constantly made and remade through what sociologist Jason Moore has described as "the web of life." If organized labor—and the climate—are to have a fighting chance, unions must offer real alternatives to the world of "shared sacrifice" and dead zones, of poisoning by austerity, of cheap fuels and cheap lives. What would it take for today's coal-belt communities, channeling the Miners for Democracy, to fight not against EPA regulations but for jobs restoring lands destroyed by mountaintop removal mining? What would it take for union activists to have a meaningful say at the next international climate talks?

This work is just beginning. But with a shared vision to guide it, labor environmentalism can take us far. Its core demand is simple: to build a world that all of us, not just the rich or white, can actually live in.

After Act 10: How Milwaukee Teachers Fought Back (2019)

Eleni Schirmer

Eleni Schirmer (1985–) was born in Madison, Wisconsin. While completing graduate work at the University of Wisconsin– Madison, Schirmer's political outlook was shaped by the labor movement's 2011 mobilization against then-governor Scott Walker's radically antiunion Act 10. Later co-president of TAA, the UW graduate worker union, she has studied the political economy of public education and completed a doctoral dissertation on the Milwaukee school system and the teachers' union there. A prolific writer whose work has appeared in the New Yorker *and the* New York Times, *Schirmer is also an organizer with the Debt Collective, the nation's first union of debtors.*

In 2011, as the Great Recession hit public coffers, Wisconsin's Republican governor Scott Walker addressed a purported budget crisis by attacking public workers. Walker's signature bill, Act 10, struck down public-sector unions' ability to automatically collect dues and limited bargaining to wages capped at inflation. Teachers could no longer negotiate class sizes. Nurses were forced to accept mandatory overtime. Unions lost money and members. Similar anti-union legislation quickly spread across the United States. These state-level offensives culminated in a national policy shift in the summer of 2018, when the Supreme Court's *Janus* ruling made it illegal for public-sector unions to automatically gather dues from employees. Critics wrung their hands and pronounced it a nail in the coffin for public unions. What started as a Wisconsin union problem has now become a national one.

Over the years that followed, however, a wave of teacher militancy swept the nation. In 2018, teachers from West Virginia's fifty-five counties filed onto picket lines, and strikes have surged across Oklahoma, Arizona, Colorado, and California. Chicago charter school teacher unionists have fought against the racist project of education privatization. Amid this burgeoning resistance, Wisconsin unionists appear a cautionary tale of defeat, the concussed victims of a brutal first round. Union members made up less than 14 percent of the state's workforce before Act 10; four years later they were barely 8 percent. Teachers were hit especially hard by the bill. Many fled the profession; more than 10 percent of teachers in Wisconsin quit the year after Act 10, a spike from the 6.4 percent exit rates the year before. This contradictory landscape raises a question: are today's teachers' unions the victorious challengers of capitalism, or among its many victims?

What constitutes success for a movement, and what constitutes defeat? The long history of Wisconsin's largest teacher union local, the Milwaukee Teachers' Education Association (MTEA), helps us answer this question. MTEA rebuffed solidarity with civil rights and labor groups in its first decades in order to secure bread-and-butter benefits for its predominantly white teachers. MTEA's narrow self-interest fueled the conservative movement that led the charge against public education and teachers' unions. Yet, starting in the mid-1980s, MTEA activists began forging a new vision for teacher unionism and public education. This vision has been exported to teachers' union's nationwide, thanks to their local activism and their nationally circulated progressive education magazine, *Rethinking Schools*. Today, MTEA proudly declares itself a social justice union, with racial justice and strong community relations central to its mission.

If we measure unions' successes exclusively in terms of the short-term outcomes—did they get the goods, did they defeat the bad politicians—we ignore the broader scope and power of union activity. Workers' collective power does not only come from these wins;

it also comes from creating and nurturing a space for future movements and activists to take root. This dimension of unionism takes time and can be difficult to detect. But such tasks are arguably the more vital project of a union: to change workers' sense of what is possible, to sow solidarity, to bring faraway aspirations into reach.

This vantage reveals a subtle but crucial truth: Unions don't organize workers; capitalism does that work. Unions, instead, reorganize workers. Our current economic system has forced education to accommodate itself to hypercompetitiveness. Teachers must prepare students for high-stakes standardized tests, quantitative measures that compress education into a market value. Schools are tasked with grooming students to become not participants in democracy, but future widget workers of the world. Public goods and institutions are depleted of resources. Teachers' unions, in this light, must do more than fight for better wages; they need to organize workers and schools and communities in order to counter capitalism's corrosive effects. Yet unions are not preordained to organize for progressive movements against capitalism—to demand investment in care labor, spaces for play, time for art, taxes on the rich, and meaningful education for people of all income levels, black and brown and white. As the history of MTEA illustrates, unions can deepen and exacerbate social division created under capitalism, but they can also bring people together in the name of a common good. They can build our collective capacity to imagine the world we want.

In MTEA's first decades, it cast itself as an organization of professionals. Teaching was one of the few paid employment opportunities available to women at the turn of the twentieth century. Many who became educators were eager to distance themselves from their working-class backgrounds. A number of teachers in Milwaukee and elsewhere had little interest in joining labor federations, preferring to seek workplace improvements by emphasizing their genteelness and professionalism rather than by forging class solidarities. Milwaukee teachers first organized under the National Education Association (NEA), which was at the time unaffiliated with organized labor. The NEA held meetings in grand ballrooms. Its leaders, many of whom were district administrators, mailed teachers dainty handkerchiefs along with membership solicitations. The competing teacher organization, the American Federation of Teachers (AFT), was a member of the local labor federation. Unlike the NEA, it encouraged teachers to explicitly use the words "union" rather than "association" and "strike" rather than "professional withdrawal program." The point of a union, AFT leaders asserted, was to draw members into political struggle. To do otherwise, as one AFT leader claimed, would be "to sterilize and fertilize the plant at the same time."

When Milwaukee teachers did eventually seek collective bargaining rights in 1963—thereby converting their association to a union—it was due to the organization's predominantly white teachers' growing fear of black students. A wave of migration of black families from southern cities crested in Milwaukee in the early 1960s, and many white teachers saw a union as a means to secure enhanced corporal punishment rights, stronger powers to remove "disruptive" students from the classrooms, and greater protections for teachers from "student attackers" in the city's predominantly black schools.

By the mid-1960s, a winnowing welfare state put schools and educators under great pressure to solve society's ills. Whereas the New Deal programs of the 1930s addressed inequality through jobs programs, minimum wages, and labor protections, in the 1960s the state rolled back its commitment to economic redistribution and instead turned to schemes to develop human capital, such as job training programs. The War on Poverty took aim at the "culture of poverty"—the behaviors and dispositions of the poor—and education became one of its main weapons. Legal rulings called on schools to desegregate but left in place the vast inequalities between black and white neighborhoods. Public schools were left to shoulder these systemic inequities. Teachers were responsible for curing the effects of rising poverty, housing insecurity, and unemployment, while earning wages that only just enabled subsistence.

As teachers were increasingly asked to solve society's problems, they understandably wanted more control of their jobs. But in

MTEA, racist fears and narrow self-interest structured their concerns. White teachers looked to gain power over black students, rather than build power with black and poor communities for better healthcare, housing, and employment. Throughout the 1960s and 1970s, the union leadership rejected civil rights movements' demands for desegregation. In 1974 MTEA disaffiliated from the state teachers' union, partially in rejection of the state union's increasingly progressive political direction. While these moves enabled MTEA to secure strong contracts for its teachers in the short-term, they crippled teachers' capacity to build broader political movements that defended public schools in the long-term. MTEA rendered itself vulnerable to the rising tide of education privatization that would soon sweep through Milwaukee.

By the 1980s, jobs were hemorrhaging from Milwaukee and incarceration rates soared. The conservative government privatized the state's basic welfare provision; Milwaukee became a laboratory for national welfare reform. Milwaukee's children, especially its children of color, increasingly came to school burdened by the traumas of poverty, their parents struggling to find work, shelter, and healthcare. The legitimacy of public schools themselves began to crack, as the growing conservative education movement took the lead in criticizing the quality of the city's schools.

In 1990, the nation's first comprehensive school voucher program opened in Milwaukee. It was created with political and financial support from conservative philanthropists invested in the ideological project of privatization and religious evangelicals interested in skirting laws preventing state aid for religious schools. The program also received support from a cadre of black community leaders who saw the free market as the solution to racial inequalities baked into public institutions. Howard Fuller, a black education reform activist in Milwaukee and former superintendent of Milwaukee public schools who had butted heads with MTEA for decades, formed alliances with the conservative philanthropies, like the Bradley and Walton Family Foundations, to become a national leader of the "school choice" movement. (Years later, Fuller supported Betsy DeVos in her nomination for U.S. Secretary of

Education.) Thanks to Fuller and others' leadership, a number of black families were drawn to school choice to circumvent a teachers' union that had turned their backs on them, and to seek quality education for children of color, be it publicly or privately provided. The private financial investment combined with the claims for racial justice made the Milwaukee voucher experiment a political triumph in its early years, incubating the national conservative reform movement. By the 2010s, education privatization had become a major rallying point for Wisconsin's conservative movement against the public sector, helping Republicans secure the state legislature and governorship in 2011.

Despite the increasingly politicized landscape of education in Milwaukee, MTEA saw its primary function as negotiating and administrating teachers' benefit packages rather than fighting for students and teachers in defense of public education. Members had very little say or stake in the union's operations, much less its vision and priorities.

In 1981, a feisty group of progressive teachers came together to form a caucus that challenged the MTEA leadership's apolitical posture. They saw their role as unionists as integrally connected to fights for communities and schools, especially when it came to racial justice. Though predominantly white, this group of teachers articulated a vision of public education that grappled with stark inequalities and sought to inspire the movements necessary to transform them. Their caucus was explicitly critical of MTEA's leadership, its heavy reliance on union staff to execute the union priorities, and its failure to address racism. To augment their work, these educators, along with other community activists, founded *Rethinking Schools* in 1986, which now serves as a leading voice in progressive educational reform around the country. The progressive caucus distributed copies of *Rethinking Schools* to building representatives at MTEA's monthly meetings. Its issues chronicled Milwaukee's specific challenges, from curriculum adopted by the school board, to the union's negotiations, to city politics. It produced some of the earliest reporting on the Bradley Foundation, a

Milwaukee-based conservative organization that funded the city's school choice initiative.

By the 2000s, neoliberal education programs had moved from the fringe to center, as Republicans and Democrats alike adopted the mantle of "choice" and "accountability." This agenda subjected public schools to market standards, forcing competition by awarding aid to only top-performing schools and sanctioning poorly performing ones. With an eye to winning funds from Barack Obama's Race to the Top (RTTT) program, in 2009 Wisconsin's Democratic governor, Jim Doyle, and Milwaukee's Democratic mayor, Tom Barrett, began plotting the mayoral takeover of the Milwaukee public schools, a rumored RTTT eligibility criterion. The proposed takeover would dissolve the city's elected school board, causing the predominantly black and brown families attending Milwaukee public schools to lose democratic representation, and eventually the closure of many schools.

The threat of mayoral takeover spurred a new urgency among those fighting for public education in Milwaukee. Despite support for the takeover from key power players—the Democratic mayor, the Democratic governor, state legislators, business alliances such as the Metropolitan Milwaukee Association of Commerce, and the national group Democrats for Education Reform—many teachers, students, and community activists fought back. Some two dozen community groups, spearheaded by the teachers' union, formed a coalition to demand a democratically governed, public school system. This coalition organized protests, including at the homes of obstinate Democratic legislators. They attended hearings. They wrote letters to the editor. They picketed the press for failing to report on the plan. In the process, disparate groups became unified. Together, they articulated a grassroots, pro-labor, pro-democratic, anti-racist vision for public education. Within months, the "Stop the Takeover of MPS" coalition, as they called themselves, had indeed stopped the takeover. But their work was far from over.

In 2010, when Act 10 was still a twinkle in Scott Walker's eye, *Rethinking Schools* founder, leader of MTEA's progressive caucus, and anti–mayoral takeover activist Bob Peterson decided to run for MTEA president. When he won the election in April 2011, shortly after Walker's Act 10 passed, MTEA found itself guided by people accustomed to organizing. Immediately following the law's passage, Peterson and his allies set to work re-organizing their union. In lieu of collective bargaining, Peterson declared, MTEA would embrace collective action. Instead of contract protections, community alliances would strengthen schools and classrooms.

Today, when asked how they got involved in their union, many Milwaukee teachers hiss through gritted teeth, "I'm here because of Scott Walker." One teacher I spoke to in 2017, as the MTEA geared up for more budget cuts, pushed up her sleeves and told me, "Oh it's Scott Walker. He organized us here. He's woken the sleeping giant." Milwaukee teachers managed to defeat another attempted takeover in 2016, this time from the state of Wisconsin. Working with community coalitions, the teachers have mobilized to oppose unregulated charter school expansion. They have successfully advocated to build a community schools program that provides wraparound services for students and families and operates through community decision-making, rather than by command of private management companies. Teachers have joined with students to fight against bringing more police into schools, demanding instead more funding for educational resources. The union, in other words, has come to life.

This revitalization has happened in part because of the loss of legal protections for Wisconsin unions. Milwaukee teachers have been forced to give up their all-too-common understanding of a union as an insurance company–cum–vending machine: put in dues, jimmy out legal protections if things go bad with the boss. Act 10 dismantled the laws that enabled unions to passively accumulate resources and powers. In today's Wisconsin, if teachers want a union, they have to show up and fight for one by actively organizing.

It's an uphill battle. Simply to be recognized by the state under Act 10, each union must conduct an annual recertification election and win support of 51 percent of all eligible members. Imagine if

Governor Walker had been held to the same standards, forced to win an election every single year with 51 percent of the possible electorate. It would prove an impossible threshold that would occupy all of his administration's time and energy.

But following Act 10, MTEA committed to training teachers to organize. Teachers regularly gather in the union's conference room to discuss strategies and skills at the building level. But they have also taught themselves how to organize for the struggles outside of classrooms through popular education workshops on topics like political economy and its effects on schools. "Working in public education is political," MTEA vice president Amy Mizialko told her fellow teachers during one organizing meeting in 2017. "It's a fight about our taxes, it's a fight about our communities, it's a fight about what our kids are going to do, what they're going to learn. . . . Whether we want it to be political or not, we are. And our union is engaged . . . we have a voice and power that move us forward."

In addition, the union has brought new focus to the work of educational assistants (EAs), the unsung, low-wage workers, predominantly women of color, who provide vital classroom support to students and teachers yet often live paycheck to paycheck, working several jobs to make ends meet. In 2014, MTEA embarked on a campaign to raise EA wages, linking up with local Fight for $15 activists. As part of this campaign, school board members spent a day walking in the shoes of EA members, to see and feel what life was like for someone earning $12 an hour. Board members were picked up at their homes at 5 a.m. to bring them to an EA's first shift job, then to their second, even third. Thanks to their organizing, EAs earned themselves a wage increase. In 2017 MTEA also made a small but radical change to its by-laws, allowing EAs to hold union officer positions for the first time (they had previously only been allowed to serve as officers in their own sub-unit). With near-unanimous support, MTEA representatives voted to ensure the organization's most vulnerable members had the power to lead the organization, bringing rank-and-file democracy to a new level in the union.

Now, when Milwaukee teachers want to win demands, they don't send a cadre to closed-door bargaining sessions. Instead, a throng of teachers gathers in MTEA's "war room," a sprawling basement lair with butcher paper taped to walls charting support at each building. They crowd around folding tables, phoning their fellow teachers late in the evening to tell them about the plan to pack the school board meeting the next week, or to wear their "Black Lives Matter" T-shirts to school. They hold community events to build support for their demands. One February 2017 weekend, for example, in anticipation of Walker's 2017 budget, MTEA hosted a community "art build" to make banners, signs, and parachutes for the upcoming protests. A local graphic designer, a thirty-something Latino man with warm eyes, told me some of his artist friends asked him to join. "It's a good use of my built-up rage," he smiled at me. An elementary-school student showed me their hand-drawn sign, bright scribbles that read, "$9999 for Schools." Dozens of screen-printed canvases were hung up to dry from a clothesline stretched across the room, fluttering like prayer flags. One read, "Public Schools Are the Heart of Democracy." Another said, "Organize Students, Workers, and Immigrants," with a woodblock image of people huddled under an umbrella; deep chisel marks made their faces look weary and fierce. Like the struggle had made them strong.

It is a good problem that, today, when people talk about teachers' strikes, they want to talk about success. Recently, teachers in Los Angeles won a charter school moratorium, fewer cops in schools, legal support for immigrant families, and promises for more social workers and librarians. Many are energized by the prospect of taxing billionaires to fund smaller class sizes, art classes, and playgrounds with grass. No doubt, these are successes. But what makes each of these victories a success isn't simply that teachers got the thing they demanded—the raise, the moratorium, the better funding plan. They are successes because the organizing that achieved those demands created space for future movements to grow. Each action brought people together. Each demand brought closer the dream for a better world.

A union can succeed on these terms even when winning

short-term goals remains out of reach. Conversely, a union can make short-term gains while failing to achieve these movement aims. The early generation of MTEA won strong contracts for its teachers but sacrificed broad solidarity and political analysis. Though MTEA lost key labor rights in 2011, they also reasserted their power to organize movements, to foment big ideas, to build bonds among disparate groups. Over three decades of political attacks on public schools and unions, Milwaukee teachers have developed the ideological architecture of social justice unionism. Their vision has fertilized movements for progressive education across the country, despite their short-term defeats. They remind us that while laws can protect unions, it is people dreaming and fighting together that make them strong.

West Virginia Teachers Walk Out (2018)

Sarah Jaffe

Sarah Jaffe (1980–) is a longtime labor journalist and among the first to report on Occupy Wall Street and the Fight for $15 campaign. A columnist at The Progressive *and a contributing writer at* In These Times, *her work has also appeared in the* New Republic *and the* New York Review of Books. *Jaffe is also the longtime co-host of the* Belabored *podcast (with Michelle Chen) released by* Dissent, *and the co-host (with Craig Gent) of* Heart Reacts, *an advice podcast for those dealing with life during the collapse of late capitalism. She is the author of* Necessary Trouble: Americans in Revolt *(2016) and* Work Won't Love You Back: How Devotion to Our Jobs Keeps Us Exploited, Exhausted, and Alone *(2021).*

When Logan County special education teacher Leah Clay Stone entered the West Virginia capitol building on February 2, 2018, she saw a sea of teachers from the chamber doors of the Senate and House all the way back to the rotunda. Her county was part of the first work stoppage this month that saw public school teachers flock to the capitol building in Charleston to protest continued low wages, spiking insurance premiums, and poor working conditions.

The teachers flooding the galleries that day came from schools in just three counties. But after February 2, the rebellion spread. Within three weeks, it had become a statewide work stoppage, with schools closed in all fifty-five counties. The teachers—who don't even have legal collective bargaining—wear red T-shirts with the outline of West Virginia and the word UNITED emblazoned across them, a visual that calls to mind not only the Chicago teachers' strike of 2012 but also the Wisconsin capitol occupation in 2011, against Governor Scott Walker and the Republican legislature's move to take away collective bargaining rights from the state's public employees. Now West Virginia public employees are showing that even without collective bargaining rights, they too can make a heck of a lot of noise.

On the morning of February 22, 2018, thousands of teachers headed to the capitol, carpooling because the walkout included bus drivers. Others stayed close to home to make sure they had a presence in their schools, where they were met with support from students and parents. That support had built over weeks: Ashlea Bassham's ninth- and tenth-grade students and others had already held their own walkout in Logan County, wielding signs that read "I'm in the bleachers for my teachers." Parents held informational pickets and walk-ins, standing outside schools in the cold and the snow to support the teachers. The movement has spread from county to county, neighbor to neighbor, as teachers who live in one county and work in another talk to friends at home and on the job. "It literally was like a fire just catching and going," says Stone, who is the local vice-president for the Logan County Education Association, one of the two associations in the state.

At the beginning of the legislative session, the executive committee of the Association called an emergency meeting to discuss changes to their insurance plan and other bills being introduced in the legislature. The teachers called for a vote to walk out. "I don't think there was anybody still seated. It was a resounding yes," Stone said. She then put her production-management background to use pulling together a voting process, getting representatives from every school to collect ballots. "We managed to get ballots into every school and all three bus garages and had them back into my hands and counted in twenty-four hours," she said. "I literally was creating a ballot as I was walking out the door of the building. I was like 'somebody else needs to drive, I need to take care of this.'"

The teachers were trying to avoid the district getting an injunction to halt their action, but instead the superintendent closed the schools, a pattern that would repeat itself in every county across the state as teachers stood up to join the statewide day of action. A movement organized by teachers on the ground was able to spread in part through existing networks, in part through social media. "A lot of people blame Facebook for all the bad things in 2016 with the election, but it has actually been really helpful here because West Virginia is so rural and spread out," said Jay O'Neal, who teaches in Charleston.

Like other teachers who have resorted to stopping work in recent years, the West Virginia teachers have emphasized that their goal is to make education better for every child in West Virginia. "Teachers' working conditions are students' learning conditions" has become the byword in these campaigns. The West Virginia teachers have demonstrated this commitment not only with their demands—for filling teacher vacancies, for smaller class sizes—but with immediate action. "As soon as we called the work stoppage, our locals took it upon themselves to start working with churches and food banks and different places to provide day care for the parents who needed it, to provide meals for the many students who get their hot meals at school," said Dale Lee of the West Virginia Education Association (WVEA).

The teachers began to notice trouble in January 2018, right at the beginning of the legislative session. In that first session, Bassham noted, there were over thirty bills introduced that seemed ominous. With respect to salaries, West Virginia teachers were already some of the worst off in the country—forty-eighth, according to Lee—and their health-insurance premiums had increased so much over the last year that it amounted to a pay cut. "I keep seeing this number thrown around—$45K is the average teacher salary. I've been teaching for seven years and I am nowhere near that," Stone said. O'Neal added, "I moved here in 2015 and my second year teaching, I made less than my first."

That pay cut came from a change to how PEIA insurance was calculated—it shifted from being based on the individual teacher's income to total family income. That could effectively double the already-high premiums for insurance that used to be seen as a counterbalance to low wages. On top of that, the teachers would be penalized if they did not participate in a wellness program.

Those issues already left teachers feeling undervalued and disrespected. And that came on top of legislators proposing bills that threatened public education—such as introducing charter schools, "education savings accounts" (giving parents public funds to spend on educating their children, or a "backdoor voucher" in Lee's words), so-called "paycheck protection," which restricts the ability for automatic deduction of union dues, and other attacks on the already deeply restricted unions. Anger at the anti-union proposals opened the door to bring up other issues that had been frustrating teachers for much longer, like sky-high class sizes in secondary schools and a lack of electives for students.

Despite it all, Lee noted, "We have great schools. We're right at 90 percent graduation rate, and for a rural state that is exceptional." To him, legislators' complaints about spending are disingenuous— the state is paying for past underfunding of retirement benefits and counting those dollars as education spending. Because West Virginia's population is quite spread out, that also means that transporting students costs more than it would in more densely populated states—more dollars that aren't going to the classroom but are still necessary to spend.

Meanwhile the state had a shortage of certified teachers because it's hard to convince people to enter a job when starting salaries for people with advanced degrees are still in the $30–35,000 range. "You're sold the idea of, hey, go to college, get a degree, get an advanced degree, and then you still really can't make ends meet," Bassham said. "Obviously we do it because we like the kids, but I also like to be able to pay my bills and not have $8 to last me six days until payday."

Leah Clay Stone is a second-generation member of the West Virginia Education Association (WVEA)—she walked picket lines with her mother during a 1990 teacher strike. Her father was a coal miner through the 1980s. West Virginia is a state with a proud labor history that gets lost in the "Trump Country" profiles. Many of the teachers in this fight have personal experiences like Stone's. It was not lost on anyone I spoke with that the first teachers to stop work were from coal country, from Mingo and Logan Counties, the sites of the great mine wars.

Stone also recalls, as a teenager, going to party with friends on top of the infamous Blair Mountain, the site of what historian Elizabeth Catte, in her new book *What You Are Getting Wrong About Appalachia,* calls "the largest show of armed resistance in the United States since the Civil War—and the most significant labor uprising in the United States." Immortalized in part in the 1987 movie *Matewan* and in memorable labor ballads, the Battle of Blair Mountain pitted workers and their allies—like venerable labor agitator Mary Harris "Mother" Jones—against a "private army" that would later be praised by the National Rifle Association (yes, the same one that currently wants to arm teachers against school shooters). It is a stark reminder that West Virginians died to organize the unions that the state's officials are currently bad-mouthing in the press.

Today's action is the first statewide walkout of teachers in almost thirty years. "If you look at what teachers and their allies are posting on social media, you can see that they are connecting the upcoming action to the state's important history of labor uprising, from Blair Mountain to Widen," Elizabeth Catte told me via email. She pointed to a tweet from Richard Ojeda, a candidate for Congress from the state, who posted a photograph of himself in a red bandanna with the caption, "The term redneck started when WV coal miners tied red bandanas around their necks during the bloody battle of Blair mountain to unionize. Today, our teachers channeled their history. #UnionStrong"

"It's rather impressive to me that people don't have the knowledge of what it means to be union proud. Or what it means to be involved in an organization," Stone, who recalled doing a school project on Mother Jones, said. "For the past few years we've struggled to keep membership even in our organization. But in this moment and this movement people have been finding out that they are the movement. If they want something done they have to speak up."

These days, of course, the labor movement is a shadow of its former self in terms of both militancy and membership. With collective bargaining banned for West Virginia teachers and public-sector workers, unions are voluntary associations—meaning that teachers at any given school might be members of the WVEA or the American Federation of Teachers-West Virginia (AFT-WV), or neither. Without collective bargaining, the WVEA's Dale Lee explained, mostly the associations fight to get work issues that unions might bargain over—like duty-free lunches and planning periods—written into state law.

There is a separate association for school service personnel, the West Virginia School Service Personnel Association, who also backed the job action—cooks, custodians, maintenance workers, and bus drivers. Beyond that, Bassham told me, they are standing for all public employees who are struggling. "It's not just a teacher issue, it's not just a school issue, it's our state not wanting to take care of the people who are trying to make our state a better place."

Their message is a reminder that despite pollsters' tendency to make a college degree the dividing line between "working" and "middle" class, the categories are often not so clear cut. The reality is that college-educated workers too have to fight for decent wages and benefits. That the teachers all cite Blair Mountain's miners as inspiration is an act of class solidarity and a reminder that the so-called knowledge economy we have been told to prize over manual labor doesn't come with a guarantee of good pay any more than coal mining did.

West Virginia's government has long been dominated by coal and other extractive industries. In fact its sitting governor, Jim Justice, is a second-generation coal tycoon and a billionaire who owes his own state millions in back taxes. But Jay O'Neal is heartened that teachers and their supporters—including the mine workers' union—are now calling for raising taxes on those extractive companies in order to fund education. In a literal sense, the teachers are fighting the same companies that the coal miners were, decades ago.

During this mobilization, all three education workers' associations took to the streets and the capitol halls, dressed in red, bearing handmade signs, some of them wearing those red bandannas.

They waved to passing drivers and marched with other unionists. As schools throughout the state remained shuttered, union representatives said they were prepared to continue the walkout until the state commits to address their demands: higher pay, fully funded insurance benefits, and rejection of the regressive bills.

Teachers had already driven to the capitol on snow days, on treacherous mountain roads. "Our colleagues in the northern panhandle and the eastern panhandle have to come so much further," Bassham said. "They drove on some crazy mountain roads to holler at legislators, and it was fabulous."

Those legislators are slowly beginning to take action, Stone said, though there is also "quite a bit of grandstanding. . . . They want you to think that they're doing everything they can for you but their voting record doesn't show that."

Public-employee strikes in West Virginia, as state Attorney General Patrick Morrisey has stated, are illegal. And yet the teachers have gone out anyway, taking the risk because it can't get much worse for them. With the *Janus* case looming before the Supreme Court, potentially decimating every public-sector union in the nation, and right-wing governors looking for additional ways to punish unions, the West Virginia teachers' situation is a bellwether.

These teachers recall that there were no laws protecting the mine workers in the 1920s either. Stone said, "West Virginians have a long background of doing what's expected until it gets to be too much, and then we make sure we do what's right, and we really want our legislators to do what's right instead of what's expected."

Mother Jones would be proud.

A Seat at the Table: Sectoral Bargaining for the Common Good (2019)

Kate Andrias

Kate Andrias (1975–) was born in New York City. A Yale graduate, she worked as a union organizer for SEIU 1199 NE before returning to take a law degree from her alma mater. Andrias then clerked for Justice Ruth Bader Ginsburg on the U.S. Supreme Court and worked as associate counsel to President Barack Obama. Thereafter, she taught law at the University of Michigan and Columbia Law Schools. Andrias has published widely on the failures of U.S. labor law and how it can be reformed to better serve the needs of working people.

There is growing consensus among left-leaning union leaders, scholars, and public policy experts that fundamental labor law reform is necessary, not only to fix a broken labor and employment regime but also to address the nation's staggering economic and political inequality. According to conventional wisdom, however, more social democratic approaches to labor relations—for example, enabling bargaining for all workers on a sectoral basis—are in deep conflict with American traditions.

A largely forgotten moment in U.S. history draws that conventional account into question. The Fair Labor Standards Act (FLSA), first enacted in 1938, a few years after passage of the National Labor Relations Act (NLRA), empowered tripartite industry committees of unions, business representatives, and the public to set minimum wages on an industry-by-industry basis. For about ten years, industry committees successfully raised wages for hundreds of thousands of Americans while helping facilitate unionization and a more egalitarian form of governance. Though the committees were limited in their scope and power, they were an important component of a broader struggle to democratize the economy, the workplace, and the government itself. Recovering this history can help inspire more ambitious alternatives in the future.

As many observers have noted, the rise of inequality over the last few decades is closely related to the decline of unions. More than a third of U.S. workers once belonged to unions, helping to raise wages and benefits throughout the economy and giving workers a collective voice in the workplace and in politics. Now, unions represent roughly a tenth of the labor market, and only about 6 percent of the private sector workforce. While any number of factors help explain the drop in union density, it's clear that the U.S. system of labor law bears significant responsibility for the withering of unions in this country.

The NLRA promises to protect the right to organize, to bargain collectively, and to strike. But the statute fails to offer meaningful protection in practice: enforcement mechanisms are weak, penalties are minimal, delays are lengthy, and employers are legally permitted to engage in a wide range of anti-union activity, like "predicting" negative consequences of unionization, closing down in response to unionization, and permanently replacing striking workers.

Moreover, although the economy has become increasingly globalized and fissured, labor law still channels bargaining and concerted activity to the worksite level. Workers at a single workplace have little power when negotiating with multinational employers, and even less ability to transform conditions along a supply chain or throughout an economic sector. In addition, the law excludes from its protections many of the most vulnerable workers, including domestic workers, agricultural workers, and independent contractors, who make up a growing portion of the workforce, at least as classified by employers.

Employment law, which protects workers on an individual basis, doesn't fill the void left by a broken labor law. Most non-union workers are employed "at will" with few rights at work and few protections against termination. Federal law and most state laws lack guarantees of paid family leave, vacation, or sick time; statutory minimums do not provide the wages or benefits necessary to keep a family out of poverty. Government enforcement of employment law is lax and violations are rampant, particularly in low-wage workforces. Effective private remedies are often unavailable because of mandatory arbitration clauses and the difficulties of class certification. As with labor law, many workers are excluded from employment law's coverage. In short, both labor law and employment law have failed American workers.

Against this backdrop, there is growing support among union leaders, policymakers, and academics for a different approach to labor law—a system that would protect all workers' rights to organize, strike, and bargain for a decent livelihood, not just at individual worksites, but across each economic sector. Scholars have shown through a number of comparative studies that power-sharing over decisions about wages, benefits, and the economy through comprehensive systems of sectoral bargaining achieves more egalitarian outcomes than firm-based bargaining alone.

Still, many argue that such a system is out of step with America's more minimalist approach to labor relations. According to the conventional account, the United States has always been committed to government neutrality on unionization, required bargaining only at the enterprise level, and kept labor and employment law as distinct regimes (except briefly during wartime emergencies and under the failed National Industrial Recovery Act of 1933). It's a system in which workers have little say over the direction of the political economy.

The history of FLSA challenges this account. Today, FLSA guarantees minimum wages and overtime rights. It is a relatively modest statute. But FLSA's original ambition was much greater. The statute was designed to operate in tandem with the NLRA by implementing a system of tripartite industry committees. These committees were tasked with negotiating minimum wages on an industry-by-industry basis. In short, FLSA's backers aspired not just to ensure subsistence wages, but also to empower unions to negotiate for all workers, to build a more egalitarian political economy, and to remake the very structure of American democracy.

The enactment of the FLSA's industry committees followed a multi-decade effort by unionists, feminists, socialists, and progressive intellectuals to resist turn-of-the century laissez faire economics and to democratize the political economy. They were convinced that political problems and economic problems were inextricably linked, and that treating the latter required addressing the former. In their view, democracy could not function in the context of great disparities in wealth and required institutional commitments that went beyond the franchise. To that end, Progressive Era reformers sought to rebalance the power of labor and capital. They believed that the working class needed to be organized and that the state needed to ensure the ground rules to enable such organization.

FLSA's industry committees grew out of these ideological commitments. The bill's strongest backers in Congress and the executive branch saw the minimum-wage law as a way to ensure a system of basic equality that extended into the political, economic, and social realms. Tripartite industry committees were one way to further this goal; they would engage unions in governing the political economy, while helping to expand the reach of union-negotiated rights to unorganized workers, particularly in the non-union South.

The American Federation of Labor (AFL) had previously resisted universal minimum-wage laws on the ground that labor conditions, at least for "able-bodied" men, were better left to private negotiation than to governmental supervision. But the organization eventually came around to support the bill. Meanwhile, the newly founded Congress of Industrial Organizations (CIO), welcomed a more universal approach to labor relations. Leaders of industrial unions, like Sidney Hillman of the garment workers union, embraced the idea of intertwining labor and employment law; in Hillman's view, the FLSA could serve as a mechanism to enhance collective bargaining and help reduce downward wage pressure on organized shops and the related problem of capital flight.

Unsurprisingly, industry groups like the Chamber of Commerce and conservatives in Congress, many of whom objected to any legislation on wages, vigorously opposed using FLSA to support tripartite bargaining. They argued it would create a morass of government bureaucracy and would be controlled by particular interests that could not possibly provide fair representation for all.

Despite business opposition, FLSA passed by a vote of 291 to 89 in the House and a similar margin in the Senate. President Roosevelt signed the bill into law on June 27, 1938. The new statute required the administrator of the Department of Labor's Wage and Hour Division to define different sectors of the economy, and then to appoint representatives from labor, business, and the public to committees that represented each of these sectors. The committees were tasked with proposing industry-specific minimum wage standards, which could be greater than the universal minimum though they could not exceed the upper bound set by the statute. The committees were to be evenly divided among labor, business, and public representatives.

In practice, the industry committees' work was a mix of bargaining and administrative decision-making. The committees conducted fact-finding missions and grounded their conclusions using statutory criteria. But the decision-making emerged from compromise between business and labor, with the public committee members acting as referees, albeit usually ones supportive of labor. Committee recommendations did not have the force of law until the administrator approved them after a public hearing, but the scope of his power was limited. He could not alter a recommendation; he could only veto it, and only for failure to meet statutory standards. Public hearings were collective events, with union members and business leaders showing up and testifying in large numbers.

In the end, the industry committees were a great success at their admittedly limited task. They were widely deemed efficient and effective. Seventy industry committees were established between 1938 and 1941, and their wage orders covered 21 million workers. Unions used the process to launch organizing campaigns and to raise awareness about workers' plight. They took seriously their responsibility to represent non-union workers, viewing the process as a way to undertake a form of collective bargaining for unrepresented workplaces. For example, when a forty-cent minimum went into effect in the millinery industry, Max Zaritsky, president of the United Hatters, Cap and Millinery Workers International Union, AFL, commented that he considered it "one of the most significant gains of our organization and our people in recent years." The forty-cent minimum wage spurred a new organizing drive among the hatters. Union organizers visited homes of workers and "pointed out that for the enforcement of the order they must depend not only on the government whose facilities are limited, but upon a strong union which would see to it that there were no violations or that if there were violations, those guilty would be punished." The CIO was similarly aggressive in capitalizing on FLSA to promote organizing. Its weekly newspaper regularly featured stories about FLSA, and locals created a system for educating workers about the wage orders and enforcing them. They urged workers to submit any FLSA complaints through the union, emphasizing that such a method would trigger protections provided by the NLRA. The CIO initiated wage recovery suits on behalf of large groups of employees and organized picket lines and strikes to oppose violations of FLSA.

By the mid-1940s it looked like the United States might expand its tripartite system to give unions formal bargaining power over an array of economic and social welfare policy questions. War boards established during the Second World War provided a potent model. But the AFL revived its longstanding opposition to governmental involvement in labor relations and opposed making the National War Labor Board's tripartite sectoral bargaining permanent. Business and conservative forces, particularly white Southerners hostile to the empowerment of black laborers, mobilized even more forcefully in opposition. In 1947, Congress decisively changed the statutory and regulatory landscape by passing the Taft-Hartley Act over President Truman's veto, significantly curtailing labor rights.

Against this background, a proposal to expand FLSA's industry committees was soon rejected. In 1949 the tripartite approach was abandoned. FLSA's industry committees were not accused of self-dealing or inefficiency, as had been the case with committees under the earlier National Industrial Relations Act. But rising hostility to unions, the opposition of Southern Democrats to the extension of labor rights to African-American workers, and divisions within the labor movement meant that there was insufficient support for a continuation or expansion of government-facilitated sectoral bargaining. A weakened Democratic Party and an embattled, divided labor movement were willing to trade the committee system for a new minimum wage increase. Tripartism and sectoral bargaining all but disappeared from core federal labor and employment statutes.

The FLSA industry committees show us that within the broad statutory framework that still exists today, worker organizations were once granted formal power in policymaking and the capacity to bargain for all workers in an industry. Their history also blurs the line that today exists between labor and employment law. At the outset, unions were given a role in the implementation of FLSA, and FLSA was seen as a way to advance unionization. In the current moment, which bears so much similarity to the vast inequality, concentrated political power, and corporate-friendly judiciary of the Gilded Age, we should revisit the ideas that workers, sympathetic political leaders, and intellectuals advanced during the New Deal.

For now, it's unrealistic to expect any move to empower workers to negotiate over expansive labor and social welfare regulation at the federal level. But reforms along the lines of the early New Deal are possible at the state and local level. Federal labor law preemption forecloses nearly all state and local labor law legislation, but employment law does not face the same hurdles. Several states, including California and New York, already have tripartite commissions vested with the power to set wages and other standards. These commissions have existed for generations and have intermittently operated to bring labor and management together under state administrative supervision to set standards on an industry-by-industry basis. For example, in 2015, after growing protests and strikes organized by Fight for $15, the New York labor commissioner exercised his authority to impanel a wage board to recommend higher wages in the fast-food industry. The board members—representatives from labor, business, and the general public—held hearings over the next forty-five days across the state. Workers organized by Fight for $15 participated in great numbers at these hearings. On July 21, the board announced its decision: $15 per hour for fast-food restaurants that are part of chains with at least thirty outlets, to be phased in over the course of six years, with a faster phase-in for New York City. The wage board order was a significant victory, followed by another victory: a bill to raise the state-wide minimum wage to $15.

Support for such reform is growing across the country. Since 2012, over two dozen states and many more localities have raised their minimum wages. Even during the election that brought President Trump to victory, minimum-wage increases prevailed when they were on the ballot. So too have regulations providing for paid leave and other benefits. These new laws have emerged out of organizing campaigns that frame the demand for better employment rights and social welfare benefits as part and parcel of the demand for union rights. Some, like the 2015 restaurant worker wage increase in New York, have even emerged from sectoral bargaining among unions, employers, and the state.

Meanwhile, the teacher strikes in Los Angeles, West Virginia, Arizona, Colorado, and Oklahoma represented another form of worker-driven sectoral bargaining. Teachers are organizing not just at one school, or in one neighborhood, but across their cities and states. Like the early New Deal efforts, the new teacher union movements collapse traditional divides between areas of law while offering an ambitious vision for reform. That is, the teachers demand not just fair wages and good benefits for themselves, but also adequate education funding for their students. And they demand the right to negotiate about those matters on a sectoral basis. Hotel workers, Google employees, and airport workers also are engaging in broad-based collective action at levels not seen for several de-cades. These movements, too, are not just seeking better conditions at individual worksites; they are demanding change across their sectors, while challenging the basic assumptions underlying cur-rent workplace law. From this on-the-ground organizing, the out-line of a new, or revitalized, model of labor law is emerging that would allow workers to build strong unions at their worksites while also giving them a seat at the table in decisions about the di-rection of the broader political economy.

The precise contours of any future labor law remain uncer-tain, but the need for reform is clear. Taking a cue from the early twentieth century, we might once again begin to imagine a legal regime that both encourages workers' collective activity and gives their organizations real power in the governing process. We might begin to imagine a more enduring democratic and egalitarian political economy.

Release the Wage (2024)

Veena Dubal

Veena Dubal (1981–) was born to immigrant parents in Houston, Texas, just as Ronald Reagan launched his crusade against organized labor by breaking the air traffic controllers' union. Dubal's family history of involvement with anti-colonial struggles on the Indian subcontinent together with her upbringing in the post–Jim Crow South shaped her early political and intellectual development. As an undergraduate at Stanford, Dubal's antiwar activism led her to the movements around global worker rights. Holding a PhD and JD from UC Berkeley, Dubal is the author of a number of scholarly and popular publications on labor and employment law, technology, and organizing. She currently teaches at the University of California, Irvine School of Law.

How can workers be kept in a state of "tolerable immiseration" such that they will continue to meet the demands of firms—and do so without agitation? This repugnant question, labor movement actors appreciate, reflects the governing philosophy of many employers and their political and economic representatives. Less clearly acknowledged within the movement and its everyday discourses and discontents, however, is that "tolerable immiseration" is also an unstated driving ideal of the neoliberal capitalist state—achieved in large part through structural monetary and fiscal policies calculated to counter wage gains of the working class.

I write this in 2024. Considering the last four decades of lost ground and the contemporary moment of historic, renewed organizing energy, I contend that the labor movement must actively prioritize the cultivation of a political economy platform that re-appropriates state power for equitable distribution. Unions, as institutions that represent the laboring classes, must develop a sophisticated political strategy that extends well beyond advancing law and policy to grow membership. The fight, after all, is not just for workplace power, but for sustained working-class economic power.

For this to materialize, political economy questions cannot be left to technocrats. Labor advocates, too, must integrate a smart macroeconomic policy platform into broader organizing analyses and strategies. Central to this platform should be to release wages from the stranglehold of austerity politics in favor of a more democratically planned economy. One promising idea, I argue below, is to restore and unite behind the central postwar demand of Black unionists and tie job creation to human need and not to capital accumulation, through—perhaps—the right to a voluntary, *good* job.

Integrating popular political economy education into organizing campaigns, both in the workplace and well beyond it, is an essential step on this path. While union leaders and rank-and-file workers have a well-informed, critical awareness of the ways in which bosses can leverage the law to suppress organizing, they have a more tenuous comprehension of the role of state actors in affirmatively countering the bargained-for gains of the working class through monetary and fiscal policy. Just as unionists explain labor's relative powerlessness with familiar and frequently told truths about Taft-Hartley's ills, including, for example, the secondary boycott ban, and of Ronald Reagan's brazen union-busting the Professional Air Traffic Controllers' Organization, so, too, they should be able to articulate how and why federal spending policies of the 1930s, which grew working-class power (particularly for white workers), were rapidly unraveled in the late 1970s.

One way to accomplish this is to compel people to query the structural constraints of their own life conditions, in comparison to other people in other historical moments. Why are so many workers in the U.S., the highest income country in the world, surviving in a state of "tolerable immiseration," without access to once achievable homeownership and retirement? What, in addition to a strong and dynamic labor movement, were the driving political economy factors behind the three decades of mid-century, (mostly white) working class economic security—one that generated low unemployment, strong unions, high wages, and social distribution—and its dramatic demise in the early 1980s? Incorporating lessons from this macroeconomic history, the labor movement can build an intelligible political economy narrative to make the "invisible hand" more visible, to broaden the current moment of labor agitation, and most importantly, to sustain tangible wins that may come of it.

As is well-known, the postwar regime of empowered (white male, breadwinning) workers resulted in exceptional wage gains for the working class. From 1947–1979, the average real hourly wage grew 2.2% each year. But, firms and financial asset holders blamed these significant advances (what they called "wage push inflation"), foreign competition, and rising oil prices on the downward pressure exerted on industrial profits. The story, as explained by conservatives, was that because U.S. workers were taking more home, firms had to raise prices on consumers to make up for the redistribution of profits. In this supply-side analysis, unions (and emphatically not the affirmative decisions of price-raising capitalists) were to blame. Accordingly, unions reverted from being considered partners in the delicate balance of Keynesian capitalism to antagonists of shareholder wealth and trickle-down economics.

A subsequent maelstrom of legal, political, and economic factors combined with the 1979 "Volcker shock" (the decision of Paul Volcker, then Chair of the Federal Reserve) to raise interest rates and orchestrate high unemployment. The 1980s subsequently saw the destruction of the fruits of New Deal state planning and the Keynesian dialectic, propelling a four-decade economic spiral for the working class. Between 1979 and 2018, inflation-adjusted hourly pay for the vast majority of workers diverged dramatically from productivity gains. At the same time, according to the Economic Policy Institute, "the top .1% of earnings grew fifteen times as fast as 90% of earnings," resulting not just in wage stagnation, but also in rising inequality. In the face of years of state-induced regression—specifically designed to arrest any widescale wage gains for the bottom 90%—workers continued to agitate against the odds, but in shrinking numbers and with too many losses.

For only the second time since the late 1970s, this dynamic shifted meaningfully after the global coronavirus pandemic lockdowns and ensuing crises. Following nation-wide orders to stay at home, which prevented people from earning, the U.S. Congress together with the Executive Branch passed fiscal laws and policies, including expanded unemployment insurance, income payments, child tax credits, and eviction protection, which, combined, provided momentary financial reprieve to many people. Even as the Federal Reserve once again raised rates in 2022 and 2023 to combat inflation and return workers to a state of "tolerable immiseration," wages continued to rise, bolstered by income injections directed into the pockets of workers through temporary spending bills. People who were previously living paycheck to paycheck suddenly had the power to reject bad jobs—and the time to look and bargain for better ones. In 2023, while top wage earners captured .9% growth, low wage earners—lifted by this moment of financial stability—experienced a 12.1% increase in real wage growth: the highest in decades.

The wage growth and tight labor market of the early 2020s have both facilitated and reinforced an exciting political and ideological renaissance among many U.S. workers who are mobilizing to organize their workplaces, to critique the greed of capitalists, and to express their discontent with the broader economic order. In seeking to form and join unions, young workers in particular are rejecting decades of "tolerable immiseration" that emerged with the expansion of outsourcing, subcontracting, temporary labor, and gigification. Their rejection comes with a strong desire to evaluate and critique what the generations before them did wrong. This entreaty poses a tremendous political opportunity for labor strategists to push well beyond building power to fight the boss and to develop support for radical macroeconomic solutions.

But, of course, this will not be easy: despite the surge in leftist organizing and thinking, union growth and power continues to see many practical obstacles. Though the private sector has seen an upsurge in unionizing efforts, due to the nature of U.S. labor law, this careful, painstaking organizing has necessarily been slow and site-based—a single warehouse, university, and factory at a time. As Eric Blanc has documented, typically, one-on-one conversations between colleagues have led to an organizing drive, which, in turn, possibly, eventually results in a union and a contract.

Legal impediments to this process, alongside the growth of non-union jobs, have limited the impacts of labor's revitalization on the overall number of unionized workers. Notwithstanding the tangible revival of radical labor politics, with a few promising exceptions, successfully bargained for union contracts have been won mostly at smaller companies. Nevertheless, firms long unmoored from the Keynesian compact have responded to the rise in worker militancy through robust anti-union campaigns and with an ideological political economy nod to the cruel spirit of Townsend. As Laura Ingraham suggested out loud to an industry representative in a televised interview, "What if we just cut off unemployment? Hunger is a pretty powerful thing."

A great deal of thinking, debate, and organizing has gone to eliminating the barriers involved in securing a positive union vote and bargaining for a successful contract. Indeed, much, if not most, of labor's active political strategy has recently focused on amending or maneuvering around federal labor law to grow union membership. The widely supported Pro Act, for example, seeks to amend the National Labor Relations Act, to expand the pool of workers eligible for federal organizing protections and to remove legal barriers (like the ban on the secondary boycott) to worker direct actions. More controversial strategies have pursued shortcuts through compromises with capital that constrain labor rights while growing union membership, including, for example, a widely criticized Washington state sectoral bargaining law for ride-hail drivers, jointly proposed by Teamsters Local 117 and Uber.

But the radical ruthlessness of what Laura Ingraham daringly verbalized—a ruthlessness that quietly undergirds much fiscal and monetary policy—must be met with equally revolutionary ideas for material distribution. In the words of Michal Kalecki, full employment is the best way to remove the "powerful indirect control [of capitalists] over Government policy." As labor continues to resuscitate itself and its power, while navigating new and old obstacles (and debates), the time is ripe to enliven our political imaginations and steadfastly introduce, debate, and promote policies that not only grow membership, but also pursue social and economic distribution schemes that extend "beyond the limits tolerable to the capitalist state." History from the last century, after all, suggests that even broadscale collective bargaining wage wins are often difficult to sustain—especially during periods of high unemployment and ideological fluctuation, as occurred in the 1970s. In this time of increased agitation and popular willingness to critique capital, labor must seize the moment and rally behind ideas that make the growth of working-class power difficult to reverse.

One promising way to permanently "release the wage" from the stranglehold of the anti-inflation wand of the undemocratic Federal Reserve and other austerity-driven fiscal policies designed to leave working-class people "tolerably immiserated" is to endorse and promote a policy of full employment. By full employment I do not mean just a goal of low overall unemployment (otherwise known as NAIRU or the Non-Accelerating Inflation Rate of Unemployment), but rather a law that mandates an affirmative right to a good, government job. Distinct from workfare models, this should be a right—a mandate for the state, not for individuals. This right and the jobs attached to it should be purposively designed to address human needs and hardships arising from climate change, disaster relief, unaffordable housing, and lack of healthy food access.

While utopian sounding, the goal of full employment (however ambiguously defined) has been part of U.S. political debate for some time. It has long been a rallying cry in Black Freedom struggles, starting, per historian David Stein, as early as Reconstruction. In the Great Depression, versions of a direct hiring program, including the Works Progress Administration and the Civilian Conservation Corps became the most successful programs of the New Deal. And later, the Negro American Labor Council (part of the

New Deal reform coalition) led by Bayard Rustin and A. Phillip Randolph in the mid-century also took on the mantle of guaranteed good jobs as a way to achieve economic equality and freedom for racial minority communities.

Due in no small part to these efforts, the aspiration of full employment is already embedded in existing law. One year prior to the Volcker shock, and because of the continued efforts of Black unionists and civil rights activists, Congress passed the Full Employment and Balanced Growth Act of 1978 (also known as the Humphry-Hawkins Act). But rather than guaranteeing access to good jobs, the Act committed the Federal Reserve to a target of 4% unemployment. Advocating for a better version of the Act on the seventh anniversary of her husband's death, Coretta Scott King took political economy and supply-side economics head on. In her testimony before Congress in 1975, she stated,

> It [has been] very calmly assumed that greater numbers of American workers must lose their jobs [to become] frontline soldiers in the battle against inflation.... [But] full employment, a job for every American who needs [and wants] one, is a real and possible goal if we would choose to make it a national priority.

The Act in its final form did not fulfill the vision of Scott King or the Black liberation fighters before her, but it was nonetheless completely ignored the year after its passage.

Despite the on-the-books mandates of the Act, we are of course unlikely to see fundamental transformations of monetary policy without concomitant ideological shifts. As leftist scholars of political economy battle for a sea change in conventional economic thought, labor movement strategists, too, should be aggressively prioritizing distributivist political economy narratives and solutions. A worker's right to a good job—just like their right to a minimum wage or to protected collective bargaining—can and should be mainstreamed as an integral part of any moral capitalist economy, one that prioritizes racial and economic justice.

But in this aspirational fight, we must reject proposals that make the government an "employer of last resort" and that set fixed minimum wages. To be sure, a true revolutionary job guarantee should be voluntary, provide skills training and other benefits, attach to important and desirable government jobs, and be accompanied by increased support for people who cannot or do not wish to engage in paid labor. It should grow the bargaining power of workers throughout the economy, while solving other crises of the working class by ushering the nation towards a green transition and providing state-supported health and care work for children and the elderly. And in doing so, it can create a virtuous cycle of labor union legitimation and strength.

To get to a place where the guaranteed right to a voluntary, good job is legislatively possible, and to where it can become a naturalized expectation in our moral order, labor strategists need to channel the spirit of Black labor and civil rights leaders to build worker power not just within firms and sectors, but also in the very legal structuring of the political economy. More recently, some public unions have embraced "bargaining for the common good," coordinating campaigns that combine workplace organizing with advocacy around government budgeting, thus raising worker wages and generating the fiscal conditions that make those raises possible. As Melinda Cooper argues, we can learn from these public sector campaigns the efficacy of "seiz[ing] the reins of fiscal and monetary power from below" and transform how we think about our future struggles for upward social distribution.

Not only would a properly executed right to a good government job "release the wage" from the tight fists of the neoliberal capital state, but it would also help to co-create fairer, safer, and more stable worlds, freeing the working class from "the obedience and subjection" brought on by the otherwise ever-present threat of hunger.

PART VI

The *Dissent* Tradition, Then and Now: A Roundtable Discussion on the Labor Movement and Democratic Socialism

Luis Feliz Leon is associate editor of *Labor Notes*.

Sara Nelson is president of the Association of Flight Attendants–CWA.

Daisy Pitkin is deputy organizing director of Workers United, national field director of the Starbucks campaign, and author of *On the Line: Two Women's Epic Fight to Build a Union* (2022).

This conversation, held in May 2024, was moderated by Samir Sonti and Mark Levinson.

SS: To start, can you talk about how your past experience in the labor movement informs how you think about the current moment?

LFL: As an associate editor at *Labor Notes*, which has a larger project to support and help build rank-and-file reform currents in the labor movement, I see myself as what Antonio Gramsci calls an active or permanently active persuader. I'm permanently persuading people to build fighting unions and workers to take the fight to the bosses. That sometimes entails being a morale booster for workers who feel isolated in their unions, if they're trying to fight not only the company but also their own entrenched union leadership. My role is to help cohere networks of rank-and-file workers so that they can build on each other's lessons from their fights. When I report on the labor movement, I try to hold up a mirror to workers to say: you see, lonely worker in South Carolina who's feeling hopeless, here's another worker in Texas fighting to build a union. You can learn from their struggle, you're not alone, you're part of a larger social movement.

SN: The only reason that I'm here is because women formed my union and made one of the most democratic unions in the labor movement. I was a dissident when I started in 1996–97, and I didn't know anything about the labor movement at that time. I didn't know anything about being in a union. I learned about unions the day that the Association of Flight Attendants came to one of my last days in training and told me about it and asked me to sign the union card.

My first day on the job, a thirty-five-year flight attendant told me that management thinks of us as their wives or their mistresses, and in either case, they hold us in contempt. Your only place of worth is with your fellow flying partners, she said. And if we stick together, there's nothing we can't accomplish. I was twenty-three, fresh out of company training from Oregon, thinking that I was going to be a teacher, having gone to a small liberal arts school in southern Illinois on a country club–like campus. That was a lot. But the message of solidarity resonated with me, so that got me involved. Through that dissenting voice and wanting the union to be better, but also having a union that had celebrated dissent and debate, there was space for me already. There was also space for me because I was a woman in a union that was created by women, which is very rare. The fact that I'm here today as the international president of our union is only because that democracy was laid out. There were times when it was not used, and there were times when people allowed it to go dormant, where we became more of a service model union, as opposed to a fighting union. But all in all, it was incredibly democratic.

I gained a firsthand experience with the horrors of capitalism after 9/11 and the airline bankruptcies, and the tearing up of contracts that had just been built up and had just become something that could create a career mostly for women and the LGBTQ community, people who didn't necessarily have a place or a voice in other places in society. These contracts are being torn up, and people's lives are being turned upside down, and I'm seeing this on the heels of incredible grief and all these messages of patriotism, "We've got to pull together, let's roll," and all that shit. I was seeing firsthand the conflict between the national narrative and the patriarchal narrative and my experience of having to fight like hell against all odds with a group of scrappy people who shouldn't be able to win, but who were making bankruptcy attorneys who charge $25 million for lunches have to really work. We were running in circles to make it really hard for them. That experience informed my entire arc, as well as seeing that what we went through was so similar to other unions that had already been on the decline and under attack in every different industry, and seeing how the system is set up against workers.

Now I'm president of the Association of Flight Attendants. More than twenty years later, we still haven't negotiated the contracts that I wanted to negotiate way back when the crisis capitalists were taking everything from us. We still have to organize Delta flight attendants who are one of the last groups sitting out there, setting the standard for the industry, working for the airline that is making enormous profits. When we went for payroll support during COVID, Delta was the only airline against it, because they thought they had enough cash to outlast everybody else and they would be the last one standing. When people become desperate, they're more likely to accept something less than they are due. I feel a tremendous pull to fight for all of that—from what place, I don't know. I have a lot of work to do within my own union. We will continue to challenge societal ideas about what was traditionally women's work for flight attendants, for nurses, for teachers, as well as work that has been marginalized or undervalued because it is done by immigrants or people of color. We need to push on the idea of what is working and what is our power.

I'm incredibly happy that I'm still directly tied to the rank and file as a union president, and as a worker myself. I'm also thinking about what we need to do on a grand scale to make the most of this moment as workers. Younger generations especially are waking up to the fact that rugged individualism is our path to ruin and collective action is our road to freedom. I'm thinking about an organization that would supercharge the Emergency Worker Organizing Committee [EWOC] and make it possible for every single worker who wants to form a union to have the support to do that, as well as the support to fight for a first contract, which is not possible today with the current unions that exist. We need to lock in long-term power for workers.

DP: In the Starbucks campaign, I'm working every day with incredibly inspiring, mostly young, but not all young, mostly queer, but not all queer, people who are fighting a massive, multinational, multibillion-dollar global corporation and winning. I come to this as someone who has been accidentally but uniquely positioned inside this fight. I've been in the labor movement for about twenty years. I've led and won big things before, and I had enough credibility inside our own union to be able to say, you have to fund this, and you have to stay out of it. You have to let this be worker-led and worker-driven, and it has to be worker-to-worker organizing, but you need to back it with real resources. And then you need to, no strings attached, get out of the way. Through the last two years, we've been able to build an incredible model for organizing that I hope gets replicated by other unions and other places, because the kind of worker-to-worker organizing that happened on this campaign helped it scale beyond what any resources and backing might have allowed it to do. Speaking to what Sara was saying during her introduction—that we need to supercharge EWOC—I really agree with that, but also, we need resources in the labor movement to back organizing on a massive scale. We need to let workers lead. That's difficult to maneuver right now. But I hope that the Starbucks workers campaign can be a model for how to do this at scale, moving forward both in the food service industry and in other industries.

SS: Since its founding, *Dissent* has served as an outlet for intellectual debate on the uneasy relationship between a vision of democratic socialism and the institutional labor movement. In what ways, if at all, do you see your roles as trade unionists as connected to a broader project of social transformation?

LFL: I'm a big fan of William Foster, the communist organizer who founded the Trade Union Education League. One of his ideas about the trade union movement is that the left wing must lead. Socialists have traditionally understood that in the labor movement, there are moments of upsurge that offer us the chance to win workers over to a program of social transformation. Socialists try to bring together these shop floor fighters for the next fight, because there's always a next fight. The material effect of an upsurge is that it produces a layer of worker-leaders or creates the conditions for them to emerge. When I think about the founders of *Dissent*, I think about Marshall Berman, who was very influential to me as a young person. His book

Adventures in Marxism was one of the primary texts I read when I first started exploring what it meant to be a Marxist. And Alfred Kazin, Irving Howe, and other New York intellectuals came up in the 1930s, when there was an upsurge in the labor movement that shaped them as students at City College in what was then an industrial New York City. In our time, what's the shared context that has produced fighters and organic intellectuals?

I see a through line that connects Occupy Wall Street, the Bernie Sanders campaigns, the Black Lives Matter movement, and the current upsurge around demanding a ceasefire in Gaza. Each of those fights has produced leaders, and we are beginning to kind of cohere our fighting forces. I think of projects like EWOC, the Southern Workers Assembly, or the Rank-and-File Project, which is supporting young workers organizing in key sectors, as being the culmination of these efforts coming to a head. Right now, the class question has become an exclamation point for many people. *Labor Notes* is popular. When in the past the labor officialdom treated us as persona non grata, now they attend our biannual conferences in large numbers. The labor movement is one of the few glimmers of hope as the far right is on the ascent, but the labor uptick won't last forever. The antiestablishment sentiment in the country cuts to the left and to the right. Reform currents are growing, while the far right consolidates its forces globally. So what do we do with the uptick in labor activity? The key question for socialists is to identify the fighters and support them. The fight is just beginning.

There is one additional point I would like to add. I came up through 32BJ SEIU as a researcher and organizer. When the labor movement was at its weakest point and talk of an independent working-class politics was not in the cards, there was SEIU training organizers. SEIU is top down and undemocratic with the exception fo some locals. Despite these faults, unions like SEIU and UNITE HERE provided an organizing orientation to a lot of young people, serving as an entry point into the labor movement. But even at that time, the comprehensive campaigns were limited because the top leadership had an aversion to taking risks. That's why the campaigns were concocted as if in a lab by teams of researchers, not workers themselves. What we are doing right now is creating institutions. In 2013, around the time that I graduated from college, there was this quote I kicked around in my head: "When leftists don't know what to do, they start a magazine." It's telling that right now, workers are starting independent unions; workers are launching their own organizing drives—not magazines. Think of Amazonians United, a minority union at the logistics giant, and the Amazon Labor Union, which recently affiliated with the Teamsters. We are in a different moment. Socialists are not starting *Jacobin* in 2024. They're starting campaigns, like the heroic work of organizers with Starbucks Workers United. These workers have dragged the labor movement along with them. The UAW is trying to learn from the momentum that Starbucks workers and Amazon workers have unleashed, while also learning how to institutionalize worker-led efforts with the backing of a deeply resourced, established union. But what happens when momentum runs out? This is where you need fighters. This is where you need the left, because momentum will eventually run out, and you need the courageous true believers who will stay the course. There is a relationship between organization and permanently active persuaders.

SN: I immediately think about what the label "socialist" means, and what the corporate elite and the capitalists have tried to make it mean. I think about how we remove obstacles between workers talking to each other about our demands and how we're going to build power to win. It's my experience that when you get people into those fights, their own politics change. I never really worried about it on the front end, but I do worry about alienating them. Unions naturally have the principles of socialism. We're trying to get our fair share. We're trying to have the economy shared with workers. We're trying to have security, health care, retirement, and a living wage. We're all socialists. I can say that right here, but there's no way I'd walk into the middle of a flight attendant union meeting and start with that. I'd be done. The conversation would be over. I think about it from an organizing perspective, considering what we're trying to accomplish and how we accomplish it as two different things. We need leaders who are always going to fight.

For example, one of my earliest fights as a union leader was the 2002

United Airlines bankruptcy. In the middle of those negotiations, we had what seemed like 90 percent of our members telling to us give them everything: "Don't let United go out of business, give them everything, take my house, I don't care." Ten percent of people were saying, "Buckle down, we're not going to let them take this from us, we can fight that with everything we have." While I really wanted to stand with those people, I felt responsible for taking care of everyone. I had already become a union leader, and I had great ideas about how to change it. And then I got into that leadership position and suddenly I had to be responsible for everyone. I remember telling one of the activists—and I'm probably being generous saying that 10 percent of our members were in that camp—"Keep saying what you're saying, but we aren't there. When we get the other 90 percent to come to where you are, then I'm going to tell you to push this fight forward." But with that said, it was really important he was there, for my own ability to even go on and have conversations with people who were demoralized and had given up. You need those fighters.

DP: I think about my role as helping people see power and its current structure. As organizers, we don't start the first general meeting of a campaign and talk about socialism and the broader project of social change. But organizing is transformative. And people's lives and identities and ideas about who they are and the kind of agency they have in the world change through an organizing campaign, through a fight with each other. Part of my role inside that fight is to lay bare the current structures of power, and to allow people to get a clearer vision of power and its various alignments and shapes inside of capitalism, and then to help them figure out how to work together—collectively, collaboratively, and creatively—to disrupt it enough that people will pay attention. In the process of doing that, and in going through that kind of fight together, people create something that they care about. Through the process of a fight, you create a beloved community that is worth defending. If you're doing the campaign the right way, it starts with anger at the current power structure and a desire to change it. Then you realize "we've built something that we love and care about" and the project becomes a community defense project. And the shift in that during a fight is transformative. People's lives change. Their capacity for fighting changes. It grows. It's the magic of solidarity or class struggle. It happens every time.

Right now, on the Starbucks campaign, we have 10,000 mostly young folks who are building a political home for themselves by creating a community with each other, building a beloved community that is worth defending, and going through this transformation. They're mostly of a generation that has been saddled with multiple interlocking global crises. They're wondering whether there will be another round of global forever wars, a livable planet in twenty years, or democracy in this country in ten years, or whether there is democracy in this country now. They're wondering whether they will be able to take their kids to the doctor if they have kids, or if they'll be saddled with student debt for the rest of their lives. All of these crises are laid on their laps. Right now, they are going through a transformative process, understanding power and their own ability and capacity to fight. This is a project about social transformation, because like it or not, we now have 10,000 young people that know how to fight and know how to win who are faced with crises left and right. They're going to figure out how to build things with each other that can combat them moving forward. The project that we're engaged in is the project of unionism, but it is also the project of broad social transformation. And it will result in broad social transformation.

ML: Each of you have stressed the role or position of the organizer. Can you elaborate upon how you think about what it means to be an organizer?

DP: As organizers—maybe this is also true for other leadership roles in unions— we are not taught to interrogate our own positions of power inside the organization. I know how to debrief an action like nobody's business, because I was trained to do it. But we're not trained to think about our positionality inside of an organizing campaign and our roles as leaders, and to interrogate that role as one of power. In my book, I tried to think about that a lot, because I had been away from the campaign I wrote about for several years, and had some time to reflect on what it means to fly in a bunch of organizers from some-where else and put them into a community to organize workers.[1] In my case, I was a young white person who barely spoke Spanish and was sent to organize mostly undocumented Mexican immigrant laundry workers in Arizona. I didn't know anything about industrial laundries. I learned a lot while I was there, but what does it mean to have that model of organizing?

This connects deeply to the issue of democracy and unions. I think a lot about the role of expertise and experience inside unions. What does it mean to have experts inside the union? We have tons of them, and they're important. We have economists inside unions who are experts. We have researchers who are experts at uncovering patterns of power inside companies. We have lawyers and we have communications specialists. The union is full of experts. What good does that expertise do? What can we do about the fact that experts end up sitting in positions of power and making calls about campaigns based on their expertise and their knowledge and making decisions for people who are fighting because they're experts. In this way, expertise ends up being a de facto power structure inside unions. What do we want to do about that? The answer, of course, is not to get rid of all the experts. But we need to be able to examine and interrogate power where it exists.

As organizers, we're trained to have organizing conversations, and our job is to train worker leaders to have organizing conversations with their co-workers. We're trained in this transfer of knowledge. But I don't think that should spill over into other parts of the union. What would it look like to structure a union where the entire communications operation entailed training worker leaders on communications, and research was about training worker leaders on research, and all of the departments of the union and all of the pieces of a campaign were geared toward train-ing a whole army of people who are going to be able to do this in the next campaign?

SN: I think about the conversations I've had about that model and what a difference it made to those workers with the information that they were armed with, rather than being told, "This is what it is" with no

connection to it at all. Having discovered it and given it meaning themselves totally changed the situation. I'm also thinking about our Delta
campaign right now, which has been going on, off and on, since the forties, and more recently since the late nineties, with fits and starts and
three different elections and two different unions at points. We launched
the campaign without any worker committee faces, which is the opposite of what you would want to do. It ran for several years without having a national committee. We had leaders in different locations, but not
a national committee of Delta flight attendants. We just announced the
national Delta steering committee last week [May 2024] and put the
campaign in their hands. The campaign has been supercharged in a week
because their flying partners are now believing it, and they're making
the right decisions about the campaign. We're stuck in an organizer-led
world where people say, "You couldn't possibly be an organizer if you
weren't trained by me," as opposed to finding talent within the rank
and file.

A couple of years ago at AFA, we put together a budget to do exactly what Daisy was talking about with communications. We brought
communications people from different locals to our international office
to shadow and help out, and it was very hard—for one, because people were connected to their locals and wanted to be back there. But
also, it was difficult because there's always a lot to do in unions. And
it's always hard to mentor people and give that time and share that
knowledge rather than doing things when there's so much to be done.
It's crucial to ground the union in the idea that, in every which way and
in everything we do, it's the members' union. It doesn't belong to anyone but the members. It is theirs to own and run and lead and change.
That's the kind of mentoring that I got from the people who trained me
when I got involved. But we don't have direct membership elections at
AFA and that is a problem. I'm actually proposing that right now, and
we're going to talk about that at our convention and hopefully I'll get
it through.

We have to constantly examine our policies. Are they actually reflect-
ing the values we're trying to promote? That's constantly in conflict or in
struggle with democracy and dissent and agitation and debate and the institution. There's a constant push and pull. At what point does everyone

come together and administer the agreements? There are certain things that have to be done to take the next step for the union to get stronger. It's an overarching question about how we're engaging people in the union, how the union is running, but then also just the push and pull of democracy and decision making. That is always going to be really hard. A lot of people say that democracy is messy. I think that's a little bit lazy. Democracy is awesome if you allow it to live. But people have to be committed to the idea that we're going to make decisions together and we're going to support each other in those decisions in order to get outcomes and constantly be having that fight.

SS: The question of union democracy is a theme that has run through all of the labor coverage in *Dissent*. In a selection reprinted in this volume, Steve Fraser provocatively argued that "Unions, unlike other popular formations, are compelled to assume multiple and not always compatible roles: as vehicles of democratic expression and mobilization, as a kind of diplomatic corps engaged in closeted negotiation, as combat organizations imposing a solidaristic discipline with which to confront a centralized enemy utterly unconcerned with niceties of democratic procedure." He continued: unions "depend upon a fanciful and historical polarity between a virginal rank and file and a venal bureaucracy." What do you make of this?

DP: In that list of the disparate roles that unions play, or projects that they have to engage in, my job is always the third. I'm the combat; you want to have a war, I'm there. I know how to lead people through a war, and sometimes, I know how to win it. That tends to be the space in a union where there's the most democratic engagement—or at least the most engagement. I won't say that it's always democratic. It requires the most engagement from workers because the workers have to be engaged in order to win recognition for the union. Whether they're voting in an NLRB election or running a militant minority campaign, workers need to be involved to win.

In my career I've worked for a bunch of different unions: UNITE, which became UNITE HERE, and then became Workers United; I've also done stints with steel workers and smaller unions. You are often lectured—at least I was as a young organizer—that when you're in the middle of the war, you can't raise the expectations of the workers too much because they are going to have to settle a contract, and then they have to live inside the union. After the war, you hand the members over to the second item on the list, the diplomatic closeted negotiation. You hand over these leaders that you've mentored and taught to fight into this process, and you don't really know what it is. Organizers are often a bit disappointed about the life these workers are going to have in the union afterward having led the war. The union is always mad at us, because we lead the war and build militancy, and it doesn't always want militant members at the end of the day.

This is where the question of union democracy comes up, because members participate in forcing a change in their workplace, from an authoritarian regime to one that is more democratic. They have decided that their agency in the workplace fucking matters, and they are going to make it matter in the workplace. And then it's handed over to a part of the union that exists to administer the peace. As administrators of the peace, you become really invested in the life of the union. You're in charge of it. At that point, workers are meant to live under peace for the next three years or so. And then you send the organizer back to rally the troops for another round of contract negotiations, and so you stand up, and then sit down, stand up, and then sit down. That's the message to the members.

I'm thinking a lot about this right now. Because we will get a contract at Starbucks. The fight is not over; we have a lot of work in front of us, but we will get a contract. But what will the life of these workers be like in their union? How do we do something different? How do we create a truly fighting union? We are going to continue fighting, and the fight is going to fuel new organizing, so that we build power inside the company over the life of the contract. There's not going to be any sit down. We're going to keep fighting, because the fight is what creates the thing that people care about, the union that they care about. If you have a whole bunch of workers who care deeply about the union that they built and that they continue to fight for, then you can't help but have a democratic union, because you've got

10,000 workers who are deeply invested in the sort of daily life of the union.

The calculus is: don't ever lay down the fight. There should never be a moment when you're administering the peace or handing things off to the experts in the union who know how to solve the grievances, while your job is just to chill out until the next round of contract negotiations. That level of disengagement turns all of the power in the union over to the hands of people who are just administering the union. It's not that they're power-hungry people who are trying to take power away from workers. It's just the way it works culturally inside the union. It's going to be hard to change, but I think we have to.

LFL: I think of an essay by the labor educator, A.J. Muste, in which he described unions as at once being an "army" and a "town hall."[2] We live in a profoundly undemocratic society, and by their structure, workers from disparate backgrounds are thrown together into these mass organizations we know as labor unions. Whatever rough edges they bring with them into the union are going to rub up against those of other workers. They're going to be transformed by being together in this institution that is their own. But there's also the picket line, when, like Daisy mentioned, unions have to function as combat organizations. When we think about what a union is, ultimately, it enforces picket lines. With that comes discipline and organization, but we also have membership meetings, and members vote on their contracts. A union ranges from business unionism solely focused on servicing members to class struggle unionism where the life of the union revolves around members being on a permanent war footing because a contract is a temporary truce. But the reality in most unions is far from that ideal. Sometimes, unions can't meet quorum, because members don't show up to meetings because they don't see the union as a vehicle for change. So, people throw their hands up and say, we're just going to, as Daisy put it, "administer the peace." We select managers to administer and manage the bureaucracy of the union, as opposed to building up a fighting membership equipped with the know-how and confidence to run the union. The goal is that every cook can govern.

Similar to what Daisy said, I was trained to find a pressure point, to be a smart person that designs comprehensive campaigns. That's very disempowering because it leaves members as bystanders in their own organization. A different approach is to recognize that democracy is power. The boss knows when members are indifferent to the union. That apathy reduces the union's power in bargaining and in the everyday match up against the tyrannical control supervisors exert over the shop floor. The winning at all costs mentality promotes risk-aversion and sidelines union democracy. That's corrosive to the vitality of any union. Which is the members. Winning at all costs exacts a heavy cost: a weak labor movement.

That's beginning to change. The UAW has recoupled labor power and democracy. For a long time, especially in SEIU, under Andy Stern, the model was: it's power, we're going to grow, and these mega locals are going to give us the density that we need to take the class struggle to the employers. What UAW has recently shown is that militant strikes can transform a union, which in turn can spur new organizing, and that is part of a virtuous cycle. The weirdos at Labor Notes have been saying this for forty-plus years. It's another thing to have a national demonstration of worker power that brings those two things together in a very profound way, which is what we saw in the "Stand Up Strike." That dynamism is at the center of our labor movement, because as socialists, we want workers to rule. The first step in doing that is transforming their unions.

It's also key to talk about the question of member expectations being raised. While walking the picket lines during the UAW Stand Up Strike, I was struck by how high their expectations were. I thought, it's Flint in the 1930s. What does that mean? How do you go back to your membership and say, "We fought, but we didn't win everything"? What does that look like? Or do you go out and stump for a vote yes, and say to the membership, "This is the best contract that we can get"? Some members say, "No, unions should not do that." I'm not of that opinion. I believe that if you go out and fight, you have to lead, and you own what you fought for, and you say what the merits of that contract are and then leave it up for the members to decide. Members have a say; they can reject it or they or they can endorse it. I don't think leadership is about refusing to take a stance on things. It's quite the opposite.

SN: One hundred percent, there's always a fight to be had. It doesn't matter if it's about a uniform policy. But there are people who don't want to fight all the time, who want to have peace. A criticism I have of Walter Reuther is that he was working to create peace, even though they kept trying to kill him. But it's also a natural human occurrence that we have to grapple with. We need young people leading our labor movement. We need young people in all of these fights. But they're less likely to have the experience to form a strategy, so everyone has to be at the table. Sometimes that's helpful, though, since many older workers, for their whole lives, have been accustomed to thinking, as Luis said, "This is the best we can get from the company," as opposed to something like "We fought, and this is what we got." But there is a natural arc of the worker's life. There is more to lose, typically, when they have more life experiences, like having a family, or having children, or being responsible to other people, or building up some kind of security. Hopefully, this is not the case right now, which is part of the reason we have so many fights going on.

What Daisy was saying about taking 10,000 people, creating their union, and continuing to fight is so true. There will be new people who come in who want to do something different. But sometimes the people who built the union are proud of how they've built it, and they want to keep it exactly the way it is. These veterans might feel that the new people come in and have no idea what they're talking about—they didn't go through the fight. Those tensions can occur too. We have to teach people from the beginning that they need to be spending at least 5 percent of their time on coming out for someone else's fight or thinking about how they're inviting someone else to their fight. But it's a difficult thing to fight through that security arc, that age arc, that desire for peace arc. Not everybody is a fighter and an agitator, and we have to figure out how to keep people with us even while giving them what they feel like is a little rest, so they can be ready for the next fight and are never sent out to pasture.

DP: People don't want to go to work every day and be in a combat zone. People want and need peace when they have built something that they can live inside of peacefully. There's a real tension between those two things: the need to keep a union fighting to maintain its democracy, and the need to create a life inside of the union that people want to live. Luis, I appreciated what you said about leadership. The power inherent in leadership is an interesting thing to have to think about and interrogate all the time, inside the various positions that staff and elected leaders have inside unions. I had a meeting with the staff on the Starbucks campaign a few months ago. We had two signs on the wall. One of them said, "I work for the workers," and the other one said, "I lead the leaders." We asked organizers to stand next to the statement that best represented their role as an organizers, and the group was about exactly split in half. Then, we had a four-hour-long conversation about what it meant to be a staff person who is leading the leaders versus one who works for the workers. What does that mean about the worker-driven nature of the campaign? Is that an abdication of leadership and responsibility? Is leadership and responsibility a way to take control of some ungranted power over the campaign?

ML: You've all been around a long time. You've seen bad times for the labor movement. We seem to be in a different time now. Why did that happen and what should the labor movement be doing in the future?

DP: I absolutely came of age in a dark time for the labor movement. As a young, radical organizer, I didn't think of myself initially as having a home in the U.S. labor movement, because I thought it wasn't radical or democratic enough. Frankly, I had disdain for the labor movement. And then at one point I thought: This is the largest pool of resources anywhere in the world that is devoted to, or at least can be used for, anticapitalist organizing. It's a means to an end, and we need to make sure that we're using it for that, because we live in a moment where economic disparity is at an extreme is only accelerating. In order to create a shift, we need resources and massive organizing.

I'm not willing to cede the ground that this upsurge will end. Audacious fights beget audacious fights. We have to keep having them one after another after another after another, because people want on board, not because the labor movement is "cool," although it is. They want on board because they want to win, and they see that we're having audacious fights and we're winning. The moment we stop having those fights is when we'll stop being on the front page of the newspaper. People will stop paying attention and turn their backs on labor only when we've stopped fighting in smart, audacious ways that are winning victories for the working class.

SN: I'm so glad you said that, Daisy. This doesn't have to end. The way we keep it going is by finding leaders that we're not used to seeing as leaders. There are more fights than we can possibly say that need to be had. We have so much to win. If we keep inviting people to tell their stories and talking about the struggles and talking about all of the places where we have to win freedom, then this can continue. We can continue to build because the solidarity of this moment and the power of this moment is that people are feeling connected; they're recognizing it's a "Which Side Are You On" moment. If we continue to show the pitfalls of capitalism and connect that to other people's fights, with new voices and new conversations between people who previously have not had the platform or the ability to do that, then I think that we can extend this moment.

But we need a diversity of experience and background in order to make that possible. That is the urgent work of this moment: to see leadership in all kinds of different places. We need to recognize that there are important fights in jobs that we're not traditionally used to fighting for. That's the power of the Starbucks campaign. I heard so many people say, "That fight isn't strategic. They should be thinking about supply chains, or they should be thinking about all these other things." But that fight was the most strategic thing we could possibly do in this moment, because it showed people that the jobs that most people said weren't worth fighting for are worth fighting for, because there are human beings occupying those jobs. That's who we're fighting for. If we can shed light on that and connect with each other, we will win. The human spirit naturally connects. It's the union busters who have tried to make us believe that's not the case.

LFL: Historically, the labor movement has only grown in upsurges. It hasn't happened gradually. It's hard to tell if we're in the crest or the beginning of the wave, or where exactly we are. But I wholeheartedly agree that we need to build worker-led movements. In the 1970s, after the upsurge of the militant strikes and civil rights organizing, we saw a surge in organizing. That happened in the context of the Black Power movement, the Vietnam War, and the feminist movement, all of which had a profound impact on municipal workers' organizing. A lot of African Americans came into the public sector—the public sector that is now under attack from the right.

As much as I would like to be a proud syndicalist, the labor movement is only one player in a larger social dynamic. Our fortunes as a labor movement are tied to political dynamics. For example, the UAW election filings in new organizing drives at Volkswagen and Mercedes have been possible with an NLRB that followed the letter of the law. The state plays an important role—the best we can hope for is to have it on our side or to beat it back to neutrality, but we ignore it to our detriment. Just like during 1936–37 Sit-Down Strike, had the Michigan governor Frank Murphy called in the state troopers to crush the strikers, the UAW might not have won recognition at General Motors. As proud as I am of being a fighter in the labor movement, the labor movement won't be the revolutionary force, as much as sectarians would want it to be at the end of the day. We have vast membership and democratic potential within our unions, but it's not going to be the revolutionary driver. That's the role of a party.

But it's crucial to ally ourselves with the forces seeking social transformation to grow the strength of our movement. I came of age in a moment when people had given up on the working class. I came from the working class: my dad was a taxi driver, and my mom was a steelworker. I knew that we still mattered. I knew that we still labored and that our labor created society and produced the bounty that people enjoy. The labor question is back at the center. We're showing the structural power that unions can have in calling for a ceasefire, in calling for Medicare for All, in calling for broader social demands that will help us put class struggle writ large on the national agenda. Not the narrow horizon of sectional interest about one union's members or another's members, but all of us. I am hopeful that we can continue to do that transformative work, that we'll create more good trouble and lead more struggles, and that in the process, new fighters will enter as other fighters are tired and need to play a different role. The struggle continues and carries forward so long as we are furnishing those ranks with new members. The revolution may not be permanent, but the truce is temporary.

Acknowledgments

This book would not have been possible without the encouragement and generous support of Jules Bernstein, whose longtime service to the labor movement and working-class struggles exemplifies the very best of the *Dissent* tradition. We are also grateful to Lyra Walsh Fuchs and Gemma Sack of *Dissent*, who graciously shepherded the project from start to finish, providing invaluable assistance in the most timely fashion. *Dissent* co-editor, Natasha Lewis, and book review editor, Mark Levinson, also played indispensable roles in helping us to conceptualize and shape the book. Interns Eli Frankel, Jahnavi Mehta, and Django Spadola offered important research assistance. We appreciate, as well, Cathy Ramsey Dexter's close reading of the completed manuscript. Finally, thanks to Marc Favreau and Gia Gonzales of The New Press, for believing in the project and for making it happen.

Notes

Introduction

1. "Editorial Statement: Our Country and Our Culture," *Partisan Review*, vol. 19, no. 3 (1952), 282.

2. An immense literature exists tracing the anti-Stalinist left during the mid-twentieth century. Among the key works: Alan Wald, *The New York Intellectuals: The Rise and Decline of the Anti-Stalinist Left from the 1930s to the 1980s* (Chapel Hill: University of North Carolina Press, 2017); Judy Kutulas, *The Long War: The Intellectual People's Front and Anti-Stalinism, 1930–1940* (Durham: Duke University Press, 1995); Peter Drucker, *Max Shachtman and His Left: A Socialist's Odyssey Through the "American Century,"* (New York: Humanity Books, 1993); Brian Palmer, *James P. Cannon and the Emergence of Trotskyism in the United States, 1928–1938* (New York: Haymarket Books, 2023); Kent Worcester, *C.L.R. James: A Political Biography* (Albany: State University of New York Press, 1996); Michael Wreszin, *Dwight Macdonald: A Rebel in Defense of Tradition* (New York: Basic Books, 1994); and Irving Howe, *A Margin of Hope: An Intellectual Autobiography* (New York: Harcourt Brace, 1982).

3. Maurice Isserman, "Steady Work: Sixty Years of *Dissent*," *Dissent*, January 23, 2014.

4. Irving Howe, "Forming *Dissent*," in *Conflict and Consensus: A Festschrift in Honor of Lewis A. Coser*, eds., Walter W. Powell and Richard Robbins (New York: The New Press, 1984), 62.

5. Maurice Isserman, *If I Had a Hammer. . . The Death of the Old Left and the Birth of the New Left* (New York: Basic Books, 1987), 85.

6. Howe, "Forming *Dissent*," 62.

7. Ibid., 63.

8. Irving Howe, "A Word of Introduction," *Dissent*, Fall 1959, 371.

9. Irving Howe, *A Margin of Hope: An Intellectual Autobiography* (New York: Harcourt Brace, 1982), 294.

10. Irving Howe, "New Styles in 'Leftism,' " *Dissent*, Summer 1965, 314–15.

11. Irving Howe, *A Margin of Hope*, 314.

12. "A Talk with Victor Reuther," *Dissent*, Spring 1983, 142.

13. "Shall We Call a General Strike?" *Dissent*, Summer 1981, 289–99.

14. Irving Howe and Michael Walzer, "Soviet Transformation," *Dissent* (Spring 1990), 1.

15. "We Thank You," *Dissent*, Spring 1985, 129.

Part VI: The *Dissent* Tradition, Here and Now

1. Daisy Pitkin, *On the Line: A Story of Class, Solidarity, and Two Women's Epic Fight to Build a Union* (New York: Algonquin Books, 2022).

2. A.J. Muste, "Factional Fights in Trade Unions: A View of Human Relations in the Labor Movement," in *American Labor Dynamics in the Light of Postwar Developments*, ed. J.B.S. Hardman (New York: Harcourt Brace, 1928).

About the Editors

Nelson Lichtenstein is Research Professor of history at the University of California, Santa Barbara. He is the author of *Labor's War at Home: The CIO in World War II*, *State of the Union: A Century of American Labor*, and a biography of Walter Reuther. The New Press published his edited collection, *Wal-Mart: The Face of Twenty-First-Century Capitalism*. He lives in Santa Barbara.

Samir Sonti is an assistant professor at the CUNY School of Labor and Urban Studies, an institution designed to serve working-class adults in New York City. He has worked in multiple capacities in the labor movement and continues to collaborate with various unions on research, policy, and educational efforts. Sonti is currently completing a book on the historical politics of inflation in the United States. He lives in New York City.

Publishing in the Public Interest

Thank you for reading this book published by The New Press; we hope you enjoyed it. New Press books and authors play a crucial role in sparking conversations about the key political and social issues of our day.

We hope that you will stay in touch with us. Here are a few ways to keep up to date with our books, events, and the issues we cover:

- Sign up at www.thenewpress.com/subscribe to receive updates on New Press authors and issues and to be notified about local events
- www.facebook.com/newpressbooks
- www.twitter.com/thenewpress
- www.instagram.com/thenewpress

Please consider buying New Press books not only for yourself, but also for friends and family and to donate to schools, libraries, community centers, prison libraries, and other organizations involved with the issues our authors write about.

The New Press is a 501(c)(3) nonprofit organization; if you wish to support our work with a tax-deductible gift please visit www.thenewpress.com/donate or use the QR code below.